NATIVE FOOTSTEPS
ALONG THE PATH OF
SAINT KATERI TEKAKWITHA

NATIVE FOOTSTEPS
ALONG THE PATH OF
SAINT KATERI TEKAKWITHA

MARK G. THIEL & CHRISTOPHER VECSEY
Editors

MARQUETTE
UNIVERSITY

PRESS

E
99
.M8
T4586
2012

LIBRARY OF CONGRESS CATALOGING-IN-PUBLICATION DATA

Native footsteps : along the path of Saint Kateri Tekakwitha / Mark G. Thiel
& Christopher Vecsey, editors. — [First edition]
    pages cm
Includes bibliographical references and index.
ISBN-13: 978-0-87462-089-4 (hardcover : alk. paper)
ISBN-10: 0-87462-089-9 (hardcover : alk. paper)
1. Tekakwitha, Kateri, Saint, 1656-1680. 2. Mohawk women—Biography.
3. Christian saints—New York (State)—Biography. I. Thiel, Mark G. II.
Vecsey, Christopher.
E99.M8T4586 2012
282.092—dc23
[B]
                                                    2012039082

This project was accomplished with the help of the Black & Indian Mission
Office, 2021 H St., NW, Washington, DC. 20006, 877-237-1605.
info@blackandindianmission.org
With special thanks to the Bureau of Catholic Indian Missions.

Cover Image: Ca. 1685: Painting of Saint Kateri Tekakwitha by Rev. Claude
Chauchetière, S.J., St. Francis Xavier Church, Kahnawake, Quebec.
AMS K02-23.

Association of American
University Presses

MARQUETTE UNIVERSITY PRESS
MILWAUKEE

The Association of Jesuit University Presses

CONTENTS

Foreword by Reverend Wayne C. Paysse 9

Acknowledgments 11

Introduction by Christopher Vecsey 13

DOCUMENTS 37

1. Remembrance of Kateri Tekakwitha, the Saintly Mohawk, Reverend Pierre Cholenec, S.J., 1696 39

2. Indian Petition to Rome, 1880s 45

3. Our Tekakwitha Club, Sister Providencia Tolan, S.P., 1940 47

4. Kateri Circles: A Native Saint in Community with the People, Rebecca Hernandez Rosser, 2012 49

5. Blessed Kateri Tekakwitha: The Prophetic Spirit of Kateri Tekakwitha within Our Indian Churches, Reverend Edmund Savilla, 1981 53

6. Blessed Kateri and the Turtle Clan, Siggenauk Center's Spiritual Day, Milwaukee, Wisconsin, Sister Kateri Mitchell, S.S.A., July 11, 1987 61

7. In Her Footsteps, Sister Kateri Mitchell, S.S.A., and Reverend John Brioux, O.M.I., 1995 65

8. Statement of the Association of Native Religious and Clergy, Distributed at the Tekakwitha Conference, Orono, Maine, August 4, 1992 67

9. Kateri's Dream and Its Fulfillment, Sister Mary Ewens, O.P., 2012 71

10. A Lily Among Thorns: The Mohawk Repatriation of Káteri Tekahkwí:tha, Presented at the 30th Conference on New York State History, June 5, 2009, in Plattsburgh, New York, Darren Bonaparte 87

11. Healing and Pilgrimage among Native Americans: The Devotion to Blessed Kateri Tekakwitha, James J. Preston, 2000 97

12. Jake Finkbonner and the Miracle at Seattle Children's Hospital, Mark G. Thiel, 2012 121

13. From the Desk of the Tekakwitha Conference Executive Director, Sister
Kateri Mitchell, S.S.A., 2012...129

INTERVIEWS 131
Mary Bordeaux Hunger, in Mission, South Dakota, on the Rosebud Indian
Reservation, May 24, 1994 133
Bertha Shaw, in Mission, South Dakota, on the Rosebud Indian Reservation,
May 24, 1994 137
Theresa Poiznee, in Mission, South Dakota, on the Rosebud Indian Reservation,
May 25, 1994 139
Kathryn Clairmont, in Mission, South Dakota, on the Rosebud Indian
Reservation, May 25, 1994 145
Rosalita Roach-Avery, in Red Scaffold, South Dakota, on the Cheyenne River
Indian Reservation, May 26, 1994 149
Deacon Harold E. Condon, in Red Scaffold, South Dakota, on the Cheyenne
River Indian Reservation, June 2, 1994 153
Sister Anthony Davis, O.S.B.S., in Marty, South Dakota, on the Yankton
Indian Reservation, June 4, 1994 159
Deacon Francis Hairy Chin, in Rapid City, South Dakota, June 24, 1994..163
Ambrose V. McBride, in Rapid City, South Dakota, June 25, 1994 167
Marvin Clifford, in Rapid City, South Dakota, June 26, 1994...................171
Delores J. Schumacher, Doris M. Giles, Cecilia Montgomery, Mabel Hawkins,
Geraldine Sherman, and Gloria Fiddler, in Rapid City, South Dakota, June
26, 1994 173
Deacon Victor Bull Bear, in Kyle, South Dakota, on the Pine Ridge Indian
Reservation, June 29, 1994 181
Reverend Collins P. Jordan, in St. Francis, South Dakota, on the Rosebud
Indian Reservation, June 30, 1994 185
Deacon Marlin Leneaugh, in St. Francis, South Dakota, on the Rosebud Indian
Reservation, July 1, 1994..191
Kathleen Lawson, Lily Richards, and Sister Gloria Davis, S.B.S., in Fort
Defiance, Arizona, on the Navajo Indian Reservation, June 22, 1995 ...195

Anna Marie Sandoval, in Lukachukai, Arizona, on the Navajo Indian Reservation, June 23, 1995 205

Victoria Blair, in Lukachukai, Arizona, on the Navajo Indian Reservation, June 23, 1995 211

Deacon Daniel Nez Martin, in Window Rock, Arizona, on the Navajo Indian Reservation, June 23, 1995 215

Joe and Juana Pecos, in Jemez Pueblo, New Mexico, July 11, 1995 225

Mark J. Cheresposey, in Laguna Pueblo, New Mexico, July 12, 1995........229

Reverend Diego Mazon, O.F.M., in Gallup, New Mexico, July 17, 1995.....233

Joseph W. Thomas, in Sacaton, Arizona, on the Salt River Indian Reservation, July 22, 1995...239

Maseline Albring, in Milwaukee, Wisconsin, June 6, 2012........................245

Larry Richmond, in Milwaukee, Wisconsin, June 6, 2012.........................249

John Clifford, in Milwaukee, Wisconsin, June 20, 2012 251

PHOTOGRAPHS...255

INDEX 273

FOREWORD

Wow! What a blessing and a joy to immerse one-self into these pages where Saint Kateri comes alive and speaks to our heart about Jesus, faith, American Indian spirituality and miracles through the lives and experiences of others. Let us join them along the path of Saint Kateri Tekakwitha!

The prophet Isaiah reminds us "how beautiful upon the mountains are the feet of him who brings glad tidings, announcing peace, bearing good news…" (Is 52:7). In her daily life, Kateri Tekakwitha was a joyful spirit in the midst of a normal life filled with extraordinary experiences. In these pages you will find many individuals who are captured by some of these experiences. Maybe you have already experienced the gentle and powerful presence of Saint Kateri?

Since 1874, the Bureau of Catholic Indian Missions has engaged Native American communities in the work of evangelization, as did the missionaries in Saint Kateri's day. By the dedicated lives of our missionaries, bishops and many, many lay people, the Catholic Church continues to bring the Good News and announces Peace throughout Indian Country and across the globe.

United in spirit with Saint Kateri, I am pleased to recommend reading and rereading of this publication as a light and witness to the many miracles God gives us in our daily lives. Share this volume with your family, friends and associates. Use the book as a springboard to gather others to share how Saint Kateri has impacted their lives. Use the book for quiet reflection and remember "thy word is a lamp unto my feet, and a light unto my path…" (Psalm 119:105). **Blessed are the feet of Saint Kateri!**

Lastly, I wish to express my heartfelt gratitude to Sister Mary Ewens, O.P., Mark Thiel, archivist for the Bureau of Catholic Indian Missions at Marquette University, and Dr. Christopher Vecsey for their openness to the spirit in making this publication a reality.

In the Joy of Saint Kateri,
Reverend Wayne C. Paysse
Executive Director
Bureau of Catholic Indian Missions

www.blackandindianmission.org

info@blackandindianmission.org

ACKNOWLEDGMENTS

Grandma Rose Miner, and her daughter's family of Alberta and Richard Day, who in Mark's formative years adopted and took him into their Catholic Ho Chunk family in Wisconsin, the experience which steered him towards his path of service to Native American people.

Sister Genevieve Cuny, O.S.F., who requested that Mark interview Native Catholics regarding their devotions to Blessed Kateri, the results of which grace this book; the Archdiocese of Milwaukee Development Fund, which funded the interviews of Native Catholics; and the interviewees devoted to Blessed Kateri, who enthusiastically consented to be interviewed and welcomed Mark into their homes.

Sister Marie Therese Archambault, O.S.F., who as a colleague while editing *The Crossing of Two Roads. Being Catholic and Native in the United States* broadened our perspectives about Native Catholics.

Orbis Books and the University of Notre Dame Press, for publishing earlier variants of some ideas and documents in this book.

Reverend Wayne C. Paysse, Executive Director, Bureau of Catholic Indian Missions, for funding this book and writing its Foreword as an introductory message about Saint Kateri Tekakwitha.

Sister Kateri Mitchell, S.S.A., Executive Director, Tekakwitha Conference, for her support of, and contributions to, this book project.

Darren Bonaparte, Sister Mary Ewens, O.P., James J. Preston, Rebecca Hernandez Rosser, and Reverend Edmund Savilla, contributing authors.

Colgate University, which funded the index for this book.

Herman D. Ray Collection (Herman D. Ray, photographer)—HDR.

INTRODUCTION

CHRISTOPHER VECSEY

Any substantive history of American Indian Catholicism (Vecsey 1997; see Vecsey 1996, 1999; Archambault, Thiel, and Vecsey 2003) must focus on Kateri Tekakwitha, the seventeenth-century Mohawk (the easternmost nation in the Iroquois Confederacy), whose conversion to Catholicism under Jesuit auspices and heroic austerities have inspired both Native Americans and non-Indians to this day. On October 21, 2012 the Roman Catholic Church will canonize Saint Kateri, thus recognizing her miraculous sanctity.

On that day she will join St. Juan Diego Cuauhtlatoatzin, the legendary Mexican Indian (d. 1548), canonized in 2002, as the only two Native Americans declared as saints by the Catholic Church. The Russian Orthodox Church glorified Peter the Aleut, Martyr (d. 1815) as a saint in 1980, and in 1985 the Episcopal Church named David Pendleton Oakerhater, Cheyenne (d. 1931) the first American Indian Anglican saint. In 2010 the Episcopal Church added Rev. Samson Occom, Mohegan (d. 1792), to its calendar of saints.

In Roman Catholicism it is a "constant tradition" (Cunningham 2009: 70), a living symbol of faith, "to venerate the saints, to name our children after them, to dedicate churches under their patronage, to invoke their names as we pray, to honor their memory in the liturgy, and to seek out their example for our own way of life."

Many Catholics already regard Kateri as a model and intercessor, especially Native Catholics, for whom she serves as a symbol of their dual identity. Scores of Catholic Indians will attend Kateri's canonization. That day should provide emotional fulfillment for many who feel kinship with her and who express devotional piety toward her.

Kateri's footprints have been trail markers of spirituality along the path of Native American Catholicism. The aim of this book is to document the relationship between Indian Catholics and their beloved Kateri Tekakwitha: to tell her saintly story as her Jesuit mentors recorded it, but more to the point, to tell the stories of her Native devotees with their eyes on her as guiding exemplar. Hence the title: *Native Footsteps along the Path of Saint Kateri Tekakwitha*.

In 1667 the missionaries of the Society of Jesus encountered a young Mohawk girl in the village of Ganadawage (near Fonda, New York) in the Mohawk River valley. The Jesuits entered Iroquois territory in order to contact Huron converts captured and adopted by the Iroquois in fur trade warfare between 1649 and 1654. The priests were agents both of the Roman Catholic Church and the government of New France; in both capacities they hoped to pacify, and perhaps transform, the Iroquois through ambitious evangelization.

The girl, Tekakwitha—"She-pushes-with-Her-Hands" or "Who walks groping for Her Way" (Béchard 1994: n.p.; Weiser 1972: 36-37), a description of a youngster pockmarked, partially crippled, and nearly blinded by a 1660 smallpox epidemic that killed her Christian Algonquin mother and Mohawk father—was born in 1656 in a nearby village, Ossernenon (not far from Auriesville, New York). In 1667 she was living in the household of her uncle, a Mohawk trading ally of the Dutch at Fort Orange (now Albany) and opponent of French Catholic incursions.

Despite Mohawk reluctance the Jesuits built a chapel at Ganadawage, hung a painting of Christ crucified over the altar, flanked by portraits of Mary and Joseph, and said daily masses. While attending to the captive Hurons, the Jesuits attracted interest among some Mohawks, including Tekakwitha, who received baptism from Father James de Lamberville, S.J., in 1676, at the age of nineteen. She received the Christian name of Catherine (Kateri, in Mohawk), after Saint Catherine of Siena.

Although for a time Kateri maintained aspects of a Catholic life—observing the liturgical calendar, resting on the Sabbath, attending mass—her christening aroused hostility among members of her extended family. At the urging of an older sister who had fled the Mohawk homeland to the French stronghold along the St. Lawrence River, Kateri made her way in 1677 with a "breakaway group of Iroquois" (Greer 2005: 99) to St. Peter's Mission at La Prairie, near Montreal. The Jesuits called this community a "reduction," a site for gathering in potential converts and neophyte Christians under clerical rule, set apart from undue influences, both French and Native.

Here Kateri met Father Pierre Cholenec, S.J., the reduction's mentor. Here she joined the rounds of piety—mass, catechism, the stations of the cross, the singing of hymns, the recitation of the ten commandments, the telling of rosary prayers—and soon earned repute as an "angel of charity" (in Weiser 1972: 149). She was known to care for the sick, the aged and the indigent; her acts of kindness were matched by her words of charitableness. Only a year since her baptism she appeared remarkably devout; therefore, Father Cholenec heard her first confession and she received first communion at Christmas in 1677.

Over the winter of 1678 Kateri went with an Indian hunting party, during which she was falsely accused of sexual impropriety. She determined to prove her purity when she returned to St. Peter's. Back at Kahnawake Kateri joined a circle of Iroquoian women, including Marie-Thérèse Tegaiaguenta, an Oneida widow, who engaged in ascetic disciplines—fasting, flogging one another with willow shoots, pricking themselves with thorns, exposing themselves to the elements, and wearing iron belts as implements of chastisement (see Béchard 1976: 159-198), as a means of expiating their sinfulness in an ethos of Catholic Indian self-sacrifice.

Following the model of the Hospitalier nuns at the Hôtel-Dieu in Montreal and other sisters of Québec, the sodality of women—the Holy Family confraternity, or the "Slavery of the Blessed Virgin," as they called themselves (Béchard 1994: 104), "scourged each other, 'intermingling prayer and penance,' after which they ran to the church, their hearts overflowing with joy" (108). Father Cholenec provided them with spiritual direction, yet their impetus seemed their own as they sought their special form of Christian identity.

Soon Kateri exceeded the others in self-abnegating imitation of Christ and identification with the Blessed Virgin Mary. She trod barefoot in the snow and ice. She ate ashes and whipped herself until she bled. She took a vow of perpetual sexual abstinence, like those of nearby nuns. While persisting in her acts of charity she became a "great penitent" (109), dedicating herself to the mortification of the flesh. In so doing she drew upon Iroquoian—as well as Catholic—paradigms of self-torture and female virginity. She was "no mere passive spectator in this unfolding of her life story: she embraced what the missionaries and other converts held out to her" and she engaged in a "revitalization" of Iroquois culture through her conversion and asceticism (Koppedrayer 1993: 294-295; see Blanchard 1982: 94).

When her privations weakened her, the Jesuits attempted to moderate her practices, to no avail. Indeed, she seemed to augment her discipline until she died during Holy Week in 1680, following last rites, at the age of twenty-four.

Perhaps Kateri would have passed into obscurity; however, several Jesuits recorded the details of her life and death, and then her astounding afterlife. Although she left behind no writings and only her bodily relics and personal effects, she is said to be "more fully and richly documented than ... any other indigenous person of North or South America in the colonial period" (Greer 2005: [vii]), because of the extensive hagiography penned by Father Cholenec [see Document 1] and his confrere Father Claude Chauchetière, S.J. Because of their literary memorials, today there are some three hundred books written about Kateri and her heritage.

At her death Cholenec was amazed by the transformation of her appearance. Her smallpox-scarred face became clear and beautiful, a miraculous sign of her sanctity according to the Church in later years (and sufficient for her beatification three centuries later, in 1980). Due to her transfiguration and the holiness of her behavior before death, the Iroquois gazing upon her corpse "began to 'regard her body as a precious relic,' kissing her hands and treating all her personal possessions as sacred objects" (Greer 2005: 17), at least according to the Jesuits. Cholenec wrote that "her death had inspired those in mourning to emulate her sanctity" (Bonaparte 2009: 221). He continued:

> There was no delay in seeing the effect, for the next day, on Good Friday, all hearts were so touched at the sight of the cross which Katharine had so loved and which the priest showed them after his sermon on the Passion, that I think that never was seen so piteous a spectacle, or rather, one so devout and touching, for suddenly everyone began to burst forth with such loud cries and sobs that it was necessary to let them weep for quite a long time.... The fruit of all this was that they no longer talked of anything but of being converted and of giving themselves entirely to God. That same day and the next and for eight days running, such excessive penances were performed in the settlement that it would be difficult for greater to be done by the most austere penitents in the world. (In *ibid.*: 221)

Thus, Native devotion to Kateri began immediately upon her death, in emotional mourning and emulation of her.

In Cholenec's account Kateri appeared shortly after her death to her dear companion Marie-Thérèse, telling her, "I have come to say goodbye. I am going to Heaven" (Bonaparte 2009: 228). In subsequent years

Kateri took the apparitional form of the sun in mid-heaven, informing Chauchetière of God's will that the Jesuits should make pictures of Kateri, to be used in their missionary efforts.

Surely the Jesuits played a significant role in fostering devotions to the late Kateri, who made spectral visits to them in the 1680s. Despite Chauchetière's misgivings about broadcasting her saintliness—because "she was an Indian" (Greer 2005: 22)—he came to see her as "the instrument of his salvation" (86). Thus, he and Cholenec extolled her virtue in print and perpetuated her memory. Chauchetière even painted her likeness, as she appeared to him in visions. This image, completed around 1690, still hangs in the rectory of St. Francis Xavier Mission at Kahnawake, Québec.

About six months after her death and for years to come in the vicinity of La Prairie, the Jesuits facilitated miracles attributed to her. They employed earth from her grave, rotten wood from her coffin, pictures of her, ejaculations of her name, water drunk from her cup, pieces of her clothing, and other relics associated with her, in order to cure local French *habitants*, and a Puritan boy-captive suffering from smallpox—whose New England community rejected such cures. The word "miracle" spread throughout the region and "the healing cult soon spread" (Greer 2005: 151, 152).

However, not among the Mohawks, even though the Jesuits moved Kateri's remains to a new wooden chapel in 1684, in order to accommodate, as Chauchetière put it, "so many good savages" (Bonaparte 2009: 244) who offered their "devotion" to her. Advertised by a small monument to her, Chauchetière wrote, "Some savages have since been seen to go to pray at the place where she lies, who had begun to go to visit her on the very day when she was buried." The Natives made pilgrimages to her remains, and moved her each time the Kahnawake Mohawks re-settled their community, but they did not seek her healing help in the decades after her death. As an historian notes,

> The Tekakwitha curing cult never caught on among the Christian Iroquois of Kahnawake. In spite of the Jesuits' promotional efforts and even though the cult centered on one of their own, the people of Kahnawake showed much less interest in saintly curing than did their French-Canadian neighbors. Iroquois Christians honored the memory of Tekakwitha, but they were not accustomed to seeking cures and other 'favors' from the dead. (Greer 2005: 157)

To the contrary, contact with dirt from her grave seemed to hurry Iroquois Christian patients to death and heaven. "At a time when Tekakwitha was being hailed by white settlers as the source of health-giving magic, she was ill equipped to fill that role for native people, and for one basic reason: she was dead" (*ibid.*: 159). To this day some Mohawks, even those whose family members have "experienced the powerful presence of a Káteri relic," regard its use in healing as "a ghoulish, medieval practice" (Bonaparte 2009: 268).

In the eighteenth century Iroquois devotion to Kateri never ceased in the Christian communities of Québec and New York. When a group of Kahnawake families formed a colony at St. Regis (Akwesasne) in 1755, they took with them half of her body; however, it was destroyed in a church fire in 1762, thus diminishing her impact among the Akwesasne Mohawks until the twentieth century. At Kahnawake, however, the cult of Kateri was continuous, sponsored by Jesuits and engaged by Natives and non-Natives alike.

At the same time the Jesuits broadcast her name to their mission stations across North America, heralding her as an archetype of evangelical transformation. In 1724, for instance, Jesuit hagiography regarding Kateri had spread to Mexico City, where her extraordinary virtue was used to justify a convent for Indians. In Baja California in 1771 a German Jesuit gave tidings of the Mohawk maiden, "whose grave with its many miracles shines brightly in Canada" (Baegert 1979: 86). Thus her story grew. The suppression of the Jesuits worldwide in 1773 diminished the attention paid to her, but in the nineteenth century the Jesuit revival resurrected the legendary Kateri on an international Catholic stage.

In the meantime some Mohawks had followed the fur trade west to the Rocky Mountains, spreading their Catholicism with them among American Indian peoples such as the Salish-speaking Flatheads, with whom they intermarried. Kateri's renown, however, was still limited to the Mohawks around Kahnawake. There are undocumented reports that around 1880 these Mohawks submitted to the Vatican—through Jesuit couriers—a petition requesting her canonization. When the Third Plenary Council of Bishops met in Baltimore in 1884, the Catholic officials received at least one appeal [see **Document 2**], forwarded by the Society of Jesus, from the Flathead Indians of Montana, where the Jesuits had established a mission. The missive called for Kateri to become "an object of ... veneration in the church" (Walworth 1891: 313;

see Walworth 1908: 5) in order to promote more Indian conversions to Catholicism and to inspire the Catholic Indian faithful.

The Third Plenary Council responded by fostering two shrines for Kateri—one at Kahnawake and the other at Auriesville, amidst the newly established pilgrimage site honoring the Jesuit martyrs of the seventeenth-century Iroquoian missions—and by submitting a request to the Vatican for an investigation into Kateri's possible sanctity and eventual canonization. In 1885 pilgrims began to arrive at Kateri's birthplace in Auriesville; however, the emphasis there was on the Jesuit martyrs, who also received priority in Vatican proceedings toward canonization.

Only in 1932—two years after the Jesuit martyrs were canonized—was Kateri Tekakwitha formally presented to the Vatican for consideration of sainthood, according to the rubrics codified by Roman Catholic canon law in 1917 (see Woodward 1990: 77-86), procedures dating to the Middle Ages. In order to determine her sanctity, orthodoxy, virtue, and miraculous intercession, the curial Sacred Congregation of Rites (now called the Congregation for the Causes of Saints) produced in 1940 a required *Positio* (see Sacred Congregation of Rites 1940)—a collection of biographical evidence regarding Kateri. Based on the positive recommendation of the Sacred Congregation, Pope Pius XII declared her Venerable in 1943, and her shrine in Fonda (established in 1938) was further separated from the Jesuit martyrs, once she was declared worthy of veneration.

By this time devotion to Kateri had spread to many Jesuit missions among American Indians in North America. Catholic missionaries named some of their stations after her, such as one among the Navajos in 1921. Catholic schools honored her life story through plays, pamphlets, prayer cards, and other traditions, including the naming of newborn babies. On several occasions during the 1930s the Jesuits at Holy Rosary Mission in South Dakota, among the Lakota Sioux, produced devotional pageants of Kateri's life, emphasizing her resistance to the indigenous beliefs and practices of her Mohawk relatives. The dramatic denouement consisted of Kateri's escape to Kahnawake, saved by the blackrobes. Although the script, "Princess of the Mohawks" in 1938, was the work of a non-Indian man, a local Jesuit enthused:

> Every feature was Indian, the cast of mission pupils, stage scenery
> painted by an Indian, Indian saint, Indian band playing Indian airs
> under its Indian leader, ... and costumes of old tribal paraphernalia

borrowed from our Indian homes. It is doubtful if this display of authentic regalia could be duplicated. (In Scott 1963: n.p.)

Catholic clerics were already evoking the saintly Mohawk for their own purposes. A Jesuit in Oregon in 1933 called on Kateri's aid to help pay mission bills and another priest in Minnesota erected a local shrine to the Lily of the Mohawks, "for whose beatification the Indians are eager, having formed a Tekakwitha League" (*Our Negro and Indian Missions* 1939: 42; see 1933: 41), where they read Catholic devotional literature and recited prayers and hymns. Similar developments were taking shape among the Salish-speaking Coeur d'Alenes in Idaho [see Document 3].

In the same year, 1939, the Bishop of Fargo, North Dakota, organized a support group for missionary priests and brothers in the north-central plains and northwest United States, as well as western Canada; he named it the Tekakwitha Conference. For four decades several dozen missionaries attended annual meetings, with a few Indian men participating, under Kateri's name, praying and planning strategy for the enhancement of American Indians Catholicism. With the impetus of the Second Vatican Council, 1962-1965, some of these missionaries began to consider ways of "inculturating" Catholic faith among American Indians (making it meaningful within their cultural patterns), and in 1976 the conferees discussed the symbiotic relationship between "native symbolism and Christian spirituality" (Starkloff 1982: n.p.). Only two Native Americans were in attendance among the three dozen discussants.

The following year, however, witnessed a transformation of the Tekakwitha Conference into a more inclusive organization, with some Native Catholic officers—including women—determined to attract other Indians. In 1978 fifty Native participants joined more than a hundred non-Indians at the annual meeting. At the subsequent conference, 1979, the Indians took over the proceedings, displacing most of the existing leadership and insisting upon Native participation in the Tekakwitha Conference and in the Church more generally.

Some Church authorities responded with funds and encouragement for a national institution that would promote the spirit of Kateri Tekakwitha—her Native identity and her Catholic spirituality, accommodated to one another—and, they hoped, her eventual canonization. Since that time the National Tekakwitha Conference has been an important factor in Native Catholic communities both in the United States and Canada, prompting liturgical, theological, and ecclesiological inculturation among American Indian Catholics. Not only at the annual conventions, but also through the formation of local Kateri Circles, prayer groups seeking spiritual fulfillment through the explicit intercession of Kateri. The leaders of the Tekakwitha Conference avowed loyalty to Kateri's model of developing a "Native Catholic Church, not in traditional [i.e., European] Roman Catholic ways but in Native ways" (*Tekakwitha Conference Newsletter* 9, no. 2, June 1990: 22). By the 1990s the Kateri Circles, proclaiming their kinship with and devotion to Kateri, numbered over 130 in North America [**see Document 4**].

In 1980 Pope John Paul II declared Kateri Tekakwitha Blessed. With this beatification—the second of three steps toward declared sainthood in the Roman Catholic Church—the Vatican established Kateri's feast days (April 17 in Canada, July 14 in the United States). The disappearance of her facial scars at the time of her death constituted a first requisite miracle, according to curial investigators. Canonization would require a second. When the annual Tekakwitha Conference took place in the summer of that year, the delegations of American Indian Catholics and others—numbering close to a thousand—rejoiced at Kateri's elevated title and prayed for the final miracle that would open the way for her canonization.

In the meantime in Kateri's name they sought "the inculturation of the gospel in native life" (Starkloff 1982: n.p.). Between 1980 and the present day Kateri has served as the focal point for Indian Catholic aspirations, a personage embodying both Catholic and Native identities. As a scholar wrote in 1997, "Before her beatification in 1980, Kateri was known primarily where Jesuits or Mohawks had spread her news. Now she is an American Indian saint-in-the-making, a symbol of Native American Catholic ideals and practice" (Vecsey 1997: 103). According to Reverend Edmund Savilla (2012), in 1981 "Many of the Indigenous peoples of the Southwest, U.S. knew little about Kateri." When asked to compose a working paper for the Tekakwitha Conference that year, he took "an opportunity to introduce and contemplate on the life of Kateri as a sister of Hope, for the Church of the Southwest" [**see Document 5**].

A few years afterward, it was apparent to Abenaki Bishop Donald E. Pellotte that Kateri had "virtually been adopted by all Native Americans throughout the country" (in McDonnell 1987: 19), and increasingly in Canada, too. (In the 1990s Catholic missionaries introduced devotions to Kateri among indigenous peoples in South America, adding to her fame.) Some, like Msgr. Paul A. Lenz, then director of the Bureau of

Catholic Indian Missions, even suggested that the upsurge of devotions to Kateri had "miraculous" aspects. In "the spirit of unification" since her beatification there was "a healing effect" (in *ibid*.: 22) among American Indian Catholics, and especially in the Tekakwitha Conference and the burgeoning Kateri Circles.

Some skeptics (e.g., Kozak 1991: 4-6; Martin 2010: 28, 150) have ascribed the growth of Kateri devotions since 1980 to manipulative policies of inculturation by Church officials. Other observers have suggested that the movement has bypassed her closest kinfolk, the Mohawk people. One scholar quotes a Mohawk man who regards Kateri as "a romanticized heroine, fictionalized like Disneyland. Kateri doesn't touch me," he avers. Her revered image? "It's manufactured by the Church" (in Holmes 2000: 118). Historian Allan Greer (2005) writes, "When I first visited Kahnawake in 1993, I had difficulty finding anyone interested in talking about Catherine Tekakwitha" (200). Rather, he said, "there had been talk [during a politically charged period in 1990] of destroying Kahnawake's Tekakwitha shrine as a symbol of spiritual conquest and oppression" (*ibid*.). Greer continued:

> I attended mass in the chapel and listened while Kahnawake Catholics prayed for Tekakwitha's canonization. It seemed to me that the faithful band of believers dedicated to the cause of their local saint was rather small and, on average, of advanced years. Most villagers I spoke with outside the church were somewhat dismissive of the Mohawk saint, inclined to treat her story as a myth generated by centuries of religious and cultural imperialism. (*Ibid*.)

A Mohawk intellectual, Darren Bonaparte (2009), criticizes Greer for implying that Kateri is not honored at home among her fellows, and provides a list of Mohawk "advocates" (267) for her saintly cause, as well as members of Kahnawake Catholic prayer circles. He asserts that Kateri's "own people have been her strongest advocates, attending in great numbers her beatification ceremony at the Vatican in 1980, as well as faithfully participating in the annual Tekakwitha Conference held throughout North America" (260). Observers found in the 1990s that devotion to Kateri was palpable among Mohawk stalwarts, despite strong overtones of hostility to Catholicism in Mohawk communities, where she was sometimes referred to as a "traitor to her people," and worse (in Preston 1991; see Vecsey 1997: 107-108).

No more vivid than in the person of Sarah Monroe Hassenplug, a St. Regis Mohawk woman (recently deceased) who portrayed Kateri in pageants for two decades. Residing in Syracuse, New York she often visited the National Kateri Tekakwitha Shrine in Fonda, well before Kateri's beatification, where she said, "I feel Tekakwitha's presence" (in Bandy 1974: 4). Hassenplug's likeness in Kateri's guise graced many items of devotional literature and her performances—at annual meetings of the Tekakwitha Conference, in Fonda, and elsewhere—elicited tears and standing ovations. She herself spoke of getting "goosebumps of excitement" as she meditated upon "kind, sweet, gentle" Kateri, in preparation for her monologues (Fargo, August 6, 1989). A few months before her death in 2012 she told a visitor at St. Lucy's Church of the great fulfillment she felt, having been recognized as Kateri's impersonator.

In like manner, Sister Kateri Mitchell, S.S.A., a Mohawk and presently executive director of the Tekakwitha Conference, grew up in a culture of devotion to Kateri Tekakwitha [see Document 6]. Her people, she says, have been celebrating Catholic liturgy in Mohawk language for centuries, combining Mohawk and Catholic symbols; hence, she is comfortable in both circles. She feels at home reciting the traditional Iroquois thanksgiving address, as she does in Catholic liturgy and sees little contradiction between them. She co-composed and has often performed a hymn about her spiritual ancestor, after whom she is named: "Kateri Tekakwitha, Noble Mother, Turtle Earth Gathers her people, East, South, West and North." She noted that the Lily of the Mohawks has gathered diverse Catholic Indian peoples together by focusing their devotion upon herself. It is Kateri's power, she avowed, to "inspire Indian Catholicism" (Mitchell, August 7, 1986). Significantly for this volume the hymn is called "In Her Footsteps" [see Document 7].

For Iroquois in Syracuse St. Lucy's Church has served as a locale for Kateri devotions since the late 1970s, when Sister Mary Elizabeth Lagoy—of partial Algonquin heritage—created a Native prayer group within the parish. Mohawk artists, dancers and storytellers instilled the group with Native imagery, as Lagoy established an Indian chapel within St. Lucy's, portraying Iroquois clans, with a large mural of Kateri gracing the space. Throughout the 1980s St. Lucy's Kateri Committee—made up primarily of Mohawk women such as Peg Bova, Anna Dyer, Julie Degonzack Daniels, and Sarah Hassenplug—conducted outreach to Iroquois communities throughout New York State, including St. Regis, and organized a regional Tekakwitha Conference. They venerated Kateri during Easter season, in commemoration of her death, and evoked her on All Souls' Day each year in honor of their ancestors at their Fallen Leaves Mass and Feast.

To enhance their ceremonies, Peg Bova composed a hymn, "Tewanaton Ne Kateri" ("We Sing of One Named Kateri"), which has become popular in many Kateri Circles throughout the United States:

> We sing of one named Kateri,
> A holy maiden of Mohawk tribe.
> Her one true love was Jesus the Lord,
> And chosen was she to be His bride.
> O lovely lily sweet and pure,
> Most wondrous flower of Indian race.
> The likeness of our Kateri,
> Lured by His love the Cross to embrace.
> Forbidden by her tribal friends,
> To follow Christ, her Beloved One.
> When urged to wed, she heard His call,
> And vowed her love to God's own Son.
> One day she fled from Mohawk shores,
> To Kahnawake was her flight.
> And there she felt the warmth of her Christ,
> And cared for the needy day and night.
> Still very young was Kateri,
> When pain and weakness ended her life.
> "I love you, Jesus" were her words,
> As heaven replaced her earthly strife.
> Upon her deathbed came a great light,
> Her pock-marked face was clean and bright.
> Amazed and awed were all who were there,
> And knew they saw a Maiden of prayer[.]
> Today we ask this friend of the Lord's
> To listen to our need as we sing.
> And peace the fruit of orderliness,
> Our Tekakwitha to us will bring. (St. Regis 1995)

In this way St. Lucy's Mohawks have spread the word about Kateri to their fellow Native Americans across the continent. They have also employed the National Tekakwitha Conference as a means of celebrating

Kateri, for example in 1995, when the annual convention traveled between St. Regis and Kahnawake, demonstrating the centrality of Kateri for the Catholic Iroquois and the significance of Iroquois Catholicism to Native Americans in the Church.

The 1995 Tekakwitha Conference showed the effectiveness of the Kateri Circles of St. Regis and Kahnawake—and even the benign acquiescence of Mohawk traditionalists, usually suspicious of Catholic pieties—as the litany of Catholic Mohawk elders was intoned, as the Mohawk choir sang "Tewanaton Ne Kateri," and as the long lines of pilgrims filed past Kateri's tomb in the St. Francis Xavier Church, tears in their eyes. In their liturgy at Kahnawake they prayed "that Blessed Kateri be recognized as a saint by the whole Church":

> O God, who, among the many marvels of Your Grace in the New World, did cause to blossom on the banks of the Mohawk and of the St. Lawrence, the pure and tender Lily, Kateri Tekakwitha, grant we beseech You, the favor we beg through her intercession; that this Young Lover of Jesus and of His Cross may soon be counted among the Saints by Holy Mother Church, and that our hearts may be enkindled with a stronger desire to imitate her innocence and faith. Through the same Christ Our Lord. Amen. (Kahnawake 1995; see Vecsey 1997: 134-137)

At the close of the Kahnawake Eucharistic Celebration in 1995 a narrator told of a dying Native American woman who painted a likeness of Kateri to be presented the shrine. "The Tekakwitha Conference has come home," she told her sons, "and I want my painting to be there." After her death the sons brought the portrait in their care from the United States to Canada. When they were asked at the border if they had anything to declare, they replied, "Yes. We have a saint in the back seat" (Kahnawake 1995).

For Theresa Steele, an Algonquin woman living in Syracuse and a member of St. Lucy's parish, Kateri has always been "our saint. We didn't even know that she *wasn't* a saint yet" (Fonda, July 15, 1989). Over the years she has needed to remind her Mohawk friends that Kateri was of Algonquin as well as Iroquois heritage. Perhaps for that reason Sarah Hassenplug chose Ms. Steele to recite the Kateri monologue when Ms. Hassenplug became too old to play the role.

Clearly Kateri has gained the attention of many American Indians beyond the Mohawks, especially since 1980. If one attends the annual Tekakwitha Conference meetings, one can witness Native people—especially women—praying before her statue, meditating upon her image, even touching her likeness. An observer witnessed one Indian woman caressing Kateri's face on a banner, and then applying her hand to her own facial features, "thus identifying herself with the Mohawk maiden's characteristics" (Vecsey 1997: 105).

The late Sister Marie Therese Archambault, O.S.F., a Hunkpapa Lakota Sioux, made sense of the intense Native identification with Kateri. Her "scarred but beautiful" face makes Indians think of their own experiences of suffering. Her condition as an orphan, the persecution she received from her relatives, her refugee status, her damage from disease, all resonate with situations Indians have endured. Thus, "she is a symbol of their hurt humanity, ... a first step to their healing, the raising of their self-esteem" (Vecsey 1997: 106).

> She has this power, according to Archambault, because Kateri is also an expression of divinity, a symbol of divine love, a self-offering like Christ Himself. Especially because she was an Indian, she can serve as meditational device for Native Americans. Indians can think of her to reflect upon their condition, but also to reflect upon sanctifying grace. When Indians pray for more miracles from her, when they pray for her canonization, they are meditating on her sanctified nature—which is the role of saints in the cultic life of Christians. (*Ibid.*)

Sister Archambault found Kateri's prowess especially appealing to Native women, because of her "relational, feminine" qualities (Archambault 1991: 6). This Mohawk woman has provided a useful complement to Jesus as a focus of devotion, because she was a woman, and also because she was an Indian. Even before she was canonized, many American Indian Catholics—including the Association of Native Religious and Clergy [**see Document 8**]—called her "Saint Kateri" (Orono, August 8, 1992), an ancestral, virginal matriarch with whom they could identify, a "traditional" Indian whose Catholic saintliness grew out of her "native spirituality" (Fonda, July 15, 1989).

For many decades Catholic missionaries have been encouraging devotions to Kateri among Native American populations. Especially among Indian women. In the 1890s Father Francis M. Craft, descended from the Mohawks and well aware of Kateri and the Jesuit martyrs of Auriesville, established a controversial sisterhood for at least a dozen Lakota Sioux women, one of whom—Josephine [Catherine] Crowfeather—he termed the "Lily of the Dakotas," following "Kateri's archetype" (Vecsey 1999: 267; see Ewens 1988: 12). Sister Mary Ewens, O.P. [**see Document**

9], depicts The American Congregation, founded by Father Craft in the 1890s, as the fulfillment of Kateri's dream to establish an order of Indian women religious. A century later Sister Eva Solomon, C.S.J., an Ojibway in Ontario, hoped to form a Native sisterhood, Companions of Kateri Tekakwitha. Simultaneously several Mohawk women at St. Regis considered forming a Native sisterhood under Kateri's banner, having received Kateri's visionary incentive. Neither of these latter efforts have come to fruition; however, they show the inspiration Kateri provides to Catholic Indian women.

Throughout the twentieth century the cult of Kateri blossomed. When the Church declared Kateri Venerable in 1943, Father Michael Jacobs, S.J., a Mohawk priest, re-kindled devotions to Kateri among the St. Regis Mohawks, by leading pilgrimages to her grave in Kahnawake. At the same time Catholic clerics in the American Southwest were eager to disseminate her story, for instance, among Pueblo Indians among whom she was hitherto unknown.

Following her beatification in 1980 Church authorities began to name parishes after Blessed Kateri Tekakwitha, such as one in Tucson and another on the Barona Indian Reservation in the diocese of San Diego, both dedicated to American Indians of the area. In reservation churches all across the United States and Canada, from coast to coast, one can find statues, paintings, stained glass windows, banners, and murals of Kateri. One can see these in Pala, California; Pine Ridge, South Dakota; Swinomish, Washington; and on both Passamaquoddy territories in Maine. At Laguna, New Mexico the church juxtaposes Indian and Christian cosmologies, and cornmeal offerings are made to Kateri's statue. Alex Seowtewa, the Zuni artist, has included a statue of Kateri in his syncretistic restoration of Our Lady of Guadalupe church in New Mexico, amidst his murals of Zuni kachinas.

The Southwest has been an especially receptive region for Kateri devotion. A tenth of all Kateri Circles are in New Mexico, with a robust following among Pueblo Indian women. In a dissertation Paula Elizabeth Holmes (2000; see Holmes 2001) has analyzed "an emergent Native Catholicism" (2000: 8) among these women—"devotion to Kateri is largely women's business" (20)—for whom Kateri is one of the most prominent agents of their inculturation. Thus she tells of an Isleta woman who became interested in Kateri when she was beatified in 1980. Having known nothing of Kateri, she created her own image of her (2), which she regarded as a real representation of sanctity. "*This is a saint to me*" (3, italics in original), she declared. She decided to make a shrine to Kateri. She dreamed of her. During a Tekakwitha Conference she visited Kahnawake, where Kateri is buried and had a highly emotional response: "My mouth got dry, I couldn't speak, I started to shake" (4).

She felt that Kateri was represented in a crystal she received from a woman at Kahnawake:

> This crystal had taken me up to see a great beautiful light, the holy light of God. I think that that star has a lot to do with Blessed Kateri, I really, really do. That healing part was for all people to come together believing in that same God. I promised Blessed Kateri that I would do her work—the work that she never got to do—she got sick and all those things happened to her and she died so young. I made that promise to her—to help all those people who came. (5)

In the Isleta woman's view, Kateri's "*message is unity*" (6, italics in original). Kateri's "people," she opined,

> were doing a lot of atrocities; that's why she left them. She couldn't stand the fighting, adultery, drinking. She didn't want to stay around. I think I've experienced a lot of things that she went through, like pain. She ran away from her people; she didn't want to be with her people, but those were her last days too. God has our time set and probably God wanted her to be baptized, and who would have baptized her in Mohawk country? She wanted to be baptized most in her life. Kateri was loved when she was first born, but after that, with such an Indian way at that time, such a traditional people, it must have been very hard on her. (6)

Holmes takes this testimony of a Pueblo woman to symbolize the "private and communal devotional activities that center around Kateri" (8), especially at Tekakwitha Conference meetings.

Another Isleta woman told Holmes how Kateri saved her daughter, who had been involved in gangs, drugs, and drinking. "'All I did was pray to Kateri,'" she testified. "'During that time, I got really strong with Kateri'" (157). A priest told her to say, "'Kateri, I give you my daughter. I put her life in your hands. Please take care of her and keep her safe. And I repeated it over and over, lifting my hands like this up to heaven'" (157). Then she convinced her daughter to go on a pilgrimage, and once again she gave her daughter over to Kateri. Within a week the daughter changed her ways. The mother concluded: "I bought her a statue of Kateri for her apartment. She keeps i[t] on her dresser with some little angels. I always tell her that they are all watching over her." The mother called her daughter "a miracle herself. *If it wasn't for Kateri, I don't know where my daughter would be.* That's a miracle in itself. She was ready to go off the deep end when Kateri saved her" (158, italics in original).

Indian Catholics seeking to overcome alcoholism and drug abuse often have turned to Kateri for help. In Holmes's conversations with "Kateri ladies" (154) in the late 1990s, they also spoke of Kateri's power to cure illness and they used the term "miracle" (165) to depict her efficacy. An Acoma woman married to a St. Regis Mohawk told Holmes of a "beautiful dream" in which she beheld

> "Blessed Kateri in the sky and in this big, big circle, there were all of the Native people who go to the [Tekakwitha] Conferences. I guess that's what it resembled, all different in their Native outfits. And right in the middle there was this face and it was slowly turning, turning and it was coming around and it turned towards me and it was Blessed Kateri.... All the time that she was turning she was saying to me 'It's all the same.' She just kept saying those words. I never had that kind of dream before. They say that when you have visions, that's from God, it's completely different from the dreams you have nightly. This one was so pretty, really pretty and it was in the sky." (172)

According to the Acoma woman her dream communicated a message that traditional and Catholic ways were one and the same "straight path" (173). Holmes infers that "this vision of unity and coherence and duality" (173) is common to Kateri's Southwestern devotees, especially those who participate in Kateri Circles and the Tekakwitha Conference. It is a theme of inculturation carried by a holy woman who was an Indian.

Holmes remarks, "When I asked the women I interviewed what they would tell others about Kateri, almost all began by emphasizing Kateri's Indian identity" (234). "Kateri's devotees believe," Holmes writes, "that the Iroquois convert never abandoned her 'tradition' and followed God as both an Indian and a Catholic" (212). Therefore, she walked the path where the two roads—one Indian, one Catholic—meet. In order to follow in her footsteps, these Pueblo devotees place her images, especially plaster statues, all around their homes. In particular, "these plaster Kateris are understood to be emotive beings, having the ability to inspire and evoke feelings of peace and goodness in the things and people around them" (250). The women treat their Kateri in a "familiar and familial way" (251). They make offerings of food, flowers, prayer cards, and other gifts to her, as one of their honored *santos*, along with

Our Lady of Guadalupe, Jesus, and other honored guests. Sometimes a Pueblo woman will dress Kateri's statue in Pueblo dress, "in order to 'make her Pueblo'" (252), and thus "she is physically transformed into 'one of us'" (253).

Pueblo women embrace Kateri in a manner, they say, that her Mohawk people do not. A Mohawk, Darren Bonaparte, responds that the effect of the Tekakwitha Conference and its many Kateri Circles has been the production of "shrines, statues, and chapels ... sprung up in various places to honor the Lily of the Mohawks." In his eyes Kateri "has taken on not only a pan-Indian appearance, but a New Age mysticism that bears little resemblance to the Mohawk ascetic she really was" (Bonaparte 2009: 260). Consequently he calls for a "Mohawk repatriation" (268) of Kateri Tekakwitha, saying, "She has been someone else's symbol long enough" [see Document 10].

Anthropologist James J. Preston spent fifteen years interviewing Mohawk devotees of Kateri, in order to document the making of a saint (Preston 1989). His findings, composed in 2000 [see Document 11], provide a stimulating academic counterpart to Holmes's study of Pueblo devotions. Mohawks' ambivalence toward Catholicism and Kateri is evident in Preston's essay, but so is their loyalty to one of their own.

In like manner Mark G. Thiel's 1994-1995 interviews with Catholic Indians—Lakota Sioux, but also including Navajos, Pueblo Indians, and others—give readers the opportunity to encounter Native Catholic testimonies about their Kateri devotions in the years before her canonization, without inordinate filtering [see Interviews]. These invaluable primary documents demonstrate the growth of Kateri's renown since the 1970s, and especially since her beatification in 1980. Several interviews from 2012 add to the corpus and reflect on Kateri's approaching canonization.

For the Indians in these interviews Kateri's great appeal is that she is an Indian woman, perhaps a distant relative, formerly unknown, but someone who can be called a sister, someone who listens to her fellow Natives in conversation and prayer, someone who has the power to unite all Indian peoples through common identity. The interviews show how strongly Catholic Indians identify with her life story; how much they wish to emulate her; how often they call upon her in times of need; and how responsive she is to them. Many of the interviewees tell of visiting her tomb; they memorialize those pilgrimages by bringing home dirt and other memorabilia from her homeland. They also recall her enshrinement in their local communities and the establishment of their local Kateri Circles. A key feature of these narratives consists of her dramatic intercession in healing the wounds and ills of their family members, and the outpouring of appreciation these Indians have felt for her.

The interviews also provide insight to the range of spiritual practices of contemporary American Indian Catholics. These native people are devoted to Kateri. They pray to her, and through her intercession to God. They also pray for her canonization. They are attached to Mary—especially for Indians in the American Southwest, in her role as Our Lady of Gualalupe—and the saints. But they also consider divinity in terms of their indigenous cultural expressions, and these may differ from tribe to tribe. These interviews testify to the impact of the Tekakwitha Conference in raising Kateri in American Indian Catholic consciousness; they also testify to the Conference's role in promoting Native spirituality and the inculturation of Catholic faith. These processes require conceptual adjustments and raise questions about devotional loyalties, as Native Catholics with local traditions incorporate Kateri to their panoply of venerations.

Visual evidence abounds [see **Photographs**] regarding American Indian veneration to Kateri. All across Native North America—from the Abenaki of the Canadian Maritimes to the Tarahumara of Mexico, and in all regions of the United States—one can see Indian Catholics in postures of piety concerning Kateri. Kneeling in prayer, fingering rosaries, crucifixes, hymnals, and offerings, they place themselves in the company of Kateri: the iconic statues and paintings of her likeness. Dressed in tribal and liturgical regalia, these Mohawks and Lakotas, Choctaws and Cherokees, Apaches and Navajos, Penobscots and Potawatomis, Pimas and Papagos (Tohono O'odham), Pueblo peoples from Jemez, Laguna, and Zuni, the Coeur d'Alene and the Lummi, and others, process with their banners, read the mass of the word, sing Kateri's praises, and dance in honor of their Native saint. They enshrine her image in their local communities and visit her tomb in Kahnawake. They re-enact her life story in plays and monologues and follow her example with their vows and habits. Native bishops, priests, deacons, sisters, and laypersons—old and young, male and female—gather at annual Tekakwitha conferences to exalt their saint and to commune as a people, under her aegis.

The National Tekakwitha Conference, which has reached something like 50,000 Indians in the United States and Canada (Kozak 1991: 14;

see Vecsey 1999: 328-333; Holmes 1999), has been most prominent in promoting the cause of Kateri's canonization and expediting devotions to her. Non-Indians are very active in the Tekakwitha movement, and so are some non-Catholic Indians, including Protestants, some of whom yearn for such a holy personage in their own traditions, who might be called a saint.

Sometimes the efforts of the Tekakwitha Conference have taken a political turn—as they may in campaigns for Catholic sainthood, where constituencies often vie for Vatican attention. For example, Kateri's cause has been counterposed to that of Father Junipero Serra, O.F.M., the founder of California's Franciscan missions among the Indians. When Pope John Paul II held an audience with thousands of Native Catholics at the annual Tekakwitha Conference in Phoenix in 1987, the Indians were eager that he announce the canonization of Kateri. He elevated neither Serra nor Tekakwitha, but beatified Serra shortly thereafter in a trip to California (pleasing the Franciscans but displeasing many Indian Catholics).

Over the decades there has been Native impatience with the Vatican bureaucracy in ascribing a second miracle to Kateri's intervention and declaring her an official Church saint. Some thought that Pope John Paul II "blew it" (Vecsey 1999: 372) in not announcing her canonization in Phoenix in 1987. Still, many Indian Catholics proclaimed her their saint, no matter what the curial or papal judgment.

In 2006 a five-year-old boy, Jake Finkbonner, of the Lummi Indian Tribe in Ferndale, Washington, experienced an aggressive, life-threatening infection from a cut lip. Following intercessory prayers from his family and friends to Kateri Tekakwitha, the infection—necrotizing fasciitis, or strep A—ceased instantaneously. Jake's mother proclaimed to the local press, "There is no doubt in my mind that he is a miracle" (Relyea 2009).

Two years later, following an investigation by the Catholic Congregation for the Causes of Saints, the Vatican determined that Jake Finkbonner's recovery was a medical miracle caused by the intercession of Kateri Tekakwitha [**see Document 12**]. This announcement fulfilled the last outstanding requirement, a second authenticated miracle, for her canonization. Hence, on October 21, 2012, Pope Benedict XVI is expected to name Kateri officially as a saint in the Roman Catholic Church and to promulgate her feast day worldwide.

News of her imminent canonization coursed through Indian Catholic communities. In St. Lucy's parish in Syracuse Kateri's faithful—including the dying Sarah Hassenplug—celebrated the development, noting, "To us, she was a saint long ago.... What the church did, it's just a formality" (Kirst 2012). One woman expressed her feelings for the saint: "She taught that you must share, and that's being Indian.... She was always Indian. She never forgot."

Journalists remarked on "some painful historical memories" (Smith 2012) mixed with the "joy" of American Indians, noting the continued contention between Mohawk traditionalists and their Catholic brethren. Tom Porter—a former Mohawk sub-chief who returned to his ancestral homeland in the 1990s just down the road from Kateri's shrine in Fonda, in order to "revitalize Native traditions and beliefs" (Porter 2006: 161)—said, "It breaks my heart" (Smith 2012) to see his relatives "devoted to Kateri." She was "used," he claimed, as propaganda for Christian colonialism. "That saint stuff doesn't have any value in our traditions" (LaRosa 2012), he stated, although he was "happy for the Indian natives that are Christians that have worked so long for this."

Sister Kateri Mitchell, however, is unalloyed in her happiness, and she "feels that Tekakwitha's recognition will help to heal the wounds of the past. Native American Catholics have felt that they have always been on the edge, or the fringes,' of the church," Mitchell attests. "That's why our people are overwhelmed with joy at this news." She anticipates with joy the annual Tekakwitha Conference in Albany, Fonda and Auriesville this July 18-21, and of course, God willing, she will be on hand in Rome for the canonization on October 21 [see **Document 13**].

REFERENCES

Archambault, Marie Therese, O.S.F. Interview by author, Fargo, North Dakota. August 5, 1989.

———. "The Time for Turning Around." Unpublished ms. in author's possession.1991.

Archambault, Marie Therese, O.S.F., Mark G. Thiel, and Christopher Vecsey, eds. *The Crossing of Two Roads. Being Catholic and Native in the United States.* Maryknoll, NY: Orbis Books, 2003.

Baegert, Johann Jakob, S.J. *Observations in Lower California*, trans. M. M. Brandenburg and Carl L. Baumann. Berkeley: University of California Press, 1979.

Bandy, Peg Bittel. "Tekakwitha." *Syracuse Herald-American* (November 17, 1974): 4, 6-7.

Béchard, Henri, S.J. *The Original Caughnawaga Indians.* Montreal: International Publishers, 1976.

———. *Kaia'tanó:ron Kateri Tekakwitha*, trans. Antoinette Kinlough. Kahnawake, Québec: Kateri Center, 1994.

Blanchard, David. "...To the Other Side of the Sky: Catholicism at Kahnawake, 1667-1700." *Anthropologica* 24 (1982): 77-102.

Bonaparte, Darren. *A Lily among Thorns. The Mohawk Repatriation of Káteri Tekahkwí:tha.* Ahkwesásne Mohawk Territory: The Wampum Chronicles, 2009.

Cunningham, Lawrence S. *An Introduction to Catholicism.* Cambridge: Cambridge University Press, 2009.

Ewens, Mary, O.P. "The Native Order: A Brief and Strange History." In *Scattered Steeples. The Fargo Diocese: A Written Celebration of Its Centennial*, eds. Jerome D. Lamb et al. Fargo, ND: Burch, Londergan and Lynch, 1988: 10-23.

Fargo, North Dakota. Author's fieldnotes, Tekakwitha Conference. August 2-6, 1989.

Fonda, New York. Author's field notes, Northeastern Tekakwitha Conference. July 14-16, 1989.

Greer, Allan. *Mohawk Saint. Catherine Tekakwitha and the Jesuits.* New York: Oxford University Press, 2005.

Holmes, Paula Elizabeth. "We Are Native Catholics': Inculturation and the Tekakwitha Conference." *Studies in Religion/Sciences Religieuses* 28 (June 1999): 153-174.

———. "Symbol Tales: Paths Towards the Creation of a Saint." Ph.D. dissertation, McMaster University, 2000.

———. "The Narrative Repatriation of Blessed Kateri Tekakwitha." *Anthropologica* 43 (2001). 87-103.

Kahnawake, Québec. Author's fieldnotes. August 4, 1995.

Kirst, Sean. "She Was Always Indian': Kateri Tekakwitha To Become First Native American Saint." *Syracuse Post-Standard.* January 1, 2012.

Koppledrayer, K. I. "The Making of the First Iroquois Virgin: Early Jesuit Biographies of the Blessed Kateri Tekakwitha." *Ethnohistory* 40 (1993): 277-306.

Kozak, David. "Ecumenical Indianism: Kateri and the Invented Tradition." Unpublished ms. in author's possession. 1991.

LaRosa, Nicole. "Saint Kateri." *Fordham* (Spring 2012): 16-21.

Martin, Kathleen, J., ed. *Indigenous Symbols and Practices in the Catholic Church. Visual Culture, Missionization and Appropriation.* Farnham, England: Ashgate Publishing Limited, 2010.

McDonnell, Claudia. "Kateri Tekakwitha. Native Americans' Gift to the Church." *St. Anthony Messenger* 95 (July 1987): 19-23.

Mitchell, Kateri, S.S.A. Interview by author, Bozeman, Montana. August 7, 1986.

Orono, Maine. Author's fieldnotes, Tekakwitha Conference. August 5-9, 1992.

Our Negro and Indian Missions. 1926-1976.

Porter, Tom Sakokwenionkwas. *Kanatsiohareke. Traditional Mohawk Indians Return to Their Ancestral Homeland.* New York: The Kanatsiohareke Community, 2006.

Preston, James J. "Necessary Fictions: Healing Encounters with a North American Saint." *Literature and Medicine* 8 (1989): 42-62.

————. "The Reinterpretation of Tradition: Catholic Devotions among Native Americans." Unpublished ms. in author's possession. 1991.

Relyea, Kie. "Ferndale. Boy's Recovery from Flesh-Eating Bacteria Could Lead to American Indian Saint Canonization." *Bellingham Herald.* October 11, 2009. http://www.thenewstribune.com/updates/story/911063. html?story_link=email_msg

Sacred Congregation of Rites. *The Positio of the Historical Section of the Sacred Congregation of Rites on the Introduction of the Cause for Beatification and Canonization and the Virtues of the Servant of God: Katherine Tekakwitha, the Lily of the Mohawks.* New York: Fordham University Press, 1940.

Savilla, Edmund. Email communication to Mark G. Thiel. June 18, 2012.

Scott, John M., S.J. *High Eagle and His Sioux.* St. Louis: n.p., 1963.

Smith, Sebastian. "Passions Grow Over First Native American Saint." Yahoo! News. January 17, 2012. http://news.yahoo.com/passions-grow-over-first-native-american-saint-063131518.html

Starkloff, Carl F., S.J. *A Theological Reflection: The Recent Revitalization of the Tekakwitha Conference.* Great Falls, MT: 1982.

St. Regis, Ontario. Author's fieldnotes. August 5, 1995.

Tekakwitha Conference Newsletter (Cross and Feathers). 1981-present.

Vecsey, Christopher. *On the Padres' Trail.* Notre Dame, IN: University of Notre Dame Press, 1996.

————. *The Paths of Kateri's Kin.* Notre Dame, IN: University of Notre Dame Press, 1997.

————. *Where the Two Roads Meet.* Notre Dame, IN: University of Notre Dame Press, 1999.

Walworth, Ellen H. *The Life and Times of Kateri Tekakwitha, the Lily of the Mohawks. 1656-1680.* Buffalo, NY: Peter Paul & Brother, 1891.

————. "Our Little Sister Kateri Tekakwitha, the Lily of the Mohawks." *The Indian Sentinel* (1908): 5-14.

Weiser, Francis X., S.J. *Kateri Tekakwitha.* Montreal: Kateri Center, 1972.

Woodward, Kenneth C. *Making Saints. How the Catholic Church Determines Who Becomes a Saint, Who Doesn't, and Why.* New York: Simon and Schuster, 1990.

DOCUMENTS

I

REMEMBRANCE OF KATERI TEKAKWITHA, THE SAINTLY MOHAWK

REVEREND PIERRE CHOLENEC, S.J., 1696

The most renowned of all Native American Catholics was Kateri Tekakwitha, baptized in 1676 in a Mohawk village. (Her mother was Algonquin, her father Mohawk; both died in a smallpox epidemic when she was a young girl.) She emigrated to the Jesuit reduction at Kahnawake in the St. Lawrence Valley near Montreal, where she joined the company of other Catholic Indians—mostly Iroquoians—under the leadership of Father Pierre Cholenec, S.J., and other Jesuits. Her intense devotionalism, her privations and penances, her renunciation of sexuality, her imitation of Christ, all made her legendary, especially after her death during Holy Week in 1680. Father Cholenec and his fellow priests celebrated her asceticism, even as it may have contributed to her death, and her life and death became central icons of the Jesuit missiology in North America.

Katharine sanctified her work by spiritual conferences. So holy a conversation, together with her zeal for the things of God, had the result that she always came away with new desires to give herself entirely to Him and to put into practice what she had just heard. She found God everywhere whether she was in church, in the woods or in the fields. Lest she live a moment that was not spent for Him, she might be observed coming and going with a rosary in her hand, which led her instructress to say that Katharine never lost sight of her God, but that she always walked in His presence. If rain or extreme cold prevented her from working, she passed almost all her time before the Blessed Sacrament, or she made small objects of mat work, but she did not spend her time visiting other girls in order to play or seek amusement, as those of her age are apt to do on similar occasions.

Weeks so well utilized were indeed weeks filled, that is to say, in the sense of the Holy Scriptures, with virtue and merit. Katharine nevertheless ended each week with a severe discussion in which she gave account to herself of all that had happened; then she had her sins taken away in the Sacrament of Penance, for she went to confession every Saturday evening. But she did so in an extraordinary manner, one that could have been inspired by the Holy Ghost alone, who Himself guided her, and who first had given her a love of suffering and, as we shall see later, a hatred of her body.

In order to prepare herself for these confessions, she began with the last part, I mean the penance. She would go into the woods and tear her shoulders open with large osiers. From there she went to the church and passed a long time weeping for her sins. She confessed them, interrupting her words with sighs and sobs, believing herself to be the greatest sinner alive, although she was of angelic innocence. Not only the desire to be always united with God, and not to be distracted by the people, made her love solitude so much and flee society, but also her desire to preserve herself in innocence, her horror of sin, and the fear of displeasing God.

FIRST COMMUNION

Thus lived Katharine from the autumn she arrived at the Sault until Christmas, and because she led such a fervent and exemplary life, she merited at this time a grace not granted to those who came from the Iroquois until several years later, and then only after having passed through many trials, so as to give them a high idea of it, and to oblige them to render themselves worthy by an irreproachable life. This rule did not hold for Katharine; she was too well disposed and desired with too great an eagerness to receive Our Lord, to be deprived of this great grace, so she was promised some time before the feast that she might receive Him on Christmas, after she had been instructed in the mystery.

She received the good news with all imaginable joy, and prepared herself for the great event with an increase of devotion suitable to the exalted idea she had of it. It must be admitted, however, that it was at this First Communion that all her fervor was renewed. The ground was so well prepared that only the approach of this divine fire was necessary, to receive all its warmth. She approached or rather surrendered herself to this furnace of sacred love that burns on our altars, and she came out of it so glowing with its divine fire that only Our Lord knew what passed between Himself and His dear spouse during her First Communion. All that we can say is that from that day forward she appeared different to us, because she remained so full of God and of love of Him.

All this will seem very surprising in a young Indian, but it will seem even more so when I add that, having afterwards had the happiness of receiving Holy Communion frequently, she always did so with the same disposition and fervor she had the first time, and undoubtedly she received the same love and manifold graces from Our Lord, who seeks only to visit us in this Sacrament of Love, and who puts no limits to His grace, when He comes in contact with hearts disposed to receive and profit by them, as was the case with Katharine. This fact, moreover, was so well known in the village that at the time of general Communion the most devout women hastened to place themselves near her in church, claiming that the mere sight of her exterior was so devotional and ardent at those times that her example inspired them and served as an excellent preparation for approaching the Holy Table in a proper manner.

A WINTER AT THE HUNT

After Christmas it was time to go on the hunt. Katharine also went with her sister and her brother-in-law. This was a sister by adoption only, who had been in the same lodge with her among the Mohawks. It was neither the wish to divert herself nor the desire for feasting that made Katharine take part in the hunt (which is the reason most of the women go), but only to satisfy this good sister and her husband. God doubtlessly wished that she should sanctify herself in the woods as she had done in the village, to prove to all the savages, by the beautiful example she gave, that virtue may be practiced equally in both these places. She continued the exercises of piety she had practiced in the village, making up for those she could not do there by others that her devotion suggested to her. Her time was regulated as that of a Religious.

She prayed before dawn and finished her day with the common prayers according to the praiseworthy custom of our Indians, who say them together morning and evening, and although she said the former while the others were still asleep, she prolonged the latter until late into the night, while the others slept. After the morning prayers, while the men ate and made preparations for the all-day hunt, Katharine retired to solitude to pray again, approximately at the time that the Indians heard Mass at the mission. For this purpose she had erected a small shrine on the bank of a stream. It consisted of a cross she made from a tree. There she joined in spirit the people of the village, uniting her intentions to those of the priests and prayed to her Guardian Angel to be present there in her place and to bring her the fruits of the Holy Sacrifice.

When she thought the men had departed for the hunt, she returned to the cabin and occupied herself there all day long in the manner of the other women, gathering wood, fetching the meat of the animals that had been killed, or making necklaces in the cabin. During this latter occupation she always invited the others to sing some devotional hymns, or to recount incidents of the lives of the saints and narrations she had heard at church in sermons on Sundays and feast days. In order to encourage them, she was often the first to begin these discourses.

She had two purposes in this: first, to avoid bad conversation and frivolous talk, which only distract the spirit; secondly, to preserve constantly her fervor and union with God, which was as strong in the forest as if she had been at the foot of the altar in the village. It was for this reason that her principal occupation and the one she took the most pleasure in was to gather wood for the cabin, for being alone she could satisfy her devotion, talking intimately with her Divine Spouse; and her humility, in working for the others, by acting as the servant of the cabin; and her desire for suffering, by tiring her body with continued toil of a painful nature.

She found another means of penance by a more spiritual and secret exercise. She would fast while there was an abundance of good meat, for she would cleverly leave the cabin to gather wood before the sagamite was ready and would not return until evening. Even then she ate very little and afterwards spent part of the night in prayer in spite of her extreme fatigue and her natural weakness. If in the morning they made her take nourishment before going to work, she would secretly mix ashes with the sagamite to take away any pleasure she might have in eating it, and to leave her nothing but gall and bitterness instead. She also practiced these mortifications in the village whenever she was able to do so without being observed.

She never became so attached to work, either in the woods or in the cabin, that she forgot her shrine. On the contrary, she took care to return there from time to time so as to satisfy the hunger of her soul while she subjected her body to a fast. She went there morning and evening and several times during the week. She ended her devotions by harsh chastisement which she administered to herself with rods, for she neither possessed suitable instruments nor did she know of their use, for she had undertaken this kind of penance in secret, and under the direction of the Holy Ghost alone.

Although Katharine's life in the woods was most praiseworthy, and even of great merit to herself, nevertheless she was not happy there, and it was easily seen by her bearing that she was not in her own element. The church, the Blessed Sacrament, the Masses, the Benedictions, the sermons, and other similar devotions in which she had taken so much pleasure in the short time she had been at the Sault, held a powerful charm, constantly drawing her towards the village, and claiming her heart and all its affections, so that if her body was in the forest, her spirit was at the Sault. Thus the sojourn in the woods, which generally is so agreeable to those of her sex because they think only of having a pleasant time, and amusing themselves, being far away from all household cares, soon began to be a burden to her, for which she felt a great aversion....

Katharine, having returned to the village, thought only of recovering the graces she had missed while in the woods. She recommended her visits to the church with her ordinary fervor and eagerness and joined her instructress again that she might profit by her pious exhortations during their work. Easter was drawing near; and those who were not far from the village, on the hunt, returned to the mission according to their custom, to celebrate the great day. It was the first time Katharine celebrated it with us for the great good of her soul. She assisted at all the services of Holy Week, and admired all these solemn ceremonies, receiving from them a new esteem for religion. She was so touched by sweetness and consolation that she shed many tears, especially on Good Friday during the sermon on the Passion of Our Lord. Her heart melted at the thought of the suffering of the Divine Savior; she thanked Him a thousand times for it, she adored and kissed *His* cross with *feelings* of the most tender gratefulness and the most ardent love. She attached herself to the cross that day with Him, taking the resolution to repeat on her virginal body the mortifications of Jesus Christ for the rest of her days, as if she had done nothing until then. On Easter Sunday she received Holy Communion for the second time, and did so with the same disposition and ardor and spiritual fruits she had on the feast of Christmas....

Reverend Pierre Cholenec, S.J., "The Life of Katharine Tegakouita, First Iroquois Virgin" (1696), from the original manuscript kept in the Archives of the Hôtel Dieu Monastery, Québec: Sacred Congregation of Rites, *The Positio of the Historical Section of the Sacred Congregation of Rites on the Introduction of the Cause for Beatification and Canonization and on the Virtues of the Servant of God Katharine Tekakwitha, the Lily of the Mohawks.* New York: Fordham University Press, 1940: 254-59, 262-63. Printed from the public domain.

2

INDIAN PETITION TO ROME, 1880s

Appended by Ellen H. Walworth within her book, The Life and Times of Kateri Tekakwitha, the Lily of the Mohawks. 1656-1680. Buffalo: Peter Paul & Brother, 1891: 312-314, and released online September 14, 2011 as EBook #37421. Walworth was a non-Native lay Catholic New Yorker and the first Tekakwitha biographer to use the Mohawk "Kateri" instead of "Catherine." While conducting her research, Walworth consulted leading authorities and archival repositories in Canada and the United States. This petition, which apparently dates from the 1880s, appeared as "Appendix F" and was the final item to be included. Reprinted here are its English and Salish (Flathead) versions.

Our Father the Pope:

Though we Indians are very poor and miserable, yet Our Maker had great pity on us and gave us the Catholic religion. Moreover He had pity on us again and gave us CATHERINE TEGAKWITA. This holy virgin, an Indian like ourselves, being favoured by JESUS CHRIST with a great grace, grew up very good, had a great love for Our Maker, and died good and holy, and is now glorious in heaven, as we believe, and prays for us all. This virgin, we believe, was given to us from God as a great favour, for she is our little sister. But now we hope that thou, our Father, who art the Vicar of JESUS CHRIST, wilt grant us a favour likewise; we beg thee with the whole of our hearts to speak and say: "You Indians, my children, take CATHERINE as an object of your veneration in the church, because she is holy and is in heaven."

There are also two others who, though Frenchmen, yet are as if they were Indians, because they taught the Indians the sign of the Cross and the way to heaven; and for this they were killed by bad Indians. Their names are BLACKGOWN ISAAC JOGUES and BROTHER RENÉ GOUPIL. We wish to have these two also as objects of our veneration, as our protectors and our advocates.

If thou givest us these three as our PATRONS, our hearts will be glad, our behaviour will be good, and our children will become perfect, also a great many unbaptized Indians will enter into the Catholic Church and will see the glory of heaven.

Lingua Kalispel (Anglice, Flathead.)

Lu ku Pogot lu ku Lepape.

Ue mil kaekonkoint kaeskeligu, u kaeteie, u pen kutunt kaenkonnemilils lu KaeKohnzuten lu kaeguizelils lu Sinchaumen Catholique. Negu kaelnkonnemilils lu kaeguizelils CATHERINE TEGAKWITA. Ye stuchemish pagpagt chikuilze ezageil t kaempile lu kueis lu kutunt sinkonns tel JESUS CHRIST, mil gest u pogtilsh, milgamenchis Kolinzuten, u lu Sinchaumis, gest u pagpagt u tlelil, u yetlgoa csimpiels 'ls chichemaskat, u kaesia kaes chaushilils. Shei Stuchemish kaentels kutunt kaesinkonm tel Kolmzuten neli kaempile lu kaep sinkusigu.

U pen yetlgoa kaenmuselsi t-anui, lu ku Pogot, kaeksnkonnemilils, lu ku Nilkalshelpenzutis JESUS CHRIST, t-esemilko t-kaepuus kaesgalitem kuks kolkoelt, u kuks zuti "Igu kuisigusigult kuskeligu, akaespoteem lu CATHERINE 'lsinchaumen, neli pagpagt, u 'ls'chichemaskat u elzi."

Negu telzi chesel ue Seme, u pen ezageil t-skeligu, neli meyieltem lu skeligu lu staktakenzut l'eseimeus, u lu shushuel ch's'chichemaskat, gol shei u polstem t-kuaukot skeligu shei lu eszustem KUAILKS ISAAC JOGUES, u SINSE RENE GOUPIL. Komi ye chesel negu kaekls'chitenzuten, kaeklchaushizuten. Lu ne kaeguizelilt ye checheles kaekls'chitenzuten, nem lemt lu kaespuus, nem gestilsh lu kaezuut, nem yopietilsh lu kaesigusigult, u nem chgoegoeit skeligu lu estemskoli m kueis lu Sinchaumen Catholique, u nem uichis lu'ls'chichemaskat lu simpielsten.

Printed from the public domain.

3

OUR TEKAKWITHA CLUB, 1940

SISTER PROVIDENCIA TOLAN, S.P.

Coeur d'Alene women honored Kateri Tekakwitha and prayed for benefactors at Sacred Heart Mission, Coeur d'Alene Indian Reservation, Desmet, Idaho, 1940. Sister Providencia Tolan, S.P., photographer and author, published "Our Tekakwitha Club" in The Indian Sentinel 20, no. 6 (1940): 87. For further reading about this Tekakwitha Club, founded in 1938, see "Indian Arts Up-to-Date" by Sister Providencia Tolan, S.P., with a reprinted addendum by Margaret L. Bingman, Indians at Work, December, 1939, in The Indian Sentinel 20, no. 1 (1940): 5-6, 13.

Our Tekakwitha Club was formally organized two years ago. Sixty-seven Coeur d'Alene women gathered at Sacred Heart Mission on the Feast of Christ the King and banded themselves together by a pledge composed by one of the women themselves. By it, they promised to live and serve God in imitation of the virtuous Mohawk maiden, Kateri Tekakwitha, by a model Christian life. The badge of membership is a medal bearing the image of their patroness. And what an object of pride it is to all of them.

The honor that this Indian woman is accorded by having her representation on a holy object unfailingly stirs their own Indian hearts. They look up to her with reverence as their model, and with confidence, as a helpful friend. Her intercession is invoked in troubles and difficulties. Last spring, when a group of them stood paralyzed with grief, watching the flames devouring their beloved mission chapel, sparks began to fall perilously near the girls' school. Annie Falcon braved the distance to the intervening fence and attached to it her medal of Tekakwitha. A shout of joy went up from the women as the wind suddenly veered and the building was saved.

They made a novena this year in preparation for Tekakwitha's feast, which is April 17th, for the speedy canonization of their beloved patroness. Each day they gathered about the little shrine at the mission, sang hymns and prayed to the Mother whom Tekakwitha herself loved so well. On the day of the feast they renewed their pledge after receiving Holy Communion and admitted several new members.

This religious spirit binds them together and inspires them in their efforts to promote both the spiritual and material interests of their people.

Sister Providencia Tolan, S.P., "Our Tekakwitha Club,"
The Indian Sentinel 20, no. 6 (1940): 87.
Marquette University Digital Publication.
Printed by permission.

4

KATERI CIRCLES

A NATIVE SAINT IN COMMUNITY WITH THE PEOPLE

REBECCA HERNANDEZ ROSSER, 2012

Rebecca Hernandez Rosser is the Assistant Director of the American Indian Studies Center at the University of California – Los Angeles with a Ph.D. in American Studies. She is a member of the Mescalero Apache Nation of New Mexico and an active member of the City of the Angels Kateri Circle in Los Angeles, California.

Since first contact with Europeans, American Indians have been characterized as savage enemies and noble savages, victims of atrocities and ultimate survivors. In this complicated mixture of fact and fiction, Native people have rarely fit the stereotypical ideas of what an Indian is. Instead, Indians understand themselves as part of the ever evolving American story. According to the 2010 census, there are 5.2 million American Indians in the United States, and less than one quarter of that population (22%) live on reservations. Most Native people today live just as mainstream Americans do, either on or off their reservations, in cities, small towns or the suburbs, and contribute to the communities they call home.

As a consequence of the diverse histories and current lifestyles of Indians, *home* can be anywhere in the world and *community* is often defined in varying ways. Each individual (as is the case with all people) distinguishes him or herself in relationship to those they spend time with, develop relationships with and consider their family. For American

Indian Catholics, faith often plays a key role in defining who they are, both outside and in their tribal community. One of the most significant ways that American Indians can express their unique culture, in the context of the Catholic Church, is by establishing and/or participating in a Kateri Circle at the parish where they attend church.

The Tekakwitha Conference website describes a Kateri Circle as "… a group of Women and Men and/or Youth of all cultures within a parish/mission who want to belong to a prayer circle/group for the purpose of learning and promoting the saintly life of the Tekakwitha Conference patroness Kateri Tekakwitha, a young Mohawk/Algonquin woman of the mid-seventeenth century." In 1991, there were 130 Kateri Circles registered with the Tekakwitha Conference, and that number has remained consistent to the present day. These groups "exist under the auspices of the Tekakwitha Conference …" and "consist of members who try to emulate the life of Blessed Kateri Tekakwitha."[1]

There are many reasons why Kateri Circles play an important role in the expression of faith for Native people in the Catholic Church. First and most obviously, the Circles provide a place for Indians to gather together with other Native people of the same faith; this is especially important to Indians who do not live on a reservation. Secondly, it allows Indians the opportunity to involve themselves in service with fellow Native Catholics. Lastly, Kateri Circles serve as a community of refuge for Amerindians who are seeking a place where they can be themselves and congregate with others who may have the similar lives. In interviews with Kateri Circle members from a wide cross section of communities, it is repeatedly stated that Kateri Circles are a place where they can find support through good times and bad. Non-Native Catholics may also take part in the work of local Kateri Circles and many do.

Actively participating in a Kateri Circle allows individuals to center their interests in service in four ways: **Intellectual/Educational**—studying the life of Tekakwitha and becoming more aware of Native American issues, **Spiritual**—praying and working toward a deeper spiritual life, **Social/Hospitality**—working for unity with activities that support and strengthen the Kateri Circle members, and **Physical/Service**—becoming involved in your local community, outreach to the sick, elderly and special needs in your community and parish.[2]

---

1   For more information see: www.//tekconf.org

2   *ibid.*

The life of Kateri Tekakwitha is the foundation on which Kateri Circles are built. Reflecting on the many difficult obstacles she endured and overcame in her lifetime gives hope and inspiration to Catholics living today. Moving away from stereotypes and recognizing that Christianity is a longstanding tradition in many Indian communities validates the lived experience of Indian people both in the past and in the present. Native Catholics are proud of the Indian woman soon to be a Saint of the Universal church, a Saint to call their *own* who belongs to all of us.

Printed by permission of Rebecca Hernandez Rosser.

5

BLESSED KATERI TEKAKWITHA

THE PROPHETIC SPIRIT OF KATERI TEKAKWITHA WITHIN OUR INDIAN CHURCHES

REVEREND EDMUND SAVILLA, 1981

Edmund Savilla is the first Pueblo Indian to be ordained a Catholic priest. (His father is from Isleta Pueblo and is also of Quechan Indian heritage; his mother is an Oneida Indian.) In his ministry as pastor at the Church of the Ascension in Albuquerque, New Mexico, he empha-sizes Native American traditions. He composed this essay as a working paper to stimulate dialogue at the National Tekakwitha Conference in Albuquerque in 1981. The piece originally appeared in the Tekakwitha Conference National Center Newsletter 5, no. 1 (1985): 22-26. He reflects on the meanings of Kateri Tekakwitha for American Indian spiritual life, especially in the context of contemporary struggles with alcoholism.

> Your Sons and Daughters shall prophesy
> Your young shall see visions and your Elders shall dream
> dreams (Joel 16-21, Acts 1-17)

At the gate called "the beautiful" a crippled man begged for alms from the apostles Peter and John. Peter said: "I have neither silver nor gold, but what I have I give you! In the name of Jesus Christ, the Nazarean, Walk!" Through the intervention of Peter, this once crippled man was made whole. Peter's faith was proclaimed through this healing action.

The gift of wholeness was accepted and the man danced and praised God in the Temple.

Does our faith in Jesus give us the courage to call upon Jesus' name to heal? Have we allowed the power of the name of Jesus to heal us?

With confident assurance, can we hope for wholeness in ourselves and our communities? Have we merely accepted the externals of the Catholic Church as a means of not having to face the reality of a commitment with the living Spirit of Jesus? Are the visions of our young the result of mind altering drugs instead of an encounter with the Holy? Do we dream of the material things we can possess, forgetting family and friends?

Questioning our faith life opens the gates of the beautiful. What we find is not gold or silver, but healing and wholeness. We rediscover our beauty, and the power of our faith in Jesus. We do this not just to feel good, though this is part of being beautiful. But, as Jesus and Peter, we find ourselves filled with more than we can hold. As a result, our faith moves us to intervene in the brokenness and meaninglessness we find in and around us. We have Hope.

Kateri Tekakwitha was a woman of Hope. Hope was her companion in this life. Her beauty was not as modern society would define it. Her body had been a victim of smallpox which left her frail and half blind. Her body was marked with tiny pits that the smallpox had dug into it. Kateri's beauty rested in the meaning she gave to her life. A meaning born out of an inward journey, that would lead her along the dream paths of her ancestors. Ending in a personal relationship with the resurrected Jesus. Hope and beauty were not sentimental goals in Kateri's life, but companions through her suffering and sacrifice.

Other companions with Kateri in life were her mother, Kahenta, missionaries, and a small Christian community found within her people, as well as her own people with whom she spent most of her life. Each of these relationships would influence her life. As an infant and young child, Kateri would experience the love and power of her mother's own spiritual journey. Kahenta was a Christian and during the four years she and Kateri would be together in this world, she would teach Kateri what has become known as the gentle ways. Smallpox would separate Kateri and Kahenta, death taking Kahenta and leaving Kateri physically handicapped. Before Kahenta's death, she prayed that her daughter would be given a Christian heart and the poison of smallpox would not touch her. Her prayer would be heard, for Kateri was gifted with faith in Jesus. Even though she did suffer from smallpox, she survived, witnessing to long-suffering and inner healing. An experience that would fulfill Kahenta's expectations and infinitely surpass them.

As a member of the Iroquois Nation, Kateri was taken in by her people. She would recover only to grow up intensely aware of her limitations. Blindness and a weak body did not allow her to join the other children in what we would call the normal development in her people's ways. Kateri would be faced with learning to adapt to cultural and personal situations. Her understanding would come not from culturally accepted norms, but from her own working out of new meanings for herself. Limitations would become invitations for her to discover new avenues of expression. Other senses becoming enhanced, helping her develop a genuine sensitivity to creation. Her journeys would be inward rather than along the forest paths.

Recalling these situations helps us to remember Kateri's faith in Jesus was not the result of a lightning bolt or an angel's appearance. Her faith is rooted in the experience of her family and community. Stories of her people's experience of the Creator and stories of Jesus told by her mother and other Christians, led her into a journey of day to day conversion. A journey of suffering and sacrifice often betrayed today by sweet pictures, statues, and sentimental stories.

We need to enter the real journey of Kateri if she is to help us understand our journey today. Part of Kateri's journey was her adult initiation into the Church. This points to evangelization and the Rite of Christian Initiation of Adults as essential points for our reflection.

Before asking to become a member of the catechumenate, Kateri had undergone her own pre-catechumenate which involved an encounter with the lived faith of her mother, other Christians, and the traditional spirituality of her people. Today we would call this journey into self an intra-religious dialogue. A dialogue not only with the person of Jesus, but with the silent God expressed in her people's self-understanding. Every step a conversion, a breakthrough, a celebration of life. Having encountered the silence of death as a child, her solitude would become a womb within which her silent God would become flesh.

Kateri's pre-Christian life is filled with many insights into her own life and the life of her people. As an active participant in the traditions of her people, she knew its truth. She would question abuses while affirming the spirit of truth expressed through tradition. Her vision would strengthen her sight, as she looked into the heart of matters.

Because Kateri was raised in the traditional way, she naturally would be exposed to all the social practices of her people. This included an arranged relationship that had the possibility of developing into a monogamous relationship. What is often overlooked is how Kateri's people accepted her as she was. They would not deny her the opportunity to participate fully within their lives because of her physical handicaps. When the time came for her to make a decision regarding the prearranged relationship, with her creativity and insight she suggested another option. This option would free the young man and her people from their spoken promises. Her vision would call her to risk the security tradition provided and place her on the path of living a single life-style. This decision was the first of much soul-searching and shows self-understanding and an understanding of the people in her life. We must be cautious here that we do not try to equate this life decision with Kateri's decision years later to make a vow of perpetual virginity. To do this would betray her vision and meaning she gave to her life as a single person. Perpetuating or imposing a sentimental interpretation of her life such as, "Tekakwitha rejected marriage in order to embrace virginity" blinds us to her real life long spiritual journey.

Another life decision Kateri made was to become a Christian. This decision was made at a time in the Church when initiation of adults was experiencing a renewal based on the ancient tradition of the catechumenate. Attempts to restore the catechumenate was an evolving experience, adapting to mistakes and accomplishments made by missionaries around the world. By the time these missionaries would encounter Kateri's people, they would have little over a century's experience in renewal in Latin America, Asia, and Africa. Prefabricated structures would include not just the Gospel, but a context within which it would be lived out. In Latin America, the Jesuits had set up what were called "reductions" or "mission towns." This structure would have far reaching effects on Kateri and her people.

… As [two historians] noted,

> Mission towns were designed to do more than give converts new identities and allegiances. Towns would also serve to isolate the converts from their unconverted kinsmen, thus preventing the kind of reversion to traditional belief all missionaries feared. As an added benefit, towns would conserve mission manpower while increasing the influence of the missionaries-in-residence. These benefits and more were anticipated by the missionaries as well as by government

officials, who were quick to recognize the town's value as a means of controlling Indian people. (Ronda and Axtell: 33)

Without this historical background, it would appear that Kateri abandoned her people. The glamour of seeing Kateri escape to the Christian settlement in Canada only shows that she was a victim of her times. Less glamorous, but more important for us today, would be to critique these methods of evangelization; learning the positive and negative effects. This is important because history shows that the idea of "mission towns" was transferred to "mission schools" producing and perpetuating the idea that there was only one acceptable way to embrace the Gospel. Besides the idea of having to go to a "mission town," Kateri was exposed to a theology rooted in apologetics, not evangelization. As a result, Kateri probably participated in the rite of exorcism and renunciation of non-Christian worship which was part of the ancient catechumenate. Exclusiveness and inclusivism characterized this theology's content. In other words, if you want to be saved, you have to believe and do what we do. The western church had forgotten what the word Indian actually meant, which is "In God", "in di[o]." Native peoples had already been acknowledged as being "in God." Unfortunately, many missionaries would ignore this reality and, in many cases, invent, and set up their own criteria of what is meant to be "in God." Kateri's life not only points to what has been characterized as the glories of the missionary effort, it also highlights its tragedies.

The present historical situation is leading all creation into a new stage. Vatican II guided by the Spirit has breathed new life into the Church. "How to evangelize" and the "content of evangelization" have surfaced anew as a result of the church's reflections. People who would like to become Christians no longer have to leave their homes in order to live in a Christian community. More importantly, they do not have to reject their past life experiences of the holy.

With the renewal of the Rite of Christian Initiation of Adults, we have been given the opportunity to enflesh the Gospel within our local traditions. No longer is the mission of proclaiming the Good News the sole responsibility of Father or Sister. The people of God, represented by the local church, should always understand and show that the initiation of adults is its concern and the business of all the baptized.... Therefore, the community must always be ready to fulfill its apostolic vocation by giving help to those who need Christ.... This community responsibility also extends to children and infants.

Along with the renewal of the structures of the Church, we are rediscovering the Good News. As a message of liberation, the Good News once again exhibits the profound relation between evangelization and human advancement/development/liberation and healing.

"Evangelizing means bringing the Good News into all the strata of humanity, and through its influence transforming humanity from within and making it new. Now I am making the whole of creation new" (Gal 6:15). The Church evangelizes when she seeks to convert (Rom 1:16). Solely through the divine power of the message she proclaims, both the personal and collective consciences of people, the activities in which they engage, and the lives and concrete environments which are theirs....

As Catholic Native Americans today, we are very aware of the past, but, more importantly, we are aware of the present situation of our brothers and sisters. We have to ask ourselves, do the Native Peoples have a need for Christ? Have we followed Kateri's example and journeyed along the dream paths of our ancestors, as well as immersing ourselves in the valued Gospel? Without ceasing to be a Christian, can we live out our unique identity found in our individual and tribal Indianness? Or are we content to live on one side of the river, dismissing the Gospel as the "white man's" religion?

The reality of our communities urgently calls us to answer these questions about the meaning of our own lives. Violence, vandalism, corruption, slander and prejudice are a few of the more observable situations to be witnessed in our Indian communities, whether they are reservations, rural or urban communities. Neither Native American Tradition nor Christian Tradition support or suggest this way of life as normal. Rather this type of behavior represents an inner disorder. Peter's faith and vision called him to heal the crippled man. Does our faith and vision call us to actively intervene in our own crippled lives as well as that of our crippled communities?

Family life is where these hurts are most directly experienced by our people. Like Kateri, we are handicapped, our vision dimmed by many factors. Respect for life has given way to child, adult, and personal abuse. The disease that kills us today is not smallpox, but alcoholism. Effects of this disease destroy the individual, our families, and even whole reservations. With the grace of God, Kateri was able to survive her illness, living to give renewed meaning to her life. This same grace

can also have and give renewed meaning to us. As Catholic Indians
to accept an abnormal reality as normal or to remain indifferent is a
betrayal of our faith in a loving, healing God. It is also a betrayal of the
original beauty the Creator gifted us with.

With today's knowledge of the disease of alcoholism, our communities
can learn to assist in arresting the disease as well as to prevent it. Our
Christian communities have a moral responsibility to use every means
necessary to prevent this cultural suicide. Besides actively supporting
the traditional structures of AA, Ala-non, and Ala-teen, we need to
address every aspect of prevention, treatment and ongoing recovery.
Developing parish workshops and providing programs such as parenting
for the recovering alcoholic women and men.

The survival of our peoples and the gifts the Creator shared with our
ancestors depends on our commitment. Here we are actively involved
in our own conversion and that of our communities. Every conversion
suggests a growth and a clearer understanding of the Creator's vision.
Broken homes and abandoned children no longer have to be sources
of discouragement and despair. These situations place us at the heart
of hope.

Kateri is often pictured carrying a cross, symbol of suffering and
sacrifice. Besides her physical pain, she must have gone through many
interior struggles as she journeyed into the depths of life's meaning. One
of the biggest sacrifices she would make would be to leave her people
at the recommendation of the missionary. This decision would prevent
her martyrdom. We now welcome her back home, into our hearts and
communities. The martyrdom that was denied her, is to be lived out
in our lives. Our commitment becomes our sacrifice for our people.
Her vision of hope is made clear in our awareness of those who suffer.

Tekakwitha's life is not a call into a preconceived notion of Church,
rather it is an invitation into a life long journey. A journey that will lead
us into the depths of who we are: affirming all that is holy in us and our
communities: at the same time, challenging the evils with courage and
hope. A major part of her personal journey consisted of the years before
she became a Christian. These years have value for us today, because
they point to what we now call the pre-catechumenate. We see that the
Spirit is working long before a formal discovery and commitment with
Jesus is made. The stage of the Rite of Christian Initiation of Adults
calls for our special attention. It is here that our intra-religious dialogue
enters an inter-religious dialogue. We share the power of Jesus in our

life, and the truth of that is witnessed in our daily lives and that of our Christian communities. The other three stages, catechumenate, period of purification and enlightenment (Lent) and mystagogia will come easily if we understand all the implications of a strong pre-catechumenate.

The Creator's intervention in human history is witnessed daily when we act in union with Jesus: sacrificing our lives to bring reconciliation and healing to our world. Our faith gives us the courage to transform suffering into beauty, death into resurrection. Our prayer is the same as Kateri's mother, faith and healing for our people. We engage in evangelization and the Rite of Christian Initiation of Adults, not so much to see how many people we can get into the Church, but to share the Creator's graces in the Spirit of Jesus. Being compassionate as our Creator is compassionate.

REFERENCE

Ronda, James P. and James Axtell. *Indian Missions: A Critical Bibliography.* Bloomington: Indiana University Press, 1978.

6

BLESSED KATERI AND THE TURTLE CLAN

SIGGENAUK CENTER'S SPIRITUAL DAY

MILWAUKEE, WISCONSIN

SISTER KATERI MITCHELL, s.s.a.

JULY 11, 1987

Sister Kateri Mitchell, S.S.A., is a Turtle Clan member of the Mohawk Nation and a sister of the Sisters of Saint Anne, who was raised in a family devoted to Kateri Tekakwitha. As a child she frequently visited the shrines in Auriesville and Fonda, New York, and she attended Kateri's beatification in 1980. She entered religious life in 1959 at age nineteen, and she has served as executive director of the National Tekakwitha Conference since 1998. Edited by Mark G. Thiel.

Kateri Tekakwitha is a gift of all Indian people, all Native Americans. So we share her together, and since we share her, she has done so much in our lives.

I think if each of us looks back in our spiritual journey, our journey of faith, we realize this. That is, she is leading us, she is walking with us.... The whole idea of journey, of walking.... Then if we fully realize that she is with us at all times.... Even if it brings with it some suffering, some frustrations, but they'll realize that we are always going to have her and our Savior who is Christ who walks with us each day.

Blessed Kateri is rooted in the lives of our people. Bringing so many tribes together, making us realize, helping us to realize that each one of us is gifted and are gifted because we are the gift of our Creator. God lives in each one of us. As he breathed life into the first person who was created, we share that breath of life. We share that gift of God in our own lives, which we are called to share with Blessed Kateri who belongs to the Turtle Clan of the Mohawk Nation.

… I feel very privileged that I too belong to the Turtle Clan. The eternal is very significant and very symbolic in my life. And I think that I have come to know and understand the life of Blessed Kateri a little bit more because of the fact that we share the plan to nurture life. Then as women this is extremely important to us. As mothers, you know what it means the day you gave birth, another life to share the breath of life that our Creator gives us. And as religious, we don't bring forth life physically, but we do also share in that life giving experience by—in the people.

Therefore, we are called together with much respect and reverence for the children. The birthing experience that we all experience, and men, you are also part of the life giving people here on earth. So, every one of us shares in the life-giving experiences … because we have been able to focus in on our Creator who is the center of our lives. And when we are able to do that, we reach out to people everywhere, all places, all faiths … all centered on our Creator.

…We know that God loves us and Blessed Kateri in her journey as we mediate what the journey is in our lives.…

As Native people [of the Turtle Clan] we have the reputation of moving slowly and eternal is very slowly, moving straight forward. But as that turtle moves, close to the ground, very close to Mother Earth, the turtle sees all that goes on, it's able to see and observe God's creation. So … from the tiniest little creature to the biggest, the turtle is able to see—and respect and appreciate all of creation. And Blessed Kateri, she appreciated life, because creation is where she found life, where she found peace.… We know that the turtle, even though it looks like a frail thing and we can kick it around, the turtle will always just continue slowly and [it has] … a shell, a hard shell. To me it represents the strength that the Turtle Clan has today, that determination to reach a goal. And as the turtle goes ahead very slowly, straightforward to reach that goal

[which] … is to be with the Creator…. That through slow movement
we can reach the center of our lives….

So Blessed Kateri means so much. The person, through children, can
be respected by each one of us. A person we know—that we are strangers
in a place and we see another Indian, what do we do? Immediately we
recognize another and there is a bond. It's magnetic, we reach out to one
another. As Native people, we are never strangers to one another, and I
have found that no matter where I go. I feel right at home.

… [In the] Turtle Clan—this is how we walk the earth … and that
strength is how we reach our goal. That whole strength of community
and we are God's people and he loves us all. He gives us strength. He
gives us what we need, if we give him a chance. If you move slowly like
that turtle, then just go forward, and if we can accept things as gifts, it
changes our whole lives.

A joy is gotten through a gift, just as Blessed Kateri. She just waited
for the day when she [could] … receive her First Communion at the age
of 22. Because she thought she knew what the Body of Christ meant,
that she would be sharing the life of Jesus … which makes us one….
She is walking with us to help us … to get to our goal.

There are so many of our Native people now gathering in various parts
of the country who are having circles by various names, but basically
groups … where men, women, and children gather to share faith, sharing
with the young. They pray together…. Quite often we hear that these
… circles … or groups are women's things. They are not because the
women are not alone in this world. You know that there's another half….
I know that we're the better half! (Laughter) And it is, by bringing the
two together, that's how we create community, that's how we create
family, and as husband and wife in a family, we know it wouldn't be a
family if you weren't together. And through that love comes full circle
with our children … new life comes when we're all gathered together.

Marquette University, Siggenauk Center Records.
Printed by permission.

In Her Footsteps - Song #8

Sr. Kateri Mitchell, SSA

Fr. John Brioux, OMI
with Sr. Kateri Mitchell, SSA

(In Her Footsteps, con't)

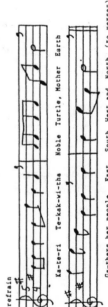
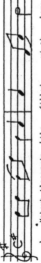

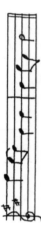

7

IN HER FOOTSTEPS

SISTER KATERI MITCHELL, S.S.A.

&

REVEREND JOHN BRIOUX, O.M.I.

1995

One of the most popular hymns at the National Tekakwitha Conference is "In Her Footsteps," composed by Sister Kateri Mitchell, S.S.A. (Mohawk Turtle Clan, just like Saint Kateri Tekakwitha) and Reverend John Brioux, O.M.I. The song compares Kateri Tekakwitha to Mother Earth and employs Native American-inspired vocal and instrumental styles to embrace Catholic and American Indian spirituality. "In Her Footsteps" was performed with special power at the Tekakwitha Conference gathering at Akwesasne in Mohawk Country in 1995. Sister Kateri has translated some verses from English to Mohawk.

CHORUS: KATERI TEKAKWITHA
                NE ONKWA TATE KENHA
                ONEN KIONKINONKS
                ONWEN TSIONHAKWEKON
VERSE 3:   TEKAKWITHA
                IAKOHARKWEN
                IAKONTSENNONNI
                KWASENNAIENS
VERSE 4:   KATSITSIANORON
                KIAKORIWAIERI
                IEIATANORON

	KWASENNAIENS
VERSE 8:	TIONKISWATHETENNI
	ROASWATHETSERA
	SATENNITERON
	TEKWANONWHERATONS
VERSE 11:	KAWHATSIRAKWEKON
	TSIKIONNHE
	TETEWAIENA
	NIAWEN KOWA

Marquette University, Tekakwitha Conference Archives.
Translation by Sister Kateri Mitchell, S.S.A., 2000.
Printed by permission.

8

STATEMENT OF THE ASSOCIATION OF NATIVE RELIGIOUS AND CLERGY

DISTRIBUTED AT THE TEKAKWITHA CONFERENCE, ORONO, MAINE, AUGUST 4, 1992

Since 1971 the Association of Native Religious and Clergy (ANRC) has served as a gathering place for Catholic American Indian leadership. Often its members have met in conjunction with the annual National Tekakwitha Conference meetings. In 1992 the Tekakwitha meeting was marked by dissension concerning Native leadership in the Conference and the future of inculturative programs. The ANRC issued a statement in which its members threatened to break with the National Tekakwitha Conference and which proclaimed their devotion to "Saint Kateri."

The Association of Native Religious and Clergy met this week. Saint Kateri has given us a new vision. We want to share it and our future direction with you.

Since 1971, our Association has met annually with a twofold purpose: to discern the spiritual direction of our lives and to follow God's Spirit moving among our peoples. We have had the privilege of visiting many Reservations. We have seen the spiritual power of our people and have experienced their hospitality.

In 1976, we were the only national Native organization that the Catholic hierarchy could turn to for help during the Eucharistic Congress.

Our contribution: Native prayers, liturgy, and spiritual leadership was a blessing for us and all who participated. Papal Legate Cardinal Knox, serving the Congregation of Rites, was Rome's representative to that Congress. It was at this time that he and the Universal Catholic Church were introduced to the power of native spirituality.

In 1978, we became involved with the Tekakwitha Conference in Yankton, SD. There we were able to sense the Spirit at work. We could see native leadership developing. We watched the people participating. We could feel our people being healed through the ministry of our Church. Two years later in Denver, the ANRC decided to become more centrally involved in our support of the Tekakwitha Conference. Over the past 10 years, we have shared many individual and collective gifts with this Conference. Our Association has lived this Conference's low and high points, moments of frustration and faith, of struggle and success.

This past week we met at nearby Indian Island. This time our twofold purpose was to discern the direction of our Association and to clarify our relationship with this Conference.

As members of our Church, we feel the present realities in this Conference make it difficult for our membership to share the truth of our traditions. In some areas the hierarchical, ecclesiastical structures no longer hear the people's concerns nor meet their needs. Our people find this a hardship. Our Elders are not being respected or listened to as they speak. Our younger people want to hope again. We need to move in a new direction—a direction that will allow for our own spiritual growth and that of our people. We have fasted and prayed. Saint Kateri has given us a new vision. In this vision, we give our support to existing and developing Regional Conferences. We encourage more areas to create their own Regional Conferences. And, as God leads us, we will help create a new National Native Catholic Conference.

The ANRC members will no longer be reactors to the Tekakwitha Conference and its Board. Rather, we will be creative initiators and [implementers] of the Vatican II documents, developing inculturation of the Gospel of Jesus Christ in our many local Native traditions and tribal spiritualities. This is how we will serve you at the regional level. Thus, the Spirit of Jesus will become ever more fully enfleshed among our peoples.

As the Association of Native Religious and Clergy, we will continue to be available to the Tekakwitha Conference whenever such is requested of us.

Finally, we are saying, "Saint Kateri." Historically, our Church has officially canonized those whom the people have proclaimed Saints. Kateri is a Saint. Our people believe this. We believe this. We will begin calling her Saint in our prayers, in our letters, our publications and our personal conversation. We invite you to join us as we move forward, strengthening our spiritual relationship with Jesus through the intercession of Saint Kateri Tekakwitha.

Marquette University, Tekakwitha Conference Archives.
Printed by permission.

9

KATERI'S DREAM AND
ITS FULFILLMENT

SISTER MARY EWENS, O.P.

Sister Mary Ewens, O.P., of the Sinsinawa Dominican Research Center, has written widely about the roles of women religious in the United States, including indigenous sisterhoods. She served as president of Edgewood College in Madison, Wisconsin, 1983-1987, and has been director of the Conrad N. Hilton Fund for Sisters, handling over a thousand projects of sisters working among the poor all over the world. She has also been director at the Jubilee Community Centre in Rome, Italy, a residence where Sisters from developing countries studying in Rome can find a supportive community.

All of the information that we have about St. Kateri Tekakwitha's life and death comes from the biographies that were written by two Jesuit missionaries who knew her: Pierre Cholenec and Claude Chauchetière. Each tried to fit the facts of her life into the centuries-old formula for writing saints' lives, called hagiography. Allan Greer, who has studied these biographies in great detail, tells us that the formula includes

progression through the stages of life, through death, and on to a postmortem glorification. The events of an individual existence had to be arranged in such a way as to highlight the subject's virtues, the signs of divine selection, and the resemblances with the lives of established saints.[1]

The "spin" put on the basic facts will be different, depending on the audience and cultural factors in a given time and place. Hence Cholenec stressed Kateri's chastity because he was writing for an eighteenth-century French audience that doubted the Indians' ability to control their sexuality. Later writers had other emphases.[2]

In this essay I would like to focus on one aspect of Kateri's life, her unfulfilled dream of starting a group of Indian nuns, and efforts two hundred years after her death to bring that dream to fulfillment. I will show how Father Francis M. Craft consciously used elements of the Kateri icon to promote the interests of The American Congregation, the Indian sisterhood that he established in Dakota Territory, U.S.A., in the 1890s. I will show how Craft used elements of the Tekakwitha hagiography to promote the interests of this sisterhood.

THE DREAM

Kateri Tekakwitha's first biographer, Father Claude Chauchetière, S.J., tells us that she and her friends wanted to have a religious community like the one at the Hôtel-Dieu in Montreal, but the Jesuits would not allow it. He describes what happened when Kateri, Marie-Thérèse Tegaiaguenta and Marie Skarichions submitted their plans to Father Jacques Fremin, S.J., superior of the mission: "The priest made light of all these beautiful plans. He told them they were as yet too young in the faith for such a singular project."[3]

He also cast doubt on their ability to keep their vows of chastity if they lived in the secluded spot they had chosen for their "cloister": "Heron Island was so far removed from the village that all the young people who were passing ... would be always at their cabin."[4]

---

1   *Mohawk Saint Catherine Tekakwitha and the Jesuits* (New York: Oxford University Press, 2005), p. 165.

2   *Ibid.* Greer discusses this in great detail pp. 171ff., and in chapter 9, pp. 193ff.

3   Claude Chauchetière, "The Life of the Good Katharine Tegakouita, Now Known as The Holy Savage," in Sacred Congregation of Rites, *The Positio of the Historical Section of the Sacred Congregation of Rites on the Introduction of the Cause for Beatification and Canonization and on the Virtues of the Servant of God Katharine Tekakwitha* (New York: Fordham University Press, 1940), p. 176.

4   *Ibid.*

Chauchetière continued, "They themselves saw that what the priest said was reasonable, and forthwith abandoned their idea of a monastery on Heron Island."[5] In writing this, her biographer, following the rules for writing saints' lives, wanted to show how virtuous Kateri was, but one wonders whether she and her companions really did accept this decision with such docility. When Father Fremin made light of the plan they had been working on assiduously, and actually living out for some time, they must have been shocked, frustrated, and grieved. The three seem to have continued living the lifestyle of nuns as they had been, though they dropped the plan to move to Heron Island.

What are we to make of this refusal to consider Kateri's plan? From the vantage point of today, it is easy to lament the Jesuit's ethnocentric bias against the Indian "barbarians," their superstitions and pagan beliefs, and decry his lack of respect for their culture and religion. No doubt such attitudes were part of the reason for the Jesuit's actions, but I would like to look at other factors that would also have influenced his decision.

Father Fremin may have shared the misogynous views of women that were reflected in the canon law, which defined vowed religious life in the Church. Women were seen as irrational, soft-brained, misbegotten males, incapable of logical thought, or of controlling their own impulses. Canon law surrounded nuns with regulations and cloister walls aimed at controlling all aspects of their lives, since they were considered incapable of governing themselves.[6] Whether he shared these view or not, he would have had to consider the canon law regulations that flowed from them. Until 1900 canon law officially required that women religious be cloistered and could not leave their convents to perform good works.

Let us look at this question of solemn vows and enclosure in terms of Kateri's plan, as Father Fremin might have done. European convents were supported by endowments from wealthy patrons, and dowries brought by their members. Kateri's group did women's work in the fields and village, and was provided with food by their neighbors, who saw their good works among the sick and needy. If they had enclosed themselves on Heron Island, and were no longer able to do their works of charity, would the public still have supported them? European communities that established convents in North America soon learned that they

---

5   *Ibid.*

6   I have discussed these matters in detail in *The Role of the Nun in Nineteenth-century America* (Salem, NH: Ayer, 1984), pp. 14ff. and *passim.*

had to adapt these rules to the new culture if they were to survive.[7] The Jesuit missionaries at Kahnawake would certainly not have wanted the responsibility of finding the resources to support such a venture.

After her death the Jesuits asked themselves why they had not allowed Kateri to take vows. Chauchetière wrote about Kateri's chastity:

> It is the most beautiful jewel in her crown…. If it had occurred to anyone to have her take a vow, the vow of chastity would not have been wanting, though she did not fail to live up to such a vow, which makes me believe that she received the merit of it. The priest was sorry after her death not to have let her make it.[8]

The priest referred to here is Father Pierre Cholenec, the chief administrator of the mission, who allowed Kateri to make her first communion without a trial period, heard her confessions, discussed marriage versus celibacy with her, and advised Kateri's little circle when they brought him questions. In his later versions of his biography of Kateri, Cholenec made up a beautiful story of how he accepted her vow of chastity.[9]

A model for the form of religious life that Kateri and her friends followed could be found in the life of her patroness, St. Catherine of Siena. Having taken the name of Catherine at her baptism, Kateri must have heard stories of her life from the Jesuits. St. Catherine belonged to a medieval alternative to the cloistered life. The Franciscans, Dominicans and others had *tertiaries*, members of the Third Order, men and women who wished to affiliate with the Order and its good works without being bound by the stricter rules of canon law for religious life. Catherine belonged to a Dominican affiliate called the Mantellate, because they wore a black mantle over their clothes. She lived at home and spent her days (and often her nights, too) in prayer, good works, and penance. (Perhaps Kateri and her cohorts learned some of their penances from her example.)[10] This is what Chauchetière wrote of the saint's influence on Kateri: "The spirit of Saint Katharine of Sienna [*sic*] and of other saints of this name, was revived in her [Kateri] by a particular guidance

---

7　I discuss these adaptations in great detail in my work cited above.

8　*Positio*, p. 211.

9　*Ibid.*, pp. 172-9.

10　For insight into Catherine's life and penances, see Don Brophy, *Catherine of Siena: A Passionate Life* (New York: BlueBridge, 2010), pp. 48ff. and *passim*.

of God, who made known to her at times, the secrets of a spiritual life. She had the spirit of penance to an eminent degree...."[11]

Both of her biographers describe Kateri's death. Chauchetière gives her farewell message to her friend Marie-Thérèse, and her final words to her, "I will love you in heaven."[12] Cholenec's long, effusive account says her last words were "the holy names of Jesus and Mary."[13] He continues his description of her death for many pages, followed by accounts of cures and apparitions.

Father Cholenec's account of Kateri's life was published in 1717, and became the basis of hundreds of biographies of Kateri for the next 170 years. Chauchetière's manuscript languished in Jesuit archives until 1887, when an American researcher, Ellen Walworth, oversaw the publication of the French document in New York City.[14]

While the Tekakwitha story was known and used over the centuries in Europe, the same was not true in the U.S. From the time of her death in 1680, there has always been a shrine to Kateri that was visited by Mohawks and other Indians. But as Indian fortunes shifted, and there were broad movements of Indians and encroachments of white settlers, Kateri's story was forgotten in many places. The Jesuit missionaries kept it alive, but the Jesuit Order was suppressed in 1773 and its impact dimmed for decades.

Finally, two hundred years after her death, the American Catholic Church had reason to resurrect Kateri's story. The Anti-Catholic and anti-immigrant forces of the late nineteenth century were battering the Church and its members. The bishops looked for a symbol that was both Catholic and American to enhance its image. They found it in Kateri Tekakwitha.[15] The bishops gathered at the Third Plenary Council of Baltimore in 1884 sent a petition to Pope Leo XIII, asking for the introduction of the causes for canonization of the Jesuit martyrs, Jean de Brébeuf and companions, and that of Catherine Tekakwitha. The following year some thirty Indian tribes sent petitions to Rome with the same request.[16]

---

11 *Positio*, p. 169.

12 *Ibid.*, p. 204-5.

13 *Ibid.*, p. 302.

14 Greer discusses the publication history and influence in Chapter 13, pp. 193ff.

15 Greer, pp. 193-94.

16 *Positio*, pp. 444-51.

Responsible for some of this flurry of interest was Father Clarence Walworth, who with his niece, Ellen Hardin Walworth, did a great deal of research on Kateri's story and Indian culture. Ellen Walworth published a groundbreaking biography of Kateri in 1891.[17] Based on solid research, the book focuses on Kateri's emotions and the development of her sense of self-worth, as well as her connections with her Iroquois culture. It was Ellen Walworth who devised the name Kateri for Catherine Tekakwitha, deriving it from the French pronunciation of Catherine and Mohawk linguistics.[18] Kateri Tekakwitha, The Lily of the Mohawks, had finally come into her own among American Catholics!

THE DREAM FULFILLED

For bishops who were trying to make their Catholicism look truly American, Central Casting could not have come up with a more perfect specimen than Francis M. Craft. Born to an Episcopalian WASP family in New York City in 1852, great-grandson of a full-blooded Mohawk Indian, a descendant of Revolutionary War heroes, he could not have been more "American." He became a Catholic in the 1870s; spent four years with the Jesuits (1876-80); catechized the Kalispel Indians; was ordained by Bishop Martin Marty for Dakota Territory in 1883; and started missionary work on the Rosebud Reservation that same year.[19]

Later he would write, "As I have become an Indian to save the Indians, I think it my duty to work as no man ever worked before to save them."[20] And work he did, first on the Rosebud Reservation (1883) then at Standing Rock (1884-89), and finally, at Fort Berthold. He rode a 300-mile circuit regularly to visit eleven missions, encountering hardships of all kinds, not to mention involvement in the political shenanigans of the reservations, involving agents, Indians, different religious denominations, and even misunderstandings with his Catholic brethren.

Craft loved the Indians and admired many aspects of their culture, attending the grass dance, wearing eagle feathers in his hat, and defending Indian rights. Spotted Tail's tribe chose him as their chief, naming

---

17   *The Life and Times of Kateri Tekakwitha, the Lily of the Mohawks* (Buffalo, NY: Peter Paul and Brothers, 1891).

18   Greer, pp. 196-98.

19   Thomas W. Foley, *Father Francis M. Craft Missionary to the Sioux* (Lincoln: University of Nebraska Press, 2002) is the chief source for details of Craft's life.

20   *Ibid.*, p. 38.

him Hovering Eagle. He opposed the sending of Native children to distant boarding schools, thus angering school and government agents. He was wounded at the Wounded Knee massacre as he tried to help the Indians. With many other people of the 1880s and 1890s Craft thought that education and citizenship would bring the Indians into full participation in American society.

There are obviously many facets to Father Craft's life, but here we want to focus on only one of them: his efforts to nurture a community of Indian nuns, Kateri Tekakwitha's unfulfilled dream. We do not know when Craft first heard about Kateri, whether from the Jesuits, from the bishops' campaign, or during his studies in Europe. However he heard about Kateri Tekakwitha, it is clear that he saw her as a patroness and example for The American Congregation, the sisterhood that he founded at Fort Berthold in 1891. Craft appreciated the Indians' abilities and their culture, and realized that women were the most effective agents for the Christianization of their people. Craft identified young women who might have a religious vocation in the mission school at Fort Yates, on the Standing Rock Reservation. He encouraged them, and saw to their further education with the Sisters of the Holy Child Jesus at St. Francis Xavier Academy in Avoca, Minnesota. There they were to learn "the rudiments of English and the ordinary manners and customs of civilized life."[21]

Craft's efforts succeeded, and Ellen Clark entered the Benedictine Sisters' novitiate at Zell, South Dakota, in 1885, becoming Sister Gregory and making her first vows a year later. Anna Pleets and Josephine Crowfeather followed her example in 1889. Josephine made her first vows and became Sister Catherine on April 21, 1890—perhaps the first woman to take a professed name honoring Kateri Tekakwitha.

Miss Crowfeather's vows were of special significance. By virtue of his investiture as a Dakota chief, Father Craft had entered into a special relationship with the Sioux, which he took very seriously. He became especially close to the family of Joseph Crowfeather, chief of the Uncpapa tribe, and he even seems to have been adopted by them. He always referred to the chief's daughter Josephine as his sister.

Josephine's Indian name meant, "They see a white buffalo woman." This was very significant. White Buffalo Calf Woman held a sacred place in Sioux mythology. She had appeared in ancient times, dressed in white

---

21   Mother St. Anthony to Rev. J. A. Stephan, Archives of the Bureau of Catholic Indian Missions, Marquette University.

buckskins, and given the Indians the peace pipe and a sacred bundle before turning herself into a white buffalo calf and disappearing. She represented a tangible link with the sacred. Accordingly, Josephine was called the sacred virgin of her tribe almost from the time of her birth, and her life was thought to be safe from all harm. Her father carried the infant into battle in his arms, thinking she would protect him, and they both came through unscathed.[22]

Years later Josephine used to say that one of her earliest dreams was to be a sister,[23] and when she was still quite young she appealed to Father Craft to help her achieve this goal. It is said that she once saved Craft's life, when some Indians threatened him. Craft used to bring Josephine candy, dresses, and other gifts at the Fort Yates School. She would share them with the other girls.[24]

When Josephine Crowfeather entered the Benedictine novitiate on Easter Sunday in 1889, the event was duly reported, not only in the regional *Dakota Catholic* (May 25 and June 1, 1889,) but also in *The New York Freeman's Journal* (June 8, 1889). The June 1 article gives the flavor:

> The first full-blood Sioux to make religious profession was received into the Benedictine Novitiate at Zell on Easter Sunday. She had been four years under the care of the Benedictine Sisters at Fort Yates, and had repeatedly asked the favor of joining the community. Under the pastoral care of the good Indian missionary, Rev. Francis Craft, she developed strong signs of a religious vocation, and her prayer was finally granted.... The ceremony was an impressive one, not only for the whites present, but also for the numbers of her tribe upon whom this event is likely to produce a marked religious effect. Her name in religion is Sister Mary Josephine.

Craft went to Fort Berthold in June of 1899 to assess the needs and possibilities. Then he wrote that he would take the mission if he could have some Benedictine sisters to help him, including the Indian novices,

---

22   Sister Mary Claudia Duratschek, *The Beginnings of Catholicism in South Dakota* (Washington, DC: Catholic University Press, 1943), p. 108.

23   "An Indian Sisterhood," *Catholic Almanac*, August 25, 1894; clipping XVII, St. John's Abbey, Collegeville, MN.

24   Interview of Sister Claudia Duratschek with two former pupils on May 25, 1943, Archives, Sacred Heart Convent, Yankton, SD.

who could do their novitiate there. "Let my sister Josephine make her novitiate [at Fort Berthold] with them, under my direction," he wrote.[25]

It was clear that money was needed for the mission at Fort Berthold. With the aspiring vocations settled in the Benedictine convent and the school at Avoca, Father Craft headed East in March 1890, ostensibly to raise money for the Bureau of Catholic Indian Missions, which would support Fort Berthold. En route to New York City he stopped at Auriesville to pray at the shrine of Kateri Tekakwitha for his Indian "daughters" and their religious vocations. There he also took some strips from nearby red willow bushes and sent them, with letters of encouragement, to each of them.[26] If we could read those letters, I think we would see him holding up Kateri Tekakwitha as a model for their religious life. (Kateri employed red willow—osier—switches to flagellate herself. Red willow bark is also a popular Native medicine, good for coughs, headaches, and other ailments.)[27]

Craft re-established ties with family and old friends, and made some new ones, particularly in the press and with James Kelly, an artist and sculptor. He made the situation among the Indians widely known, but raised very little money. And he honed his skills as a public relations marketer for the Indian missions and his Indian sisters.

Several of the newspaper articles he generated mentioned six Indian sisters, and some carried line drawings of Sisters Gregory, Bridget (Anna Pleets,) and Catherine (Josephine Crowfeather.) One in the *Irish World* for August 16, 1890, carries the caption, "The Lily of the Dakotas," under Sister Catherine's picture. Clearly he was touting her as a modern-day Catherine Tekakwitha, even at this early stage, when she had been in the convent for little more than a year.

Craft returned to Fort Berthold in April 1891, after being wounded at Wounded Knee in January, and spending some time recovering. When school closed, he accompanied his six protégées from the school at Avoca back to Standing Rock. On the way back he arranged for them to give up their Indian citizenship and tribal rights and become American

---

25 Francis M. Craft, *At Standing Rock and Wounded Knee: The Journals and Papers of Father Francis M. Craft 1888-1890*, ed. Thomas W. Foley (Norman, OK: Clark Co., 2009), p. 240.

26 *Ibid.*, pp. 81-2.

27 Internet web site for ehow, *Medicinal Uses of Red Willow Bark*, URL: www.ehow.com/list_7397961-medicinal-uses-red-willow-

citizens.[28] (American citizenship would later be required of all who entered his community.) All six of them entered the Benedictine community in the fall. At the same time Mother Gertrude Leupi, who had guided the Benedictines since their arrival from Switzerland, returned to Switzerland, leaving a 33-year-old sister in charge.

There were problems of many kinds in the community, including episcopal interference, ethnic tensions, and factions vying for power. Craft had heard of some unhappiness among the Indian sisters there, but when Catherine Crowfeather informed him that they were going to send her sister, Claudia Crowfeather, back to Fort Yates because of her ill health, Craft went himself to deal with the situation.[29] There is little evidence that he had a long-term plan to found an independent Indian community, but now he determined to do it, and to prove that Indians could be the equals of anyone in living a religious life. On November first he was at the Yankton motherhouse, armed with the authorization of Bishop Shanley to bring the Indian sisters and candidates to Fort Berthold and take full responsibility for their religious life. Those named were: Sister Mary Catherine and postulants Claudia Crowfeather, Jane Moccasin, Alice Whitedeer, Nellie Dubray, and Louise Bourdeaux.[30]

Sister Gregory (Ellen Clark) had gone off with others to start a convent elsewhere, and Sister Bridget Pleets chose to stay with the white sisters at Yankton. In the end both joined Craft's group, and were among the final three sisters with him when the group finally disbanded in Cuba around 1900. Bridget complained that Catherine "caused more trouble than anyone else."[31]

Not everyone was in favor of encouraging Indian women to become sisters. Craft wrote to Rev. George Willard of the Bureau of Catholic Indian Missions on January 17, 1890 about a meeting with Father Joseph Stephan: "He spoke strongly against my plan for Indian Sisters, and in general regards me as a crank whose views are entirely visionary." Craft defended those views, however, saying that they were the same as those of Robert De Nobili, Brébeuf and other missionaries among the Indians.

---

28   A notarized document dated June 30, 1891 contains the wording of the official document, Archives, Sacred Heart Convent, Yankton, SD. (ASHC).

29   Letter of Mother Xavier, Oct. 20, 1891, ASHC.

30   Letter Nov. 1, 1891, ASHC.

31   Sister Bridget Pleets to Mother Gertrude Leupi, November 27, 1891, ASHC.

Then Craft brought up a new subject, the persecution of Josephine at the convent:

> I knew what trials awaited me here, and took this place only because my sister had been persecuted on account of her vocation, and I saw no other way to save her than by sacrificing myself. Had she been let alone, and treated like other aspirants to the religious state, I would not have known so much about the dirty, cowardly teaching of holy people....[32]

Craft complained repeatedly about race prejudice against his Indian sisters, and it is clear that racism did exist. The Indian agent at Standing Rock was suspicious of Craft's zealous attention to the young ladies studying at Avoca.[33] In Craft's mind the exposure of his pure Indian maidens to evil and corruption in the reservations, and their persecution, were akin to Kateri's experiences. He had written in his journal on February 11, 1889: "If [Jesus] keeps souls pure, in the midst of corruption, as He did Catharine Tegakawita [sic], the Lily of the Mohawks, how can I doubt that He will save, and sanctify, and take as His spouse my Josephine Mary, the Lily of the Sacred Heart!"[34]

Even at this early stage, before Josephine had made vows and chosen the name Catherine, Craft was making the comparison with the Lily of the Mohawks. He used "Lily of the Sacred Heart" for her because that was the name of the mission at Fort Berthold. He used "Lily of the Dakotas" when he was writing in a Dakota newspaper. Surely the very recent petitions from the bishops and the Indian tribes to Rome for Kateri's canonization (in 1884 and 1885) had brought the Lily of the Mohawks to the attention of all connected with Indian endeavors.

Because of the persecution that he perceived, and the definite opposition to the idea of an Indian sisterhood among some Jesuits, Benedictines, and others, and various problems he had on the reservations (some of them of his own making), Craft thought about moving the sisterhood to the East. Again, Kateri was in his thoughts as he wrote to his artist-friend James Kelly in 1892:

> It would be a good idea if I could establish my Indian community somewhere near the settlements of the New York Indians, and try to convert them. The interest taken in the shrine [of Kateri and the

---

32   BCIM Archives.

33   Foley, *Craft*, p. 101.

34   Craft, p. 235.

Jesuit Martyrs] at Auriesville would seem to show that the people of New York would be in favor of a work like ours.[35]

Father Craft had a great imagination, and used it in giving religious names to the young women who joined his sisterhood. Josephine Crowfeather, who had been Sister Catherine among the Benedictines, was chosen the superior of the new group, and became known as Mother Catherine Sacred White Buffalo. According to Thomas Foley, the "Catherine" part of the name was taken after Catherine (Kateri) Tekakwitha.[36]

With the official establishment of the community, Craft began a national publicity campaign. An article reprinted in the *New York Freeman's Journal* on February 6, 1892, calls the sisters "Lilies of the Sacred Heart," and says, among other things: "It is worth noting that the Indian community that Catherine Tekakwitha intended to establish, had she lived long enough, has been established—perhaps through the prayers of the "Lily of the Mohawk," by Sister Mary Catherine, 'The Lily of the Dakotas.'"

He also noted that the director of the community—Craft himself—was a brother of Kateri Tekakwitha by the family and tribal relationship. Prominent in the community room of the sisters' new convent were red willows that he brought from Auriesville, and the picture of Kateri that Craft had brought back for Sister Catherine.

Claudia Crowfeather, whose illness had brought about their move, died in March 1892, having received the habit and made perpetual vows, and taken the name Sister Theresa in December. In due time the others were professed and received names related to their Indian names: Liguori Sound-of-the-Flying-Lance, Gertrude Brings Forth Holiness, Francis Regis White Eagle, Anthony Cloud Robe, and Aloysia, all preceded by "Mother."

Father Craft termed an article in a magazine called the *Poor Souls' Advocate* for July and August 1892, written by Mother Liguori Sound-of-the-Flying-Lance (Alice White Deer), "the first literary effort by an Indian Sister." Titled "Indian Vocations," it had this to say:

> After four centuries of missionary labor among the Indians, after many thousand Indian virgins passed away ... there is at last an Indian community among the Indians. What the Mohawk Catherine and her friend Theresa and their pious Indian maidens dreamed of and

---

35   Foley, p. 149.

36   *Faces of Faith* (Baltimore, MD: Cathedral Foundation Press, 2008), p. 14.

sighed for two centuries ago … the Dakota Catherine and her sister Theresa, and their companions have realized….[37]

Mother Catherine Sacred White Buffalo had had a chest cold during the winter of 1892-3, which was actually tuberculosis, and she succumbed to the disease that had also killed her sister, on May 2, 1893. Having learned, no doubt, from Kateri's biographers what a proper "saint's" death should be like, Craft made it a major event.

The nationwide publicity that accompanied his wounding at Wounded Knee seems to have propelled him to a new level of consciousness regarding his role and that of his sisters in helping the Church to be seen as American. It is as if he said to the bishops, "You want an American symbol? Kateri is your ideal icon? Let me give you some even better ones: Indian sisters in The American Congregation, who speak English and are concerned about the problems of the day, the Irish, progressive politics, the immigrants, etc." He wrote a description of Catherine's death that rivaled Cholenec's of Kateri's death, and had artist James E. Kelly make a drawing of the scene, both of which were circulated all over the world. He was poised to "out-Kateri" Kateri.

Craft used a ritual that had been used in the Indian missions in upstate New York in the seventeenth century that was NOT used at Kateri's funeral. He described it in the *Irish World* for May 1893:

> On Sunday, April 30, the feast of her patroness, St. Catharine of Siena, she received the chiefs and representatives of the Indians, and gave them her last advice and wishes for her people. Early in the morning of May 2nd, feeling that she was dying, she had her sisters carry her to the convent chapel … and lay her before the altar, dressed in her religious habit. She received the Holy Viaticum…. She directed her Sisters to sing her Latin, English and Indian hymns in honor of Venerable Catharine Tekakwitha, to the music of the Te Deum—the English version—"Holy God We Praise Thy Name."

Craft went on to describe the exposition of the blessed sacrament on the altar, the mass, and benediction after mass. She made her last adoration while they recited the prayers for the dying. With the incense still wafting in the air, she died, "holding her crucifix and praying fervently…." He went on to describe how she had put right four centuries of infamy for the Church. By the success of the Indian sisterhood, under severe trials, she has "triumphantly vindicated the Catholicity of her church and the

---

37 Foley, pp. 102-3.

spiritual and mental capacity of her race." Then he related her interests to those of the readers. She was concerned about all downtrodden people. The Irish, the Italians, Pope Leo XIII, the Progressives, the editor of the newspaper and his family, all would enjoy her constant intercession for them before God.

In a letter to artist James E. Kelly, he added more details. The habit she died in was the one she had made from "the blood-stained and bullet-torn cassock" he had worn at Wounded Knee, and the crucifix she held was the one he had used in the battle. It was a scene "never witnessed before, except at the death of St. Benedict." As if he was starting a cult of relics, he enclosed for Kelly a Sacred Heart badge worn by Mother Catherine. Then he asked Kelly if he could send some prominent person or member of the press to visit the sisters and make their work known.

He sent Kelly a drawing he made (à la Chauchetière's of Kateri?) of the death scene, and asked him to re-work it. He gave him many details and photographs to help him, and also asked him to do a sculpture, that might reside one day in Statuary Hall in the U.S. Capitol, with copies to be made for the Pope and Cardinal Satolli, the Pope's special representative to the U.S. Church. We have a photograph of a bust that Kelly sculpted, but the original has never been found. Cardinal Satolli had sent her a papal blessing, but Craft's letters inviting him to visit had probably been intercepted, Craft said.

While Catherine's death scene can rival Kateri's, the same is not true of her burial place. She was buried in the Catholic cemetery in Elbowoods, North Dakota, near a tall crucifix that was a place of much devotion for the Indians. When the Garrison Dam project flooded the area, the remains were moved to Queen of Peace Cemetery near Raub, North Dakota. Her simple Corps of Engineers marker reads, "Sister Catherine, Grey Nun."

After the death of their "foundress," Mother Liguori Sound-of-the-Flying-Lance (Alice White Deer) took over as superior. The sisters did home nursing (having learned from Father Craft, who had studied medicine), and were catechists to their people. They spent the summer of 1894 in St. Paul, studying the methods used by sisters there in teaching and nursing. New sisters joined, bringing the number to twelve by 1896.

Father Craft admitted that he had never fully recovered from his battlefield wounds. That, combined with many years of exertion, and the constant worry over supporting and defending the sisters made him irascible, paranoid, and difficult to deal with. In trying to defend the

Indians or the Church he got into public fights with Washington officials, Benedictine missionaries, and others. Though he was the sisterhood's chief supporter and defender, he was also sometimes a liability to the community. Bishop Shanley reported in a letter in 1899 that the years of work had taken their toll on Craft, and his mind became diseased. The lonely life at Fort Berthold would drive anyone crazy, Shanley said.[38]

In 1897 there were charges on the reservation that some sisters had acted immorally with some school officials. Craft said the accusation was political, Democrats against Republicans. Things were reported to bishops and to Washington; there was an investigation that cleared the sisters; people were fired and then retaliated, and life became very difficult for Craft and the sisters.[39]

Several sisters left the community and returned home. Craft and the remaining sisters departed from Fort Berthold in June 1897, and spent the summer visiting the Sioux camps. Reports that some who wanted to leave were afraid to, reached various agents and Church officials.[40]

When the Spanish-American War broke out in April 1898, Craft wrote to the War Department, offering his services and those of his sisters in the medical field. They were experienced nurses, he said, and used to working in primitive conditions. Sisters Bridget Pleets, Gregory (Ellen) Clark, Anthony Bordeaux, and Joseph Two Bears were all accepted, and Craft became a hospital orderly. They served in camps in Savannah and Jacksonville before being shipped to Havana. Sister Anthony died there, and received a military funeral. Craft's efforts to have her remains buried in Arlington National Cemetery were unsuccessful.

After the war they stayed on in Cuba and ran an orphanage, while Craft tried desperately to salvage the situation. On December 31, 1899 Anna Pleets and Ellen Clark, no longer sisters, boarded a boat for New York, from whence they returned to the Dakotas.

---

38   Shanley to Katherine Drexel, August 19, 1899, Archives, Sisters of the Blessed Sacrament, Bensalem, PA.

39   Craft to Rev. J. A. Stephan, April 20, 1897, BCIM; Craft to James E. Kelly, April 2, 1897, New-York Historical Society Archives.

40   See, for example, the letter of agent James E. Jenkins of the Sisseton Reservation, where Ellen Clark's mother lived, to the Superintendent at Pierre, Oct. 10, 1898. Record Group 75, National Archives.

Mother Joseph Two Bears and Father Craft arrived in New York sometime before April 4, 1901, the day Kelly did a portrait of her.[41] That was probably the last official record of the valiant attempt to bring Kateri's dream of an Indian sisterhood to fulfillment. Perhaps some day in the future The American Congregation will receive a modicum of the recognition and fanfare that have accompanied Kateri's failed dream.

Francis Craft returned to his home in Milford, Pennsylvania, and became the first pastor of St. Matthew's Church in East Stroudsburg on July 4, 1902, where he served with distinction until his death on September 11, 1920.

The idea of an indigenous sisterhood serving their own people may have suffered a setback, but it did not die. The 1930s saw the foundation of The Oblate Sisters of the Blessed Sacrament in South Dakota and of the Sisters of the Snows in Alaska, and the dream lives on.

---

41   For further information on The American Congregation, see Mary Ewens, "The Native Order A Brief and Strange History," in *Scattered Steeples. The Fargo Diocese: A Written Celebration of its Centennial*, eds. Jerome D. Lamb et al. Fargo, ND: Burch, Londergan and Lynch, 1988, pp. 10-23.

Printed by permission of Sister Mary Ewens, O.P.

IO

A LILY AMONG THORNS

THE MOHAWK REPATRIATION OF KÁTERI TEKAHKWÍTHA

PRESENTED AT THE 30TH CONFERENCE ON NEW YORK STATE HISTORY, JUNE 5, 2009, IN PLATTSBURGH, NEW YORK

DARREN BONAPARTE

Darren Bonaparte is a Mohawk intellectual and historical journalist from Akwesasne, whose essays have appeared in many American Indian journals. In 1999 he created an archival website, The Wampum Chronicles, in order to promote and preserve Mohawk cultural heritage. He is author of A Lily among Thorns. The Mohawk Repatriation of Káteri Tekahkwí:tha (2009), from which the following essay derives, in which he asserts the Mohawk content of Kateri's spirituality.

"Who will teach me what is most agreeable to God, so that I may do it?"
Káteri Tekahkwí:tha

INTRODUCTION

Blessed Káteri Tekahkwí:tha, the Lily of the Mohawks, was a Kanien'kehá:ka woman of the 17th century whose extraordinary life and reputation for holiness have made her an icon to Roman Catholics throughout the world.
　　She was declared venerable by Pope Pius XII in 1943, and beatified by Pope John Paul II in 1980. In 2008, the Cause for the

Canonization of Blessed Káteri Tekahkwí:tha was formally submitted to Pope Benedict XVI. She is memorialized at Saint Patrick's Cathedral in Manhattan and the Washington National Cathedral in Washington, D.C. Throughout North America, she is depicted in statues and stained glass windows that adorn chapels named in her honor.

A recent biographer (Greer 2005: vii, xi) declared that no aboriginal person's life has been more fully documented than that of Káteri Tekahkwí:tha. The writings of Jesuit priests who knew her personally became the basis for at least three hundred books published in more than twenty languages.

Reverence of Káteri Tekahkwí:tha transcends tribal differences. Indigenous Catholics identify with her story, and have taken her to heart. They have made her so much their own that they depict her in their art wearing their own traditional clothing.

The only negative in all of this is that she looks less Mohawk with each new depiction, as though her cultural background is irrelevant. The opposite is true: Káteri Tekahkwí:tha was raised with—and defined by—traditional Mohawk beliefs, and it was her understanding of them that led her to embrace a new faith, not so much as a rejection of her traditional beliefs, but as the fulfillment of them.

In recent decades, scholars like David Blanchard, K. I. Koppedreyer, Daniel Richter, Nancy Shoemaker, and Allan Greer, among others, have wrestled this subject away from the domain of more devotional writers, bringing a more critical insight into the cultural world of Káteri Tekahkwí:tha and the Rotinonhsión:ni converts of Kahnawà:ke.

The time has come for the *Rotinonhsión:ni* to take it to the next step by repatriating the story of the Mohawk maiden and liberating it from the "saint among savages" theme that was attached to it so long ago.

THE LIFE OF KÁTERI TEKAHKWÍ:THA

The 17th century was the age of contact and colonization for the Kanien'kehá:ka, the People of the Land of Flint. With the arrival of Champlain and Hudson, *The Prophecy of the Serpents of Silver and Gold* was fulfilled before our very eyes.

The Kanien'kehá:ka were part of a confederacy known as the Rotinonhsión:ni, the "People of the Longhouse," also known as the Five Nations and the Iroquois. To negotiate a treaty of peace and friendship with the Longhouse, Dutch fur traders of New Netherland had to go through the Mohawk, the "Keepers of the Eastern Door."

Wampum belts depicting this covenant sometimes have two human figures holding a chain between them. The European is holding an ax in his other hand, representing both trade and military alliance. For the Rotinonhsión:ni, the covenant with New Netherland meant conflict with the aboriginal allies of New France, the Huron and Algonquin.

Káteri Tekahkwí:tha witnessed firsthand the "clash of cultures" brought about by the colonization of Turtle Island. She was a product of it. Her mother was a Catholic Algonquin captured during a Mohawk raid on Trois-Rivières, adopted and nationalized as a Mohawk, and married to a chief. Tekahkwí:tha was their first child, born sometime around 1656. The smallpox epidemic of 1661-1662 killed her parents and a younger brother, and left her disfigured, sickly, and unable to stand bright light. The name Tekahkwí:tha, in fact, is a reference to the way she used her hands to feel her way. In the aftermath of this tragedy, she was taken in by an uncle, a leading chief of the village, and raised as one of his daughters.

While his wife made plans to arrange a marriage for the little girl, the chief concerned himself with the affairs of the nation. Mohawk attacks on their Huron trading partners had long been an irritation to the French, and a new governor arrived in New France, as one Jesuit wrote, "to plant lilies on the graves of the Iroquois" (Thwaites 1896-1901, vol. 46: 241).

The Oneida, Onondaga, Cayuga and Seneca entered into peace talks with the French, but the Mohawks refused to be a part of it. The French sent an army to Mohawk country in January of 1666, but they got lost in the woods near Schenectady, and were forced to abandon their ill-conceived mission with great losses.

Several months later, they launched another assault with an army twice the size of the first. With the herald of war drums to announce their approach, they succeeded in marching straight into our villages and burning them to the ground. We were able to evacuate before they arrived and were seen shouting at the French troops from a nearby hilltop, but we could do little to halt the progress of the Carignan-Salières Regiment. The French commander marvelled at the material prosperity evident in the Mohawk villages. It is said the French army found enough food in these villages "to nourish all Canada for two years" (Marie de l'Incarnation 1967: 326).

Tekahkwí:tha was then ten years old and living in the eastern Mohawk village, *Kahnawà:ke*, or "At the Rapids," the first to be destroyed by the French. The burning of her village must have been particularly traumatic to a child, but her Jesuit biographers rarely mention it.

Somehow we managed to survive the winter. We were probably taken in by our brother nations. In the spring, we built new villages on the north side of the Mohawk River, just in time for the French to send peace envoys in the form of Jesuit missionaries.

At first the Jesuits tended to our Christian Huron and Algonquin captives, but Mohawks began to take an interest in their teachings as time went by. With missions established in all of the Five Nations, a steady flow of Iroquois converts began to depart our homelands for *Kahentà:ke*, a new Indian mission across the river from Montreal at Laprairie. The success of this mission caused one Jesuit to remark,

> … In less than Seven years the warriors of Anié have become more numerous at montreal than they are in their own country. That enrages both the elders of the villages and the flemings of manate and orange. In a short time, less than a year or two, 200 persons were thus added to the number of the Christians at la prairie (Thwaites 1896-1901, vol. 63: 177-179 [sic]).

The Mohawk population had already suffered significant losses to disease and warfare, and on-going conflicts on other fronts meant the Mohawks had no souls to spare. Yet there was a good argument for having eyes and ears in the heart of New France, where we could watch troop movements should hostilities resume. It also gave us another market for furs, giving us leverage with the English, who by this time were running the old Dutch store under the name New York.

Jesuit accounts emphasize religious differences between the Mohawk converts and their traditional kin as the primary reason for the removal. The schism seems to have affected the home fire of Tekahkwí:tha in particular. Her uncle was one of the village elders opposed to this exodus to New France. When the renowned warrior *Atahsà:ta*—better known as Kryn, the Great Mohawk—left for Kahentà:ke in 1673, more than 40 people went with him, including Tekahkwí:tha's older sister. The chief was not about to lose another daughter, so he forbade Tekahkwí:tha from going near the missionaries.

One autumn day in 1675, Father James de Lamberville, a newly arrived priest, walked by what he thought was an empty longhouse and felt impelled to look inside. He found Tekahkwí:tha there with a foot injury. The 19-year-old was a good candidate for instruction, so he spoke to her of Christianity, and urged her to come to mass. She was baptized on Easter Sunday of 1676, and given the name Káteri, the Mohawk version of the French form of Katharine. It is by the combination of her Catholic and traditional Mohawk name that we know her today, Káteri Tekahkwí:tha.

Around this time her new parents arranged a marriage for her, but she refused to go along with it. The Jesuits tell us Káteri was persecuted for becoming a Christian, and had stones thrown at her by children. They also claim that her uncle had a warrior enter her lodge and threaten her with a tomahawk, but she only bowed her head as if to accept her fate, spooking the young warrior. The story gets more dramatic with each telling, with the terrified warrior fleeing for his life as if pursued by demons.

She would not endure these trials for long, as her older sister sent her husband on a dramatic mission back to the Mohawk Valley to bring Káteri to New France in the fall of 1677.

With the assistance of Father Lamberville, Káteri was spirited away from the Mohawk village by her brother-in-law and a Huron of Lorette. Káteri's uncle returned home to find her missing and set out in hot pursuit. The men were aware of his approach and hid Káteri in the forest. They convinced her uncle that they were hunters and not the individuals he was looking for, nor had they seen a young woman. Although the Jesuits state that the uncle was in a homicidal rage when he began the chase, he calmly turned around and went home.

Káteri and her companions proceeded on foot to Lake George, where they recovered the canoe the rescuers hid there on the way to the Mohawk Valley. After a journey of about two weeks on the Lake George/Lake Champlain/Richelieu River corridor, they reached the new Indian mission, St. François Xavier du Sault, established several miles west of Laprairie at what is now Ville Sainte-Catherine. Like the Mohawk village from which many of its people came, there were rapids nearby, so it was given the name Kahnawà:ke, the name by which it is known today.

After a long and harrowing journey, Káteri arrived at her new home. During the tour of the new Kahnawà:ke, she would have been taken to the chapel, which at that point looked more like a bark longhouse than a church, but it did have a proper altar with monstrance, chalice, paten, and candelabra. There was also a wampum belt of over 8,000 beads, a recent gift of the Hurons of Lorette to the people of Kahnawà:ke. Father Claude Chauchetière wrote of this wampum belt in his history of the Mission of the Sault, which we find in the *Jesuit Relations*:

> It was a hortatory collar which conveyed the voice of the Lorette people to those of the Sault, encouraging them to accept the faith in good earnest, and to build a chapel as soon as possible, and it also exhorted them to combat the various demons who conspired for the ruin of both missions. This collar was at once attached to one of the beams of the chapel, which is above the top of the altar, so that the people might always behold it and hear that voice. (*Ibid.*, vol. 63: 193-195)

Káteri moved in with her older sister's family, and took instruction from an older woman named *Kanáhstatsi Tekonwatsenhón:ko*. This was a woman she knew from childhood, a long-standing Christian. Kanáhstatsi became a third mother to Káteri.

When it came time for the winter hunt, she went with her sister's family out into the wilderness. There were several other families in this hunting party. One night an exhausted hunter came in after everyone else had gone to sleep. He found an empty space on the floor of the lodge and fell fast asleep. His wife woke up the next morning and saw that he was lying next to Káteri. She convinced herself that the two of them were having an affair, and accused her of it to the priest when the hunting party returned to Kahnawà:ke. Káteri was questioned about it and acquitted herself well in the matter. The priest believed her, but she swore off winter hunts after that.

Káteri made a new friend the following spring, a young Oneida widow named *Wari Teres Tekaien'kwénhtha*. They met while visiting the construction site of the new wooden chapel after the carpenters had left for the day. Káteri and Wari Teres became inseparable friends, each of them supporting the other in a celibate life devoted to Christ. They even spoke to a Huron woman about starting their own convent. When Káteri's sister and Kanáhstatsi put pressure on her to get married, she refused. She knew that French nuns were consecrated unto Christ, and decided that was the life for her. On March 25, 1679—the Feast of Annunciation—she made a vow of perpetual virginity.

This brings us to the part of the story that many of the later books gloss over or omit altogether.

According to Jesuit accounts, the *Onkwehón:we Tehatiiahsóntha'*— "Original People Who Make the Sign of the Cross"—somehow found out that the Jesuits would scourge themselves in private, and wanted to participate in this hidden aspect of Christianity. They imitated and exceeded the Jesuits in this regard. Not only did they whip themselves repeatedly, but they walked barefoot through snowdrifts, and cut holes in the ice to submerge themselves in water up to their necks long enough to say the rosary. The most fervent would wear a *cingulum*, or "penitential girdle," a leather belt with metal studs on the inside that dug into the wearer's skin.

The Jesuits made half-hearted admonitions against all of this, but they secretly admired the fervor of their converts and allowed them to continue. They even admit to supplying some of the instruments.

Káteri Tekahkwí:tha and Wari Teres Tekaien'kwénhtha were among the young women swept up in this movement. A contemporary letter written by Father Pierre Cholenec in February of 1680 undoubtedly describes Káteri, even though she is not identified by name:

> … there is one especially who is small and lame, who is the most fervent, I believe, of all the village, and who, though she is quite infirm and nearly always ill, does surprising things in these matters. And she would beat herself unmercifully, if she were allowed to do so. Something quite important happened to her lately, which Father and I could not marvel enough at.
>
> While scourging herself as usual with admirable ardor (for she exceeds in this particular all the other women, with one exception of Margaret) and that in a very dark spot, she found herself surrounded by a great light, as if it were high noon, lasting as long as the first shower of blows, so to speak, of her scourging, for she scourged herself several times. Insofar as I could judge from what she told me, this light lasted two or three misereres. (Cholenec 1966)

One night Káteri asked Kanáhstatsi what she thought was the most painful thing a person could endure, and she said, "fire." That night, Káteri and Wari Teres decided to place a hot coal between their toes for as long as they could stand it. Just the thought of it was enough to cause Wari Teres to faint. The next day, Káteri revealed to Wari Teres that she went through with it and had the burns to prove it.

The next act she did alone, scattering thorns on her bed and laying on them for three nights in a row. Wari Teres found out about this and told the priest, but it was already too late.

Káteri was small to begin with—probably no more than 4 ½ feet tall—and malnourished from frequent fasting. Her tiny frame and poor health could not endure such harsh mortification. She died in the odor of sanctity on Holy Wednesday, 1680.

Father Pierre writes of a "marvel" that he witnessed upon her death:

> Due to the smallpox, Katharine's face had been disfigured since the age of four, and her infirmities and mortifications had contributed to disfigure her even more, but this face, so marked and swarthy, suddenly changed about a quarter of an hour after her death, and became in a moment so beautiful and so white that I observed it immediately (for I was praying beside her) and cried out, so great was my astonishment.... I admit openly that the first thought that came to me was that Katharine at that moment might have entered into heaven, reflecting in her chaste body a small ray of the glory of which her soul had taken possession. (Sacred Congregation of Rites 1940: 306-307)

Not long after she died, Káteri appeared to at least three individuals, one of whom was Father Claude. The apparitions varied from a simple bedside visit, which is how Wari Teres saw her, to terrifying, prophetic visions of death and destruction, which is how Father Claude saw her.

There were whispers among the settlers of New France that a saint had been among them. Miracles were attributed to her intercession. Dirt from her grave, the utensils she ate with, the crucifix she wore—all were known to affect cures.

Convinced that he had been in the presence of holiness, Father Claude wrote the first of his many biographies of the young Mohawk woman, followed by Father Pierre, who was equally prolific. Through their writing, the legend of Káteri Tekahkwí:tha, the Miracle Worker of the New World, reached across the sea to France and all the way to the Vatican.

A LILY AMONG THORNS

Káteri Tekahkwí:tha is universally known as the "Lily of the Mohawks." A Mohawk elder told me that she is called this because after her death, lilies grew on her grave. That may be so, but there is a more mundane explanation.

The *fleur-de-lys*, or "lily flower," is a heraldic symbol of the French monarchy. Four are depicted in the flag of Québec. The stylized lily represents the Holy Trinity and the Virgin Mary. Associating Káteri with the lily was the French stamp of approval.

It was Father Claude who first evoked the lily metaphor when he wrote, "I have up to the present written of Katharine as a lily among thorns, but now I shall relate how God transplanted this beautiful lily and placed it in a garden full of flowers, that is to say, in the Mission of the Sault, where there have been, are, and always will be holy people renowned for virtue" (*ibid.*: 142).

He was borrowing from the Song of Solomon (2:2) for his analogy: "As the lily among thorns, so is my love among the daughters." By his hand, another Jesuit's words were fulfilled as prophecy: a lily was planted on the grave of an Iroquois.

Traditional Mohawks, by default, are the thorns in this metaphor, and it's not surprising that they don't go anywhere near this story, having served as the contrast to Káteri's goodness all these years. But there are other thorns to consider. There is the crown of thorns that Káteri chose to share when she consecrated herself to Jesus Christ. There is the bed of thorns that hastened her demise.

This brings me to why I believe there was something much more than a simple conversion going on with Káteri Tekahkwí:tha.

The Jesuits had to learn Mohawk. They didn't force us to learn French. They borrowed names and concepts from our creation story to teach us their story. *Karonhià:ke*, the Mohawk name for Sky World, became the Mohawk word for heaven in the Lord's Prayer. This was not just a linguistic shortcut, but a conceptual bridge from one cosmology to another.

We had something else in common: the belief that it was possible for a human female to unite with a powerful, unseen spirit, and to produce children with mystical powers from this union. This is found not only in our creation epic, but in the story of the Peacemaker and the legend of Thunder Boy. Hearing the story in Mohawk, Mary and her "fatherless boy" must have sounded like one of our own tales.

Did Káteri Tekahkwí:tha see herself in that light, as an earthly woman uniting with a Sky Dweller?

Or had she been a Sky Dweller all along?

REFERENCES

Cholenec, Pierre, S.J. "Of Two Other Women." *Kateri* 70 (September 1966): 8-9.

Greer, Allan. *Mohawk Saint. Catherine Tekakwitha and the Jesuits*. New York: Oxford University Press, 2005.

Marie de l'Incarnation. *Word from New France: The Selected Letters of Marie de l'Incarnation*, trans. and ed. Joyce Marshall. Toronto: Oxford University Press, 1967.

Sacred Congregation of Rites. *The Positio of the Historical Section of the Sacred Congregation of Rites on the Introduction of The Cause for the Beatification and Canonization and on the Virtues of the Servant of God Katharine Tekakwitha, The Lily of the* Mohawks. New York: Fordham University Press, 1940.

Thwaites, Rueben Gold, ed., *The Jesuit Relations and Allied Documents*, 73 vols. Cleveland: The Burrows Brothers Company, 1896-1901.

Printed by permission of Darren Bonaparte &
The Wampum Chronicles.

I I

HEALING AND
PILGRIMAGE AMONG
NATIVE AMERICANS
THE DEVOTION TO BLESSED
KATERI TEKAKWITHA

JAMES J. PRESTON, 2000

James J. Preston is Professor of Anthropology Emeritus at the State University of New York, Oneonta. He is interested in the role of religion in the process of social change, particularly the intersection between globalization, identity formation, and a variety of religious movements, in India, Europe and North America. For many years he conducted research on Catholic devotions among Native Americans, especially among the Mohawks. He has published essays about the process of proclaiming Kateri Tekakwitha's sanctity, both in local and Vatican traditions. He wrote the following work at the turn of the twenty-first century.[1]

1   This paper is based on fifteen years of intermittent fieldwork conducted on the devotion to Blessed Kateri Tekakwitha. I am especially grateful to the many Mohawks who have shared their concerns with me over the years. For critical help in preparing this paper I thank Dr. William A. Starna, Fr. Thomas Egan, S.J., David Kozak, and Albert Lazare. They are exonerated from any responsibility for the final results. I wish to thank the following sources for financial assistance: The Dewar Fund of the St. James Episcopal Church, Oneonta, New York; the Walter B. Ford Foundation of the State University of New York, Oneonta. I am particularly grateful for generous

A pilgrimage tradition often unites important religious events with some notion of sacred geography. Consequently, the "spiritual magnetism" of a place of pilgrimage is generated by embedded memories that, once released through reenactment, produce a source of healing for participants (Preston 1992). Many ethnic groups are represented by a particular spiritual model or saint who enshrines the highest moral and spiritual principles upheld by that community. "Spiritual magnetism" in the Roman Catholic tradition has long been associated with the bones of martyrs and saints. These relics constitute the spiritual DNA of a rich Catholic pilgrimage tradition, one that is not only dispersed throughout Europe and across the globe, but is also widely represented in the United States.

CATHOLIC SAINTS AND PILGRIMAGE TRADITIONS

While some Catholic saints have universal appeal, such as the apostles and martyrs of the early church, others are repositories for ethnic identity and the continuity of tradition. Devotions to saints encapsulate and focus some of the most valued sentiments in human communities. Here reside highly treasured remnants of language, deeply felt fragments of custom, intimate reminders of origin. Devotions to saints reflect two opposing forces, the centripetal motion centered on commitment to local community and the opposite centrifugal motion that stretches the devotee toward identity with the larger universal church. The tension between these seemingly contradictory and opposite motions is mediated in the saint who becomes simultaneously the anchor point for both universal and parochial sentiments.

At a more cosmological level, Catholic saints embody bonds of intimacy between the human world and heaven. They are mediators, friends, companions, and heroic models, venerated as supreme paradigms of Catholic spirituality. The heroic virtues of a potential saint encompass a range of highly valued religious attributes, such as a reputation for piety, intensity of faith, love for God, apostolic zeal, charity, prudence, justice, temperance, fortitude, poverty, chastity, obedience and humility. In the canonization process the Church must establish the *fama sanctitatis* (reputation for sanctity) of the potential saint. This procedure is required because the saint is an intercessor, a conduit between God

support for this project from the Bureau of Catholic Indian Missions, Washington, D.C., and the American Academy of Religion.

and humanity, heaven and earth. Saints enshrine the finest, most perfect qualities possible for humans to attain.

While some Catholic cultures have a long established tradition of venerating and communicating with saints, others rarely employ images of sacred mediation. Western European Catholics have had extensive experience with the cult of saints. Consequently, most formally canonized saints are of European derivation.[2] This uneven distribution of Catholic saints in the different cultures of the world has received a certain amount of criticism. In the twentieth century, however, there has been a gradual change of focus. It has become increasingly evident to some members of the Church hierarchy that Western Europe is no longer the exclusive heartland of Catholicism. After Vatican II, and especially during the reign of Pope John Paul II, there has been a shift toward the beatification and canonization of many non-Europeans.

While pilgrimage to shrines associated with saints is usually considered primarily a European or Latin American phenomenon, few people are aware of how extensive Catholic pilgrimage has become in the United States. There are well over a hundred pilgrimage shrines heavily concentrated in densely populated Catholic enclaves such as Rhode Island, Massachusetts, the Mid Atlantic, the Midwest and the Southwest. The range of pilgrimage traditions associated with these shrines is vast (see Preston 1990). Most Catholic ethnic groups in the United States have saints who are the focus of pilgrimage. For instance, Polish immigrant populations attend pilgrimages to Our Lady of Czestochowa and there are numerous shrines dedicated to Our Lady of Guadalupe among Mexican populations throughout the West and Southwest. Until recently Native Americans have not had their own saint.

Early Catholic missionary activity in North America was concentrated in two regions, the Southwest principally by the Franciscans and the Northeast mostly by the Jesuits (Bowden 1981). Early evangelization was accompanied by the usual incidents of martyrdom for the faith. During the first several centuries the Church hierarchy in North America was sparse. There were few bishops to advance the causes of potential saints. America's first saints, the eight Jesuit Martyrs, were not canonized until 1930. While the cases for these missionary martyrs were

---

2   Maurer (1987: 115-116) notes an exception to this general rule among the Tseltal Indians of Chiapas. These people have a long tradition of saints as guardians and protectors of their villages. It is believed the saints were once the traditional deities of Tseltal religion.

being prepared for submission to Rome, some clergy were aware that martyrdom and exemplary religious piety were strongly represented among the first Native American converts. Still, only two Indian cases have been introduced to Rome so far, those of Juan Diego (associated with the devotion to Our Lady of Guadalupe in Mexico [Ed.: canonized in 2002]) and Kateri Tekakwitha, a pious Mohawk maiden who lived in the seventeenth century. Other Indian causes are possible, since numerous Native Catholics died as martyrs alongside their clergy.

There are many reasons for the slowness of the Roman Catholic Church to advance Native American causes: 1) Over the years the vast majority of Catholic saints have been European clergy. In the last three hundred years of Catholic history among Indian populations only a handful of Native Americans have been ordained. 2) While revered and respected persons are not unfamiliar among Indian cultures, the European custom of placing some members of the community on pedestals above others is foreign.[3] 3) Even if the raising of saints had been a familiar Indian custom, until recently most Native American communities were relatively powerless.[4] The usual bureaucratic procedures for canonization require strong political support within the Church hierarchy by advocates representing the community associated with the saint. No doubt the departure of the Jesuits from Canada in the late eighteenth century greatly reduced the likelihood that Kateri Tekakwitha's cause would be introduced. Also, until 1986 Native Catholics had no bishops of their own to help advance the causes of saints in Rome. 4) The Church, like virtually all other social institutions in the Western world, suffered from a certain amount of incipient racism and ethnocentricity in some quarters. This may have contributed to the blockage of Black, Asian and Indian candidates for sainthood. The contemporary Church, however, under the leadership of Pope John Paul II, has dramatically changed this pattern, not only by canonizing more saints than all the other popes in history (Woodward 1990: 19) but by making major efforts to correct

---

3   The other reason for this uneven distribution of Catholic saints in different world cultures must include the political fact that sacerdotal power was wielded most strongly in those European countries that constituted the core of Western civilization during the last two millennia.

4   There are some exceptions among Native Americans in their hesitance to employ saints as mediators. Kozak (1991) notes an interesting example among the Papago Indians of south-central Arizona. This population has a long tradition of venerating saints.

for biases of the past. In the 1980s and 1990s he canonized a large number of non-Western European saints. The present Congregation for the Causes of Saints in the Vatican has reserved a rank of high priority for those candidates derived from cultures with few saints.[5]

THE DEVOTION TO BLESSED KATERI TEKAKWITHA

It would be a mistake to suggest that the whole Church was an instrument for the destruction of indigenous Indian cultures, In this respect the history of the Church is uneven; while some priests and religious orders dedicated themselves to the preservation of Indian customs and traditions, others were extremely intolerant and bent on imposing a European cultural veneer on all Native peoples. The lack of officially declared Indian saints has been a source of concern among some members of the Church hierarchy. They are anxious to correct for an unfortunate oversight on the part of the Church. This is also a point of contention among those critics who perceive the Catholic Church as an agent of colonialism and repression.

Catholic Indians themselves seem less concerned with formal matters of canonization. Many consider Blessed Kateri Tekakwitha to be a saint already. These individuals care little about the need of the official Church to wait for one more miracle to be approved by the Sacred Congregation in Rome. A new sense of pride is emerging as this first Native American saint begins to form an emblematic following and a source of identity for Catholic Indians from different Native cultures.

Who was Kateri Tekakwitha? Why was her case, rather than that of other Natives, the first to be introduced for canonization in Rome? Unlike most candidates for sainthood, Blessed Kateri was *not* 1) a member of the clergy, 2) the founder of a religious order, 3) a martyr, 4) a theologian, or 5) a mystic. She was merely an ordinary person with deep religious convictions who was a Catholic for only four years before she died.

The events of her life are well documented in two major monographs written by the Jesuit missionaries who knew her best. These biographies, along with a collection of letters, form a concrete basis for establishing the historical veracity of Kateri's life. Some of this documentation is found in The Jesuit Relations 1610-1791 (Thwaites 1959). Kateri Tekakwitha was born in the Mohawk village of Ossernenon (Auriesville,

5   The data on the Vatican's role in the making of saints was gathered during the summer of 1990 while conducting field work in the offices of the Congregation for the Causes of Saints in Rome.

New York) in the year 1656. Both her Mohawk father and Christian Algonquin mother died of smallpox when Kateri was only four years old. The disease of smallpox, a result of culture contact, not only left her an orphan, it scarred and crippled her for life. Kateri remained weak, pock marked and partially blind. She was baptized at the age of twenty by Fr. James de Lamberville, S.J. At that time considerable pressure was brought to bear on Kateri by family members who wanted to see her married. She vehemently resisted.

The next year, 1676, Kateri migrated, like many other Mohawks at the time, to a newly established Jesuit mission on the banks of the St. Lawrence River (located across from present day Montreal). There, at St. Francis Xavier Mission, she joined other Catholic Indians, the majority of whom were Mohawks. Her extraordinary piety and spirituality were noted immediately by the mission priest who administered First Communion to her. At that time people received communion only once per year. Newly baptized individuals would often wait for several years to be considered worthy of communion.

During the next few years Kateri developed deep spiritual friendships with other Mohawk women. In the words of the Church, she lived an "exemplary life," engaging in severe penances, proposing to found a community of Indian nuns, and taking a private vow of perpetual virginity. In 1680, only three years after moving to the mission, Blessed Kateri grew seriously ill. Her strength declined rapidly. In a matter of a few days she died in the "odor of sanctity" with a peaceful smile on her face. A few minutes later she was reported to have become radiant and beautiful, an event proclaimed by some witnesses to be "miraculous." During the ensuing months numerous miracles were attributed to her by both Indians and non-Indians alike.

Gradually over the years the cult of devotion continued to grow. An unbroken three hundred year history of miracles and favors has been attributed to this Indian maiden from the time of her death. It was not until 1931 that Kateri's cause was introduced formally to the authorities in the Vatican.[6] Twelve years later she was declared Venerable (1943),

---

6   The cause of Blessed Kateri Tekakwitha was technically introduced at an earlier date along with the causes of the North American Martyrs. Rome did not accept this attempt to canonize Kateri at the same time as the North American Martyrs. Her cause falls under a different category and must be treated as a separate case. The situation has contributed considerably to the delay.

the first stage in the long and tedious canonization process. Until then her devotion was confined mostly to Mohawks, and some non-Indian Canadians and Americans. They were aware of Kateri's heroic virtues because scattered clergy and laity kept the devotion alive, particularly at Kahnawake (the present name for the mission and Mohawk reserve on the Saint Lawrence River across from Montreal). It took until 1980, another thirty-seven years, for her to be beatified in a grand ceremony in Rome attended by 450 Catholic Indians. Today there are thousands of devotees all over the world who hope she will be canonized soon. Only one miracle is needed.[7] The Roman Catholic Church does not canonize a person without evidence of strong, unbroken support manifested in popular devotions. Also necessary is some sign from heaven (usually in the form of a miracle) that the individual is one of the saints.

During the latter part of the twentieth century the devotion to Blessed Kateri Tekakwitha has expanded dramatically. This is particularly evident at the three shrines devoted to her in the United States and Canada. Large numbers of pilgrims attend these shrines each year. The pilgrims are both Native Americans and non-Indians who are greatly attracted to Blessed Kateri's ability to heal them for a wide variety of both psychological and physical ailments.

After the beatification ceremony in 1980, Blessed Kateri's devotion began to spread rapidly among Catholic Indian populations throughout North America. Since then the church has invested two Native American bishops.[8] The National Tekakwitha Conference has expanded from a few hundred to several thousand Indians, representing over a hundred tribes who gather each year to share common interests and needs. The Tekakwitha Conference has become a Catholic vehicle for the reinterpretation of Indian traditions, a process occurring in communities all over North America. At Conference meetings Native Catholics rediscover and redefine who they are in the context of an apologetic Church that

7 The usual requirement for miracles was suspended for the beatification of Kateri. Her reputation for sanctity was judged to be a sufficient prerequisite. Rome is insisting at the present time that at least one miracle be required for the final act of canonization.

8 In 1986 Rev. Donald E. Pelotte, S.S.S., was appointed to the Diocese of Gallup, New Mexico, and ordained as the first Native American bishop [Ed.: now deceased]. A second Native American, Rev. Charles Chaput, O.F.M.Cap., was ordained Bishop of Rapid City, South Dakota, in the summer of 1988. Both bishops have been very well received by Native Catholics throughout the North American continent.

seeks to open new ways for Indians to express their ethnicity within the institutional framework of the Church. This same process of reinterpretation is very much alive among non-Christian Native populations today who are trying to retain the ancient traditions of the elders.

A study of the devotion to Blessed Kateri reveals how the reinterpretation of tradition continues to evolve new forms. For the last fifteen years I have conducted research on the devotion and pilgrimage among both Indian and non-Indian Catholics. The field work has been concentrated intensely on the Mohawks of New York State and Québec, Canada. It has involved interviews with hundreds of devotees, including a large number of Mohawks and a variety of both Indian and non-Indian Catholics. Also included are numerous nuns, priests and bishops in the United States and Canada. In addition, the field work for this project has been based on extensive participant observation at three shrines associated with Blessed Kateri.[9] The research extends even to high officials in the Vatican Curia, including Pope John Paul II who has expressed considerable interest in the progress of this particular cause.

THE REINTERPRETATION OF TRADITION

The devotion to Blessed Kateri Tekakwitha is distributed unevenly among the Mohawks of St. Regis/Akwesasne and Kahnawake. While some Catholic Mohawks are deeply and openly devoted to their now famous sister, many are more cautious and quiet about it. Some are even skeptical. This mix of responses would be typical for any community. However, in this case, it is complicated by internal divisions. Matters of religion and cultural identity have become central issues to the Mohawk people, as they seek a variety of ways to recover waning cultural traditions, to preserve a fading grasp of their own language, and to recapture an eroding land base.

While many Mohawks—Catholic, Protestant, and Traditionalists alike—respect Blessed Kateri as an historical figure, others see her as a traitor, a pawn of White colonial hegemony and an instrument of the still present expansion of that power. Several crucial questions arise. How is this ambivalence expressed in the context of Mohawk life? What is

---

9   The shrines associated with Blessed Kateri Tekakwitha include: 1) the place of her birth at Auriesville, New York (Shrine of the North American Martyrs), 2) the place of her baptism at Fonda, New York (The National Kateri Shrine), and 3) the place of her death at the Mohawk reserve in Kahnawake, Québec (St. Francis Xavier Mission Church).

the range of responses to Blessed Kateri among community members? Most important, how is Mohawk tradition undergoing reinterpretation through the growth of this devotion?

One approach to an understanding of ethnic identity is through the myths people use to define who they are, where they come from, and the meaning of life. As Malinowski has asserted so eloquently, myths are charters of ethnicity, blueprints, as it were, for tradition. Myths are fictive but not ordinary fictions (Preston 1984, 1991). In Shakespeare's words, they are the "stuff as dreams are made on." Yet myths are corporate not private dreams, pointing toward realities intuitively encountered by human communities, realities conceived to be beyond ordinary experience. Myths do many practical things too; they classify plants and animals in the environment, define appropriate or inappropriate social relations (such as kinship rules) and legitimize power structures. They may also contain a healing potential for those individuals who become integrated into their communities through shared dreams or mythos.

Myths function as "healing fictions," stimulating cures through rituals centered on key values in collective religious experience (Preston 1989: 47; Orsi 1989). For Catholics the religious imagination is expressed through a variety of avenues, including 1) dramatic reenactment of religious texts, 2) the veneration of relics, 3) pilgrimages to sacred centers, and 4) prayers for the intercession of saints. All these ritual activities tie individuals back into what their culture defines as "sacred," resolving alienation and revitalizing a sense of community solidarity. The crucial role of myth and myth making is extremely important for Mohawks as they seek to rediscover their identity, struggle for legitimate authority, and seek ways to be healed through a return to mythic origins.

ORAL AND WRITTEN INTERPRETATIONS

It is the storyteller's creative impulse and capacity to interpret and reinterpret fragments from the past that create and recreate cultural identity. For the insider, the storyteller participates in an ongoing creation, an emerging sense of corporate identity shared in cultural bonds of woven tradition. Stories are danced, sung, told, reenacted, and recapitulated in many different settings scattered throughout the year. Outsiders also tell stories about cultures. Historians and anthropologists, for instance, seek to anchor their stories in the bedrock of verifiable facts. Other outsiders—colonialists, foreign governments or missionaries—tell still other stories that sometimes do not serve the interests of the people.

The stories people tell about their own origins are often couched in oral traditions that preserve common bonds of identity. These mythic histories represent fictive insights about beginnings, insights that act as templates or models for later actions. Thus, myths and histories encapsulate paradigmatic structures that constitute the very deepest cornerstones of cultural traditions.

Fragmented cultures display fractured, sometimes contradictory mythic histories. Various stories are told in these cultures by different factions that reflect complex internal fissures. Heavily acculturated peoples are particularly vulnerable in this regard. The Mohawks are no exception. In the last decade of the twentieth century, Mohawk communities continue to struggle with deep internal rifts that heal and fester alternately as the people attempt time and again to cope with hostile and intrusive outside forces.

The sense of Mohawk identity reflects a complex double nature. At one level there is total unity in the face of hostile outsiders who threaten Indian survival. At another there are strong internal differences that reflect deep fractures in these communities. At first glance the casual observer misses the subtlety of what appear to be opposite levels, wanting to stress one or the other, and having a difficult time seeing both simultaneously.

Most of the written sources on Kateri Tekakwitha have been penned by outsiders. These consist of 1) The Jesuit Relations 1610-1791 (Thwaites 1959), a collection of letters, diary entries, journals and reports written by the early missionary priests and 2) the official *Positio* (1940), a scholarly dissertation on the life of the future saint produced by Church authorities as part of the case to be presented for approval to the reigning pope. The *Positio* for Blessed Kateri Tekakwitha documents the miracles and favors granted through her intercession. In recent years a wide variety of hagiographies have been written that elaborate on Kateri's conversion, the details of her life and her spiritual eccentricities. Many are filled with romantic stereotypes about Indians (Preston 1989: 47- 53). Almost nothing has been written about her by non-Catholics, except for a few passing references by historians and an irreverent novel or two. In recent years there have been a few plays, essays and articles about Blessed Kateri Tekakwitha written by Catholic

Indians, including some Mohawks. Otherwise the majority of written sources are by non-Indians.

The oral tradition is different. It operates at a quieter, more intimate level. Stories about Kateri have circulated for generations among members of some families. The clergy have participated in maintaining oral traditions centered around Kateri. The pilgrimage tradition and the cult of her relics extends back to the earliest years of the mission; first in the seventeenth century immediately following her death, then in the eighteenth century when the original community at Kahnawake split, resulting in twenty to thirty families (approximately 200 people) relocating upstream at St. Regis/Akwesasne. This move occurred around 1755. At that time Kateri's bones were divided in half; the upper part of her body was taken to the new mission while the lower half remained at Kahnawake (Bruyere 1952; Béchard 1962). It is difficult to assess accurately how extensive devotion to Kateri was during these early years. It was less intense at St. Regis/Akwesasne, partly due to a fire in 1762 that destroyed the log chapel containing Kateri's relics. Thus, there was no place to focus the devotion. In the twentieth century the devotion was revived there and actively encouraged by the Mohawk priest and pastor, Fr. Michael Jacobs. The devotion has been more continuous at Kahnawake. For many years the bones of Blessed Kateri were stored in a room behind the church. While the devotion there may have been considerable over the years, it would never have been allowed to become too demonstrative or prematurely formalized without permission from Rome. During interviews I found evidence that the devotion was active in some families and hardly known among others.

Beyond the Mohawks is a wider community of Catholic Indians who are spreading an oral tradition associated with Blessed Kateri in webs that radiate across North America. Before her beatification in 1980, Blessed Kateri was known in some parts of North America but not others. There were pockets where she was known, especially in Jesuit missions. Otherwise, most Native Catholics knew little about her. In the last twenty years this has changed dramatically as the devotion has mushroomed. The Tekakwitha Conference represents a pan-Indian Catholic movement organized around the devotion to Blessed Kateri. It thrives on a network of oral testimonials of healings shared at conference meetings. In the Tekakwitha Conference, Kateri undergoes a cross-cultural transfiguration, as she is raised above her Mohawk community to dwell amidst a larger Native constituency.

CONTRADICTORY INTERPRETATIONS

At the turn of the twentieth century St. Regis/Akwesasne and Kahnawake were virtually all Catholic. No doubt some were nominal rather than active in their faith. The earliest traces of Protestantism extend back to the mid 1800s, with more intense activity in the early twentieth century. Some have argued that the Longhouse Tradition never really disappeared entirely. It clearly dates to the 1880s, perhaps earlier, and begins to grow dramatically during the twentieth century. Today rough estimates would place the Catholics at about 60-70%, the Protestants at 5-10%, and Traditionalists at roughly 20-25%. For some people the Longhouse Tradition is interpreted as a religion rather than a way of life. Others have no difficulty being Catholic and Traditionalist at the same time. In recent years some Catholics have abandoned the Church and are "turning Longhouse." The dramatic rise of Traditionalism is particularly evident among young people. Most families in these communities consist of different members who are Catholic, Longhouse and Protestant. This mix can be a source of family stress, producing factions that tear them apart.

Today, partly as a consequence of these different changes, the Mohawk devotion to Blessed Kateri is uneven. No longer are all the children on these reservations raised in Catholic schools as they once were. Nor are the Catholic clergy as influential politically. At one time they were indirectly consulted about many important community decisions. Assertions of Native self determination, the influence of television, and the age of the automobile have changed reservations into communities with all the problems of suburbanism, compounded and greatly exacerbated by racism. Such changes have transformed once relatively quiet and isolated Catholic enclaves, into communities with all the problems of mainstream American and Canadian life, including alcoholism, drug abuse, and teenage alienation. As a consequence the Mohawk reservations are like powder kegs easily set off by any number of possible incidents. This same stress is a pan-Indian phenomenon found across the United States and Canada. The Mohawks have been deeply wounded in a series of losses, as their lands have become increasingly alienated by various government ploys.

The tensions at Kahnawake and St. Regis/Akwesasne are reflected in the devotion to Blessed Kateri Tekakwitha. For some she is the focus of community factionalism. Substantive interviews in these two communities have yielded five types of responses to Blessed Kateri among Mohawks. These include individuals with a) strong positive devotion, b) ambivalent devotion, c) marginal devotion, d) no devotion, or e) open hostility toward the devotion. Despite occasional feuding among factions, there is a degree of tolerance for differences that reduces the potential for divisiveness and enmity. These various attitudes are difficult to assess in terms of percentages. They should be considered more as general trends.

a) Strong Devotion:

Those individuals who are strongly devoted to Kateri see her as a "sister" who is very close to them. While they are proud that the Catholic Church is finally raising a Mohawk to the honors of the altar, their devotion does not depend on whether Kateri is canonized formally. Many strong devotees are pillars of the local church community. Most are women who have confidence about their Indian identity. At the same time, they see themselves as Catholics and are proud of it.

b) Ambivalent Devotion:

Those who are ambivalent about their devotion are often confused about their identity as Indians. Some have married Whites, others have lived away from the reservation for many years. They are devoted to Blessed Kateri but do not appreciate some versions of her life written by Whites. Occasionally they try to bridge both Catholic and Traditionalist worlds. Some think the Church is pushing the devotion to attract more Indians. Most ambivalent devotees see Kateri as an Indian who bridges two worlds like themselves. Their ambivalence stems from insecurity, rejection of the rigid Catholicism of their parents, or a sincere search for deeper and more meaningful roots.

c) Marginal Devotion:

People with a marginal devotion to Blessed Kateri have heard about her, yet know little about her life. Some may pray to her occasionally under desperate circumstances. For the most part, those who are marginally devoted are pragmatists who have never experienced religion as a central part of their lives. They live secular lives, except for those times when they claim their Catholic heritage as an emblem of corporate identity. This happens only on major holidays like Christmas and Easter, or when weddings and funerals require some ritual context at a familial level.

d) No Devotion:
While some of the Catholic Mohawks not devoted to Blessed Kateri are young people who are unfamiliar with the religion of their parents, others are active Catholics who are uninterested in saints as mediators. Also, most Protestants and Traditionalists fall into this category. They are indifferent to Kateri, except as an historical figure or a product of the Catholic imagination.

e) Hostility Toward the Devotion:
Among some former and a few contemporary Catholics who are hostile toward raising Kateri to the altars, there is a belief that the Church is using her as a means of further acculturation. These people particularly dislike the emphasis placed on Kateri's virginity. They argue that virginity is a preoccupation of Europeans and not Indians. While these people grant that Kateri may have been a virgin, they dislike the Euro-American Catholic literature that stresses this aspect of her spiritual life. Many of these Catholics feel bitter toward the Church, which is seen as having taken away the cultural integrity of the people—their intimate relationship with nature, their dignity as warriors, even their language. Some remember the pain of being torn away from their families and forced to attend boarding schools far away.[10] To these people Kateri represents one more instance of the White man's disastrous incursions into Mohawk life.

The most hostile response to Blessed Kateri is from those Traditionalists who think of her as a "traitor to her people." They perceive Kateri's journey from the Mohawk Valley to the mission on the St. Lawrence River as a distorted story made up by the Catholic priests. Some of them even question whether she existed at all. They assert that there is no record or any evidence of her in the oral tradition, and that further, if she had been a person of such great importance, some memory of her would have been preserved. Also, they question a number of elements in the priests' versions of Kateri's life. They assert, for instance, that she was unmarried and virginal, not due to religious vows she took but because the pock marks on her face made her too ugly for marriage.

Clearly the raising of Kateri to sainthood threatens the efforts of Traditionalists to return to a pre-Christian life style. Some Mohawk Traditionalists tend to insist that one cannot be a Catholic and a

10   Not all informants reported negative responses to their boarding school experiences.

Traditionalist at the same time. Many non-Traditionalists disagree emphatically.

FICTIVE HISTORIES

Disagreements over Kateri Tekakwitha represent only the tip of the iceberg. Underneath these disputes is an old set of wounds suffered by the Mohawk people, wounds rooted in problems of identity, the erosion of traditional Mohawk culture, and economic impoverishment through the increasing loss of a land base. For over three hundred years, through a constant unremitting process of acculturation, the integrity of Mohawk culture has been eroded by degrees. Although all these forms of acculturation have taken their toll, the Mohawk people have maintained an amazing resilience above and beyond the deep internal fissures in their communities.

Today Mohawk tradition faces numerous problems of interpretation. What does it mean to be Mohawk in the context of a modern industrial world? Can this way of life retain its uniqueness in the face of the assault of modernization, including loss of the Mohawk language and eroding forces of assimilation? Once traditions are gone for more than a generation, is it possible to recapture old life ways? And what about using anthropological sources to reconstruct lost customs?

Traditions are never anchored incontestably in fact. They are rooted in origin stories, the mythic structures that transmit cultural codes from one generation to another. In the Mohawk case, stories of origin are maintained as mechanisms of identity. For this reason, Blessed Kateri is perceived with much ambivalence among various factions in Mohawk communities. Each faction is committed deeply to preserving some remnant of Mohawk identity, as Catholics, Traditionalists or both.

Blessed Kateri is caught in the midst of these factional differences. Among some she is a saint. For others she is a respected figure from the past. Still others think of her as only an instrument of the White man's church. For those to whom Blessed Kateri is a saint, she is a model of Mohawk Catholic identity, a source of healing, at once both Native and a part of the universal Church. Her appeal as a saint extends beyond Mohawk communities, being particularly strong among many Catholic Ojibwas and Native populations in the American Southwest. In addition, her popularity is widespread among thousands of non-Indian Americans and Canadians.

The ways in which Natives blend remnants of older traditions with modernism pivot around concepts of "foreign" or "other." These notions vary somewhat in each community and among different factions within communities. Occasionally practicing "traditional" ways is itself considered to be "foreign" or alien. This would be true for those Native Catholics who resent attempts to get them to return to customs that their ancestors abandoned generations ago. Sometimes they refer to such efforts to return as "playing Indian." They dislike being coerced into using traditional Indian symbols in their religious ceremonies. At the other extreme are those who assume that everything associated with Whites is "foreign" and potentially threatening to the preservation of their cultural identity. Most Mohawks are located somewhere between these opposite poles. No matter what their religious persuasion may be, every Mohawk learns at an early age to identify himself as an Indian. This occurs not only as a result of pride in national identity, it is also a crucial step in order to combat the overwhelming forces of hostility and prejudice that surround them. Anything that threatens Mohawk cultural boundaries must be rejected.

SAINTS AND COMMUNITY SOLIDARITY

The Catholic Church expects its saints to inspire ethnic unity among the people who venerate them. In thousands of communities throughout the world saints embody the corporate identity of people. They are emblems of social solidarity that transcend competing elements of factionalism. For this reason the case of Blessed Kateri Tekakwitha is instructive. Several key questions are raised by this particular devotion: Will it have a healing effect on Mohawk communities? Could it have the opposite result, deepening internal differences, like salt on a wound? The matter is delicate and hard to assess.

The mission priests have difficult roles to play on Indian reservations. Those I have interviewed recognize how fragile and volatile Mohawk communities have become, especially with the spread of factionalism affecting virtually every family. To them it is evident that community solidarity cannot be imposed by outsiders. Sometimes they face the awkward problem of being asked by some Native people to introduce Indian elements into the liturgy (such as the burning of sweetgrass or tobacco as a kind of incense), while others vehemently oppose such efforts. For this reason they are cautious about how much to encourage the devotion to Blessed Kateri. Although they are reluctant to push it, the priests support spontaneous inclinations for devotional expressions by individuals or groups. The various Kateri prayer groups, for instance, are small centers of intense spirituality supported by the Church. Yet, to a certain extent, they are left alone to have an independent life of their own.

No matter what Blessed Kateri may mean to Mohawks, she is a rising star among non-Mohawk Indians as well as non-Indian Americans and Canadians. Kateri's appeal is her inner strength to stand for what she believed, despite strong forces of opposition. She extends Catholic Indian identity beyond the specifics of Mohawk culture, forging the beginnings of a truly pan-Indian catholicity. In recent years dozens of regional Tekakwitha Conferences have been held annually through-out the United States and Canada. These meetings act as forums for Catholic Indians to share common problems, seek solutions and form larger units of power and influence.

There is ample evidence to demonstrate that these regional Tekakwitha Conferences help to blend Catholic and Indian identities. Some Indian clergy are trained in both Catholic theology and Native medicines. They do not believe that one is opposed to the other. Each informs the other in an ongoing process of reinterpretation. The Catholic Church has become increasingly sensitive to the need for Native input. It must become involved in the major issues and concerns that face Native peoples. As long as the Church can act as a vehicle for reinterpretation it will survive. Otherwise it will represent only the remnant of an op-pressive past. The Pope has acknowledged this fact by his apology to Native people for the past mistakes of Europeans.

The devotion to Blessed Kateri Tekakwitha embodies a new post-Vat-ican II Catholicism. What was once in some pockets of the Catholic Church a strident, often repressive and judgmental attitude is being replaced by a renewed interest in cultural pluralism, not only on the periphery of the Church (which has always been acceptable) but at the center as well (Crollius 1987). Even as far back as the sixteenth century, some branches of the Church were deeply concerned with inculturation and the protection of Indian identity, while others were determined to completely change native people and to Europeanize them. Pope John Paul II, having canonized more candidates for sainthood than any other pope in history, has guided the Church in the direction of increasing tolerance for cultural diversity. These changes are slow in coming for

Catholic Indians. Their communities are greatly fragmented, extremely fragile and often quite volatile. Will the final act of the canonization of Blessed Kateri Tekakwitha represent a turning point for Native Americans? How far is the Church willing to become involved as an advocate for Indian causes? How much will it fight on their behalf in the face of ongoing battles against racism, alcoholism, and stolen Indian lands? What shape will Native Catholicism take in the post-Vatican II era? There are attempts now through the Bureau of Catholic Indian Missions to accomplish many of these tasks.

Since the Medieval period, and even before that, the lives of saints were employed to teach the faithful religious actions they could imitate (Heffernan 1988: 5). The sacred stories featuring the saints were paradigmatic for Catholic communities, centering individual concerns in corporate sentiments reinforced by the Church. Hagiographies were didactic devices used as models for children to imitate. They were sources of great inspiration in an environment filled with hardships. The feast days of saints were often the single most powerful means of focusing communities around the Church. Today some of these same functions persist as Catholic communities the world over celebrate the lives of local saints.

Despite the religious divisions reflected in the devotion to Blessed Kateri among the Mohawks, there have been great moments of cooperation and solidarity at the transcultural level. This is best exemplified by the complete takeover of the leadership of the Tekakwitha Conference by Native Americans. In the keynote address at the 1990 national meeting held in Tucson, Arizona, the Indian priest, Rev. P. Michael Galvan, reflected on the changing relationship between Natives and the Church:

> My brothers and sisters in Blessed Kateri Tekakwitha, My brothers and sisters in Blessed Juan Diego, My brothers and sisters in our Lord Christ Jesus, it is good to be here with you at our 51st Annual Tekakwitha Conference. With this Conference, Blessed Kateri: Hope on New Horizons, our dreams for the future broadened even further then they did last year in Fargo, North Dakota. Our gathering with the Native Leadership of the Tekakwitha Conference firmly in place gives us great satisfaction as we see a dream dreamed by our brothers and sisters in Yankton come to fulfillment. This dream has been shared by so many of our ancestors through the generations in our villages throughout these two continents now called the Americas. It is a dream of the Kingdom of God breaking into our world. It is

a dream of the Roman Catholic Church firmly planted among our people with our own languages, our own traditions, our own leadership. (Galvan 1990: 1)

This new effort by the Roman Catholic Church to anchor the faith from within through an acceptance of Indian languages and traditions is a welcome development. It contrasts dramatically with over three hundred years of external religious colonialism. No doubt there were important exceptions, such as the Jesuits who often insisted on working with the native culture as much as possible. However, this was once a minor theme that has now become the major one. For Native peoples, both Catholic and Traditional, the emerging new face of the Church is a welcome surprise. The dialogue has opened a critical chapter in the history of Indian Catholic relations. Rev. Galvan expresses the importance of this dialogue for the Native people:

> This past June marked the tenth anniversary of the beatification of Kateri Tekakwitha. I still remember the excitement many of us shared as we traveled to Rome for the ceremony. I recall the Pueblo woman who sat next to me. She had never been out of New Mexico—but for Blessed Kateri she would make this extraordinary journey. And extraordinary it was! The Roman people were curious about us—most had seen only moving images of us, often stereotypes, from Western films. Their curiosity about us amazed me and I was amazed when I realized that our presence was changing their understanding about us: a new dialogue and a new understanding were beginning. (*Ibid.*)

While the ongoing process of assimilation and syncretism are very old in the history of Catholicism, the recent willingness to enter into a dialogue on the basis of mutual respect constitutes a bright new orientation on the part of the Church. At this time the question about how much Indian culture can be brought into Native Catholic liturgies is an open one. Also at issue is the matter of whether or not a separate and special Native liturgy might evolve. Today there is clearly a trend toward increased participation of Indians as deacons, clergy and bishops. This kind of empowerment is essential if Catholicism is to survive among Native American peoples. Native Catholicism is strongly represented in the emblematic image of the Virgin of Guadalupe. Will Kateri Tekakwitha inspire a strong enough following among Indian populations to renew the roots of Catholicism in North America? Or is it too late for old wounds to be healed? Reconciliation requires hard work on both sides as the dialogue unfolds.

HEALING AND PILGRIMAGE FOR CATHOLIC INDIANS

For the Catholic Mohawks of Kahnawake the rising pilgrimage tradition to the tomb of Blessed Kateri Tekakwitha is both a source of healing and, for some, a reminder of their wounded past. Other Catholic Mohawk populations, such as those in New York State at St. Regis/Akwesasne or in the city of Syracuse, are very enthusiastic about the development of a national reputation for their "saint." One could even argue that the greatest contribution of Blessed Kateri has been among the hundreds of Native American populations who are not Mohawk. She is very popular in the Southwest and among a wide variety of Native communities both in the United States and Canada.

Among non-Mohawk Catholic Indians, Blessed Kateri Tekakwitha has become an emblem of pan-Indian Catholic identity and revitalization. While much of this has been orchestrated by the Catholic clergy, there can be no doubt that this enthusiasm is genuine as it spontaneously breaks out and expands throughout North America. Typically the annual Tekakwitha Conference held in various parts of the country attracts several thousand Native Catholics. They see Blessed Kateri as a vehicle for healing their own communities from within. Native American churches, prayer groups, and various programs to improve Indian life are dedicated to this fragile seventeenth-century Mohawk woman.

The majority of pilgrims who attend the two Kateri shrines in New York State are mostly non-Indians. The Shrine of the North American Martyrs at Auriesville, New York, is located where it is believed that she was born. Over a hundred thousand pilgrims visit this shrine per year. It is difficult to assess how many who attend are primarily interested in Blessed Kateri Tekakwitha, since three of the eight Jesuit martyrs are also venerated there. The Blessed Kateri Shrine at Fonda, New York, is located where she lived at the time of her conversion and baptism in the Catholic tradition. This shrine is run by the Franciscans and it is unmistakably dedicated to Blessed Kateri alone. Between five to ten thousand pilgrims visit there each year. These pilgrims find the Mohawk maiden to be a source of profound inspiration. They are particularly taken with her "simplicity" and, as they express it in interviews, her "purity of spirit."

While many American and French Canadian pilgrims attend the shrine church located on the Mohawk reserve at Kahnawake, Québec, most of the pilgrims there are Mohawks from the surrounding region. The prayers offered at Blessed Kateri's tomb encapsulate her meaning for Native Americans in general, and Mohawks in particular. As with pilgrims everywhere, Blessed Kateri is petitioned for the usual protection from harm, cures for physical illnesses, employment opportunities, and the return of relatives to their faith. Other requests, however, reflect a deeper longing. In these petitions Blessed Kateri is addressed as though she were a relative, someone who understands the stresses of living as a Native in an overwhelmingly White world. In these prayers she is addressed as "sister" and considered a friend who understands the special circumstances of being an Indian.

There is no question that Native American Catholics are healed when they attend pilgrimages to the shrines dedicated to Blessed Kateri Tekakwitha. Still, for most Native people these shrines are distant and mostly inaccessible. Consequently, such outward journeys are less important than the inward journey that occurs either in private devotions, in prayer circles or in the context of the National Tekakwitha Conference. The inner pilgrimage consists of a deep level encounter with a true Native Catholic spirituality, one that heals the split at the core of their experience, a wounded identity derived from a long history that sought to colonize not only their bodies but also their souls. Once again the words of the Native priest Rev. P. Michael Galvin ring true: "This dream has been shared by so many of our ancestors through the generations in our villages throughout these two continents now called the Americas. It is a dream of the Kingdom of God breaking into our world. It is a dream of the Roman Catholic Church firmly planted among our people with our own languages, our own traditions, our own leadership" (*ibid.*).

The shared dream becomes the purpose of the pilgrimage. The healing of wounds so deep can only occur when the outward pilgrimage becomes enfolded in the key values of collective religious experience. When pilgrimage is experienced in this way, it no longer needs to be defined by either spatial or temporal boundaries. Thus, pilgrimage as metaphor still retains its vibrance for Native American Catholics, even in the increasingly unbounded communities emerging during the early years of the twenty-first century.

REFERENCES

Béchard, Henri. "The Treasure of the Iroquois." *Kateri* 14 (September 1962): 7-10.

Bowden, Henry Warner. *American Indians and Christian Missions in Cultural Conflict.* Chicago: The University of Chicago Press, 1981.

Bruyere, Jacques, S. J. "1552-1952." *Kateri* 4 (June 1952): 3.

Crollius, Arij A., S.J., ed. *Effective Inculturation and Ethnic Identity.* Rome: Pontifical Gregorian University, 1987.

Galvan, P. Michael. "Keynote Address to the 51st Tekakwitha Conference." *Lily of the Mohawks* 45 (Winter 1990): 1.

Heffernan, Thomas J. *Sacred Biography: Saints and Their Biographers in the Middle Ages.* New York: Oxford University Press, 1988.

Kozak, David. "Ecumenical Indianism: Kateri and the Invented Tradition." Unpublished paper, Department of Anthropology, Arizona State University, Tempe, 1991.

Maurer, Eugenio, S.J. "Inculturation and Transculturation among the Indians." In *Effective Inculturation and Ethnic Identity,* ed. Arij A. Crollius, S.J. Rome: Pontifical Gregorian University, 1987: 99-128.

Orsi, Robert A. "The Cult of the Saints and the Reimagination of the Space and Time of Sickness in Twentieth-Century American Catholicism." *Literature and Medicine* 8 (1989): 63-77.

Preston, James J. "Empiricism and Phenomenology of Religious Experience." *Mentalities* 2 (1984): 10-20.

———. "Necessary Fictions: Healing Encounters with a North American Saint." *Literature and Medicine* 8 (1989): 42-62.

———. "The Rediscovery of America: Pilgrimage in the Promised Land." In *Pilgrimage in the United States,* ed. Gisbert Rinschede and Surinder Bhardwaj. *Geographia Religionum* 5. Berlin, Germany: Dietrich Reimer Verlag, 1990: 15-26.

———. "Spiritual Magnetism: An Organizing Principle for the Study of Pilgrimage." In *Sacred Journeys: The Anthropology of Pilgrimage,* ed. Alan Morinis. Westport, CT: Greenwood Press, 1992: 31-46.

———. "The Trickster Unmasked: Anthropology and the Imagination." In *Anthropological Poetics,* ed. Ivan Brady. Savage, MD: Rowman and Littlefield, 1991: 69-103.

Sacred Congregation of Rites. *The Positio of the Historical Section of the Sacred Congregation of Rites on the Introduction of the Cause for Beatification and Canonization and the Virtues of the Servant of God: Katherine Tekakwitha, the Lily of the Mohawks.* New York: Fordham University Press, 1940.

Thwaites, Reuben Gold, ed. *The Jesuit Relations and Allied Documents: Travels and Explorations of the Jesuit Missionaries in New France, 1610-1791,* 73 vols. New York: Pageant Book Company, 1959.

Woodward, Kenneth C. *Making Saints. How the Catholic Church Determines Who Becomes a Saint, Who Doesn't, and Why.* New York: Simon and Schuster, 1990.

Printed by permission of James J. Preston.

12

JAKE FINKBONNER AND THE MIRACLE AT SEATTLE CHILDREN'S HOSPITAL

MARK G. THIEL, 2012

On Saturday February 11, 2006, while playing basketball, the game he loves, Jake Finkbonner was knocked down and cut his lip. Immediately his face became extremely swollen, and on Monday, his parents brought him to Children's Hospital and Regional Medical Center in Seattle. Doctors determined that the five year-old was infected with necrotizing fasciitis or strep A, which annually kills 10-15% of its victims. After entering the cut, this rare flesh-eating bacteria rapidly ravaged and killed flesh across his head and upper torso in spite of a number of different treatments and interventions attempted by hospital staff. On the second day of his hospitalization, Jake's doctors urged his parents, Donny and Elsa, to call their pastor, Reverend Tim Sauer. Father Sauer visited and anointed him, and he urged his parents and the three parishes he served, to pray to Kateri Tekakwitha for his recovery. He believed Tekakwitha would be the perfect intercessor with Jesus because Jake's life resembled hers in a number of ways. Both had American Indian ancestry (his father being a Lummi Indian), and while very young, both suffered from life threatening bacterial diseases that left disfiguring facial scars. Immediately, the Seattle-area media picked up the story and many others joined the prayer chain.

ELSA FINKBONNER: He's so into basketball, he loves it—that's his favorite sport—and that's where it all began. He was playing basketball, and it was the last minute of the game, and the last game of the season.... There was strep A present on the surface of the basketball hoop. So when he pierced his lip with his front tooth—that's where the infection began.[1]

JAKE FINKBONNER: I was driving for a lay-in.... I got pushed from behind the back and I hit my lip on the base of the basketball hoop.[2]

DONNY FINKBONNER: The game ended.... I told him to get some ice cream, you know, "Get something on that lip," and I was thinking to myself, it's his first big fat lip.[3]

JAKE FINKBONNER: The swelling didn't go down. I got really sick. They took me to the hospital. Things weren't going so well.[4]

DONNY FINKBONNER: I walked in the room.... My heart sank when I saw his face and he said, "Hi Daddy!" But he couldn't see me because his eyes were swollen shut.[5]

ELSA FINKBONNER: We got to Children's [Hospital] on a Monday, and on Tuesday, we had a priest ... giving Jake his Last Rites. The doctors ... told us that they were not expecting him to live.[6] ... It was the most excruciating thing for a parent to have to listen to.... Everything just kept getting worse and worse ... it was just one grim day after the next.[7]

DONNY FINKBONNER: They were ... doing everything they could to stop it. But at that point, we knew as parents, we knew that his life was in the balance.[8]

ELSA FINKBONNER: [Father Sauer] saw how serious everything was. That's when he sat down with us and encouraged us to pray for Blessed Kateri's intercession....[9] We got letters and emails and cards from people in Japan... There was a woman from New York that sent a

---

1   Carol Smith, "Saint Kateri," KUOW News, February 8, 2010, accessed online.

2   Barbara Bradley Hagerty, "A Boy, An Injury, A Recovery, A Miracle?", NPR, April 22, 2011, accessed online.

3   Hagerty.

4   Bob Woodruff, Roxanna Sherwood, and Eric Johnson, ABC News/Nightline, "Beyond Belief: Jake Finkbonner among the Angels," August 3, 2011, accessed online.

5   Hagerty.

6   Chris Sullivan, "Ferndale Miracle accepted by Vatican," MyNorthwest.com, December 21, 2011, accessed online.

7   Woodruff.

8   Woodruff.

9   Sullivan.

letter. I remember thinking, how would a woman from New York have seen this? So, she prayed, and people just started putting Jake on their prayer chains. The news of Jake spread just far and wide.[10]

Meanwhile, some religious sisters initiated a parallel spiritual effort involving a first-class relic of Kateri Tekakwitha, which was a tiny ½-inch sliver from her wrist bone. Jewish and Christian Scriptures teach that God also accomplishes healing and miracles through relics, which draw attention to the lives of saints as models and intercessors.[11] Relics are sealed and displayed within special reliquaries. Unlike the ornate pieces in art museums, this was a thin plastic container measuring 1 ¾ x 1 ¾ inches. Sister Kateri Mitchell, a life-long follower and Executive Director of the Tekakwitha Conference, received it at the beatification from the Canadian Vice-Postulator, Rev. Henri Béchard. Since then, she has kept it in a small buckskin pouch adorned with beadwork.[12]

No doubt aware of the importance of relics in healing, Sister Mary Ann Reichlin, a great aunt of Jake's[13] and a sister in the Congregation of the Sisters of St. Joseph of Peace, first asked Sister Julie Codd, another sister in that community who has devoted many years to ministering to local Native Catholics, if she had a first class relic. Sister Julie did not, but she knew that Sister Kateri Mitchell did. On Thursday, February 27th, she called Sister Kateri and discovered that she already had plans to be in Seattle on the next Tuesday, March 4th, to plan that summer's national annual meeting of the Tekakwitha Conference, which was scheduled to be held in the Seattle area and co-hosted with the Lummi Nation.[14]

On that Tuesday, hospital staff admitted Sister Kateri and Sister Julie to Jake's room about 3:00 p.m. while staff prepared him for surgery. The sisters

10 Smith.

11 2 *Kings* 13:20-21, *Matthew* 9:20-22, *Acts* 19:11-12; *Catechism of the Catholic Church*, 828.

12 Sr. Kateri Mitchell memo on Jacob Finkbonner, September 9, 2008; interview by Mark G. Thiel, May 7, 2012; Sr. Kateri Mitchell email received May 8, 2012 with digital image of reliquary. Like her namesake, Sr. Kateri Mitchell is a Turtle Clan member of the Mohawk Nation, and she is a sister of the Sisters of St. Anne who has served as the Tekakwitha Conference's executive director since 1998. Fr. Béchard, a Jesuit priest, was based at The Kateri Centre, St. Francis-Xavier Church, Kahnawake, Québec, where the tomb of Kateri Tekakwitha is located.

13 Sr. Mary Ann Reichlin is a blood-sister of Donny Finkbonner's mother. Sr. Kateri Mitchell memo on Jacob Finkbonner, September 18, 2008.

14 Sr. Kateri Mitchell memo on Jacob Finkbonner, September 17, 2008.

joined his parents around his bed and Sister Kateri gave Jake's mother the relic to hold. Sister Kateri put her hand on hers as she placed the relic by her son's body and began to pray spontaneously to Blessed Kateri for healing. Sister Kateri then closed with the Prayer for Tekakwitha's Canonization and gave the parents a prayer card and small religious medal with Blessed Kateri's image.[15]

Sister Kateri conducted this session as she always does when there are requests to pray with the relic. It was brief and lasted only five minutes, yet it was a very moving and spiritual experience. They prayed intently over a gravely ill boy whose head was swathed in bandages, and while they were still praying, the hospital staff wheeled him off to surgery.[16]

ELSA FINKBONNER: …I pinned that relic [religious medal] to his pillow and [thereafter] I read that prayer to him every single day.[17]

JAKE FINKBONNER: Sometimes, I could hear prayers buzzing around in my head and mostly I heard my mom and my dad's voices.[18]

ELSA FINKBONNER: Donny and I went off to the chapel and just surrendered Jake back to God. We just said, "God, he is yours. Thy will be done, and if it is your will to take him home, then so be it." It was later that I found out the visit [by Sister Kateri with the relic] was the last day they [the doctors] had any further findings on the infection….[19] There's no question in my mind that it was in fact a miracle….[20] [When Sister Kateri visited] … it was something beyond coincidental. She was a messenger. It felt like it was a revelation from God.[21]

DONNY FINKBONNER: To us, it's always been a miracle whether the church recognizes it's a miracle or not. It's not up to us,

15   Sr. Julie Codd memo, "The Events Surrounding the Miracle of Jake Finkbonner," received May 8, 2012.

16   Mitchell interview.

17   Sr. Kateri Mitchell memo, September 17, 2008; Cathy Lynn Grossman, "Native American is proclaimed Catholic saint," USA Today, December 20, 2011; Mitchell interview; Elsa Finkbonner email, June 1, 2012. The "relic" was actually a religious medal with the image of Kateri Tekakwitha.

18   Smith.

19   Hagerty; Lorraine Malinder, "Holy Rivalry over Kateri," The (Montreal) Gazette, Saturday, March 20, 2010, accessed online.

20   Hagerty.

21   Kristen Cates, "Blessed Kateri to be Canonized," Great Falls Tribune, January 9, 2012, 5A.

but in our hearts, we know that Jake is a miracle. We've seen it with our own eyes.[22]

Jake drifted in and out of a coma and was completely unresponsive for over two months. Then one day after regaining consciousness, he retold his extraordinary near-death experience about visiting with God.[23]

ELSA FINKBONNER: I remember him just laying there … in the hospital bed … he sat straight up and said, "I've been raised."[24]

JAKE FINKBONNER: I was in heaven and I spoke to God…. God sat in a high chair and was very tall…. He wasn't the size of a normal person.[25]

ELSA FINKBONNER: Jake said, "Jesus' heart went into him and then back to Jesus." He said, "It was like a thousand pennies fell from the sky."[26]

JAKE FINKBONNER: I was able to look down at the hospital and then I went back to the house where I saw my family. The only thing is I didn't see myself…. I really enjoyed myself … [but God] said that my family needed me and everybody else down here … [so] he sent me back down.[27]

Much later, after his recovery, Jake began to offer advice to other young people who are very sick.

JAKE FINKBONNER: Don't be scared at all. Either way, it will be a good way. If you go to heaven, you'll be in a better place. If you live, you'll be back with your family….[28] They [the doctors] said I wasn't able to live, [but] they didn't give up…. These people are special. They kept on going. They tried as hard as they could, and they barely pulled it in.[29]

On July 21, the Tekakwitha Conference, which was meeting for five days in Seattle, gathered on the Lummi Nation Indian Reservation near Ferndale. There, Seattle Archbishop Alexander J. Brunett announced that an investigation of Jake's case was underway by the Congregation

22 Woodruff.
23 Elsa Finkbonner email, May 22, 2012.
24 *Ibid.*
25 *Ibid.*
26 Lorraine Malinder, "Holy Rivalry over Kateri," The (Montreal) Gazette, Saturday, March 20, 2010, accessed online.
27 Woodruff.
28 *Ibid.*
29 Smith.

for Causes of Saints, a committee of cardinals and bishops in Rome. The Congregation sent representatives who reviewed Jake's medical records and they interviewed Jake, his family and friends, and staff at his school and the hospital. Later, in response to a request for more details, Father Sauer sent a letter with additional information from Jake's family. After five years, the Congregation concluded, and Pope Benedict XVI approved, that Jake's cure was a miracle caused by Kateri Tekakwitha's intercession, which was announced on December 19, 2011.[30]

ELSA FINKBONNER: We look at [the work of] that [hospital] team specifically as being miraculous in itself....[31] It [the questioning by church representatives] was a little intimidating. I guess we didn't really realize just how significant it was until we saw the panel of people that came. We were like, "Oh my gosh. Wow! They mean business." They're not messing around. There was a priest, a doctor, a lawyer, and a notary. They never asked about whether the family thought this was a miracle or why they believed it was. The panel simply asked what happened and had them tell their stories. We are just so honored to be a part of this day and the making of history for not only the Catholic Church but the Native American culture. It's just such an honor for our family to be a part of such a day in history.[32]

JAKE FINKBONNER: I also thank all the people that prayed for me. Obviously, God heard their prayers....[33] I pray to Kateri now myself. Other people have asked about my story and told me their stories, and I pray to her for other people to be healed....[34]

ELSA FINKBONNER: He's very normal. He ... likes to play video games like any 11-year-old boy ... [and he plays basketball] with passion and drive. [But] he has a sense of wisdom ... that the typical 11-year old most likely wouldn't have because he has been robbed of that sense of invincibility.... In my heart, in all of us, we've always found that Jake's recovery—his healing and his survival—truly was a

30   Kie Relyea, "Boy's Recovery puts Indian Woman on Road to Sainthood," The Seattle Times, December 20, 2011, accessed online; PROMULGAZIONE DI DECRETI DELLA CONGREGAZIONE DELLE CAUSE DEI SANTI, 19.12.2011, Vatican News Services bulletin 28579, accessed online; Elsa Finkbonner email, June 6, 2012.

31   Smith.

32   Sullivan.

33   Jake Finkbonner website, posted January 30, 2012.

34   Grossman.

miracle. As far as Blessed Kateri becoming a saint, it's honorable to be a part of that process…. [Jake] is excited to meet the Pope. I think that's going to be the icing on the cake for him.[35]

Jake has undergone more than two dozen surgeries as doctors continue to repair the damage to his face. He is actively engaged in school and sports, and serves as an altar boy in church. With his family, he plans to attend Kateri Tekakwitha's canonization in Rome on Sunday, October 21, 2012.

35   Relyea.

13

FROM THE DESK OF THE TEKAKWITHA CONFERENCE EXECUTIVE DIRECTOR

SISTER KATERI MITCHELL, S.S.A.

This letter from Sister Kateri Mitchell, S.S.A., first appeared in the May-June 2012 issue of Cross and Feathers, the newsletter of the Tekakwitha Conference.

Dear Friends of Saint Kateri Tekakwitha,

The Risen Christ has entered our hearts, homes, and communities bringing joy, peace, life and hope. These gifts we welcome for our human and spiritual rebirth.

2012, a year of new awakening and many blessings for the Indigenous Catholics of this land and all peoples of the Universal Church who are filled with new life and energy with the upcoming Sainthood of our patroness, Kateri Tekakwitha in October. Even creation is rejoicing with its new array of budding trees and display of spring flowers. North America will have its own Indigenous Saint on October 21 proclaimed by our Holy Father Pope Benedict XVI.

What glorious recognition and affirmation for the once invisible and voiceless First Peoples of Turtle Island! What a wonderful celebration for the hundreds who will travel to the Vatican, the Eternal City. Our Kateri Tekakwitha, a young Mohawk/Algonquin has brought many to a deeper faith, prayer life through healing and hope for her people.

People are asking:

Will the Tekakwitha Conference end? What will be its purpose after the canonization? The Tekakwitha Conference will continue with greater impetus, conviction and jubilation. This organization exists for evangelization among the First Peoples. Kateri Tekakwitha will always be a patroness and evangelizer among her own. Through her life of prayerfulness, conviction and recognition of a Creator God in her life she has become a model for many who today are evangelizers and catechists among their own people.

Will the Tekakwitha Conference fold and die? It will become more vibrant and experience a rebirth. Signs will be very visible as we gather in Albany, Fonda, and Auriesville, New York this July. In fact, the Tekakwitha Conference National Office is busier than ever and the annual conferences are scheduled as far as July 2017. The Tekakwitha Conference is truly alive and with the welcoming back of former members and new members of the conference, we are moving forward.

Yes, we live and God lives in and among us as the Risen Christ who is alive. He will continue to bring healing, peace and hope through the inspiration and intercession of (Saint) Kateri Tekakwitha especially to her Indigenous sisters and brothers and all of their friends throughout the land.

May you have a safe and blessed summer. See you in Albany and/or Rome and together we will continue to give praise and thanksgiving.

In Kateri Tekakwitha,

Sister Kateri Mitchell

Marquette University, Tekakwitha Conference Archives .
Printed by permission.

INTERVIEWS

MARY BORDEAUX HUNGER

IN MISSION, SOUTH DAKOTA, ON THE
ROSEBUD INDIAN RESERVATION, MAY 24, 1994

Born around 1905-1910, Mary Bordeaux Hunger was an elder bilingual mixed-blood member of the Rosebud Sioux Tribe and a lifelong resident of the Rosebud Indian Reservation. She attended Catholic schools at St. Francis and O'Neil, Nebraska and was a lifelong Catholic who was active in the St. Mary's Society. A widow, she was married and raised five children. Interviewed and edited by Mark G. Thiel.

THIEL: When did you first learn about Kateri Tekakwitha?

HUNGER: See, I was in a sewing room with one of the Sisters. And then, that sewing room is for the fathers' and brothers' clothing. And so, now and then the priest[s], they come in with their cassocks to be made over or adjust the hem.... So the sister that I work with, she always visit with the scholastics or the brother or the priest. She visits with them and I'm there. But she only has one girl to help her, so that's where I was. So, that's where I got acquainted with the fathers and brothers. And that's where one of the scholastics had a Kateri, just a little pamphlet book. It isn't a big book, it's just a small, little one.

And that has the story of Tekakwitha, and he gave that to me. So I read that through. I ... read it through and through, that little book. That, I got to thinking when I get home, I'm going to make a wooden cross for myself and hang it in the trees. Which I never got to it, because I had to go out in the trees by myself, I'm scared. So that's something I never did. I was going to make a wood cross and hang it somewhere. See how long it'll hang there. And that's the story of the Tekakwitha because she was doing that, not really that way, but she lived that kind of life. So I was going to do that in the trees, too. I was going to make branches, you know, make a cross. Now I wished I had done that and hang it up....

So I read about Tekakwitha then, but I couldn't, pronounce it— Tekakwitha. The priest was telling me how to pronounce it.... And that's where I learned about her. But of course nobody in school, nobody ever know. She wasn't known. Just to the sewing room this scholastic had this book. And so I got it. I may still got it, too.

THIEL: So not many people read those pamphlets.

HUNGER: No. And it's never been mentioned. It's never been mentioned in our religion classes. And it seemed like in them days, it would be nice if it had been mentioned in a classroom, you know, the girl. But we knew the other saints, you know, the Blessed Virgin and all the women saints. We know them just all except Tekakwitha has never been mentioned, never. So, if they had known then ... more of the Indian children would know that. But it wasn't that way. Just from that sewing room where I learned about Tekakwitha. And I like her ways, the way she lived. You know, she was a very pious girl, praying all the time, and her life story, you know. It wasn't much but that's what little I know I read about her. And I like the way she lived....

THIEL: ... How often did you pray to her?

HUNGER: ... [After] I ran into her story, ... I want to live imitating her. But her real story, real life is really different, you know, the way she live and die and I couldn't live that way. But I'll think of her, that I want to be little better but I don't want nobody to see me be that way 'cause the other kids, if you're too religious, they make fun of you. So I don't let anybody know all it—put all my thinking to [the] way she act. I want to live that way without quarreling with the other kids or fighting.... I try not to, but the sisters, they know that I don't fight around like—that's all on the account of Tekakwitha. I'm trying to imitate her, but nobody knows. The children wouldn't know that. So I don't want to fight....

THIEL: Does Kateri have more followers today around here?

HUNGER: Yes. Tekakwitha is better known today. And it hasn't been too long ago, because where that came more popular about her was when, you know that statue that they put out at the St. Francis ground. That's where that really come up. More better known. And the Indians really kind of worship her. They really go there and they pray.

THIEL: So it starts with that statue.

Hunger: Mm hmm. So Tekakwitha statue is put there.

THIEL: Is that the only statue of her around here, the one at St. Francis?

HUNGER: That's the only place that I know of that's been there. Because, different reservations I think do that too. So, I know Tekakwitha quite a bit. In my young life, that student priest and then that sister that talk about it.... That's where I got to learn little more about it.

THIEL: What does Jesus Christ mean to you?

HUNGER: … He's all the church to me. And the saints. That's, when I think about the church, it seems like that makes the whole court of heaven. I think of all the saints, and I include Kateri in there. To ask her if she's there to pray for us. That's what I'm doing now. But that's about the only thing a person could ask her.… But sometimes I do something that … I've prayed for that I would want it done. And, when I go back to Tekakwitha, I ask her if she's in heaven, then to answer me. And the little thing that I want, got too puzzled about, that would kind of straighten me out that way. That she must be, and she is, in heaven. That's the way today is, to me it is. So always, if she's in heaven, to ask our Lord to help me, you know to … get well. I was sick all winter. This is unpractical and now can't live anymore.

But that kind of gives me courage to keep on, you know, thinking of living. Because at times, oh, I don't care, I don't care. That's the feeling I have: I don't care. What kind of life our Lord's gonna give me, I don't care. Just about the kind of feeling I have at times. And then I ask Tekakwitha to help me to kind of get me to think about myself, to live a better life. So, in my old age, I don't want to go astray some way, you know, crawl away. That's my main prayer now today. The last years of my life I should live more for Christ.… So that's where I am today. So I'm up and down, I'm up and down. I get sick and then, well, I give up blood. But I get better again, then. Then I have to pray that thank God that I … feel better.… That's where I'm at, too now. 'Cause I'm, everyday now I am that bad. I get weak. I give up blood. I get disgusted, discouraged. All that comes at one time. And I … really put my mind through it. I don't want to and that's when I ask Kateri to help me. To think better about myself and about the church too.

Marquette University,
Kateri Tekakwitha Project Oral History Collection.
Printed by permission.

BERTHA SHAW

IN MISSION, SOUTH DAKOTA, ON THE
ROSEBUD INDIAN RESERVATION, MAY 24, 1994

Born in 1923, Bertha Shaw was a 71-year-old member of the Rosebud Sioux Tribe, a lifelong resident of the Rosebud Indian Reservation, and a fluent speaker of Lakota. She was raised Catholic, attended a government boarding school, and attended the Episcopal Church during the early years of married life before returning to the Catholic Church. A widow, she had given birth to ten children, five of whom were still living. Interviewed and edited by Mark G. Thiel.

THIEL: When did you first learn about Kateri Tekakwitha?

SHAW: Hmm, [I] really didn't know that much until 1988. Then I read lot about her after that. I'll get materials, and read a lot about her after that. But I really didn't know until 1988.

THIEL: What did you think when she was beatified?

SHAW: Well I thought that was wonderful being she was a native.

THIEL: When do you think that she will be declared a saint?

SHAW: When? You know, you pray that she will become a saint. These summers that we go to these conferences, … maybe this summer when we go I don't know. I expect it, a year or so.

THIEL: So what do you think about the idea of having the Native American saint?

SHAW: Idea of having an American saint.... Well you can say she's a native and … she was born that way. She was born with that vision. All I can say, it's just wonderful that she is.

THIEL: How often do you feel her presence or how often do you think about her?

SHAW: Probably every night because I do have a picture. I have one hanging on the wall and I got a little one right on my … nightstand.

THIEL: So how do you communicate with Kateri?

SHAW: Pray. Do a lot of praying.

THIEL: When do you seek her?

SHAW: I seek her help…. Like I say, I went through lot of tragedies in my life. I seek for her help. I would say it has given me strength because … to me, somebody will come up and say to you that you're strong …, because I just lost my husband, not too long ago I lost a son. You're strong they say and I say, Yes—I believe in my faith and I really do. I pray to Kateri.

THIEL: When you pray to Kateri what happens to you inside?

SHAW: … I get that feeling where I'm just lonely, I guess, and it kind of hurts your back, and like that. It does me anyway. Because I can set there and think about it … and when I get that way I pray. I just go in my bedroom, all by myself and I pray. And I know when I seek her help it helps me.

THIEL: Have you ever experienced favors or miracles due to Kateri?

SHAW: No, I've never experienced any miracles but I can pray to her that I miss loneliness or whatever I have inside me will be gone. I can pray that…. It seems like I'm relieved. That's the way I feel anyway.

Marquette University,
Kateri Tekakwitha Project Oral History Collection.
Printed by permission.

THERESA POIZNEE

IN MISSION, SOUTH DAKOTA, ON THE
ROSEBUD INDIAN RESERVATION, MAY 25, 1994

Born in 1954 in Valentine, Nebraska, Theresa Poiznee was a middle-aged member of the Rosebud Sioux Tribe, not fluent in Lakota, who participated in Lakota religious traditions and Catholicism. She was married with seven children and lived on and off the reservation and out-of-state. On the reservation she earned a bachelor's degree in education at the Sinte Gleska University, and since then, she taught fourth grade in a local elementary school and served as a youth ministry coordinator of St. Thomas Church in Mission. Interviewed and edited by Mark G. Thiel.

THIEL: What would you describe as ... your earliest religious memory?

POIZNEE: Mom said I was about four, five years old. She said, "You was outside playing out in the country but then you came back in," and you said, 'Mom, when I grow up I'm gonna be a nun." We didn't go to church that often out there, ... and we didn't have no car or vehicle, no electricity, couldn't watch it on TV or anything. "You came in with this idea that you wanted to be a nun." I don't remember that part, but I remember when I was about six [or] seven years old, walking, playing with the rosary, walking like I was planning to be a priest. At that young age I'd make my little sister and brother follow me, right behind me like this with their hands behind and we pray and set that down and we bow our heads, we'd kneel and I'd make them pray with me. And that's what I remember.

THIEL: Do you have any religious articles in the home?

POIZNEE: Oh yeah. You can go in my house and every one of the kids' rooms got crucifix. They bought sage, bundles of sage hang in their room. They've got pictures of Jesus and Mary. And a lot of these, their rosaries, a lot of these they bought on their own or they got one when they come to ... the Kateri group [which] has religious articles for sale, ... the kids buy their own stuff. They've got probably every one of them have their own Bible, not saying that they read it a lot, but they all have their own Bible.… I keep a simple wooden cross with tiny thread made just out of pieces of wood we went out and gathered. To me they were something because there was a Tekakwitha Conference. I found it and we tied them together and made the crosses. It still hangs with the wreath of sage in my home next to the picture of Jesus and I got one of Mary. There is a lot. There's … pictures of Jesus Christ on the wall in the living room and kitchen. So there are a lot … plus my little altar in my bedroom … for myself. There's quite a bit.

THIEL: When you close your eyes what religious images do you see?

POIZNEE: We see things that are Catholic and of our religion. The bundles the ties make, … the cross is frequent with me, and pictures of Jesus, the rosary and the bundles of sage and sweet grass and my prayer bundle and my medicine bag.…

THIEL: When did you first learn about Kateri Tekakwitha?

POIZNEE: I've always heard the name and stuff but I never really paid much attention to it. It was a beautiful name, and then one of my friends was talking to me about it.… That's the first time I've ever really heard.… I've heard other people mention her and little bit about her, that she was Native American. And then when she start talking to me and telling me about it and stuff it was like my interest started growing a little more because she was Native American, because she became Blessed. And it was just like, to me this is the first Native American I've ever heard that was even thought about in those ways and there's probably been many more people that were really religious and really, to me, walked in a sacred way. But she was recognized for that. You think about the views that she has from not only her own people but the other religions are having a hard time accepting them fully as nuns.… I really admire her perseverance and dedication to what she believed in. And I realize how sometimes we're criticized. People say something about us, about trying to be holier than thou or trying to be goody two-shoes all of a sudden because I'm working with the church or their expectations. And I can just imagine what she went through. I can't say I know how she felt, but I can imagine what it feels, the trials that she had went through. The crosses she had to carry for her belief. And just thinking about it more and more was, like, all right! There's a Native American being recognized in the church. About time.

THIEL: When do you think that she will be declared a saint?

POIZNEE: I don't know, the way the church moves, whether … the miracles are happening or not, all the work that has to be done to clarify them. I don't know if it's clarifying them or ... to me like they're judgmental, being really critical of the things that are happening and stuff, so I don't know. I hope it's in my lifetime that it happens but I can never say.

THIEL: How often do you feel her presence or think of her?

POIZNEE: ... every two weeks we have a Kateri youth group meeting ..., so she's really on my mind then. But through working with the kids I'm usually a very prayerful person, there's times when I get so busy I forget especially the month of May and at the beginning it was all right because it was Mary's month and we really focused in on that. But with Kateri ... I think about things to teach the kids about her a lot. And try to depict her life as something you could—to me the kids say like, Oh we could never walk that way. And they're right, they couldn't be that. Because they aren't Kateri. But ... I think of her a lot and how I could get the kids to think about her more.... Especially when it comes time towards the national Tekakwitha conference I think about her a lot more than about anyone.

THIEL: How do you communicate with Kateri?

POIZNEE: We've used the chaplet but the kids have developed a kind of a chaplet ... a twelve bead chaplet. And with that they have the different colors representing the four different peoples on this earth, our earth mother here, and then they say the prayers ... for these people.... And then they pray the prayer of Blessed Kateri and ... we use that a lot. And then I have a statue of Kateri at home. And then I have a little container of sand by the statue that was taken from New York or some other place. Well it was given to me by a friend. In turn it was given to him by a friend that ... had these little containers where they go to get this dirt all the time. And so ... that's how I used them and that's what I'm praying ... whenever I'm there. And sometimes with the kids, they also ... say the prayer, my daughter ... says it regularly every night. She knows, so she kind of keeps me going. When you have a large family ... you tend to ... prayer when you have time. But it's been good, for the kids as well as for myself.

THIEL: When you pray to Kateri, what happens to you inside?

POIZNEE: It depends. If I'm in a hurry and I know it, and it's just like all of a sudden it comes to my mind, I shouldn't rush through this, ... I shouldn't rush through the prayers just to hurry up and get it done and over with and say you've said your prayers. And it's always this calming effect. You need to slow down and take it easy. Count to ten. And even in being rushed I do that. Not just when I get angry, ... but when I'm being rushed, it's like, ... prayer time is not a time to rush through it. And I used to do that with the rosary with my daughter. But now ... we sit down and [it]calms me down to think that this is not the time to be rushing through prayers.

THIEL: Have you ever experienced favors or miracles due to Kateri's intercession?

POIZNEE: No, I've never asked. I've always prayed for her. For her to become a saint, for them to recognize [her]. So I've never really asked for anything from her. I've never asked for anything from any saints. Well, Mary I have, but that's about the only one.

THIEL: What does Kateri mean to your tribe?

POIZNEE: For the people that are involved at the Church, our Native American people that involved at the church here, ... especially with the elderly people, I've noticed that they ... really respect her a lot. They wait for her to become a saint. And, with the youth, they're proud, ... there's a pride in that one of our people here on this continent would be recognized. So that's to them a pride....

THIEL: What does Kateri mean to other Indian people?

POIZNEE: Just by going to the conferences, just by observing. It pulls people together. Unity, you know. But the community, even with people you don't know, and I've noticed this especially with the kids, that they're Indian, and everybody else around them is Indian. They have no walls to put up or defenses. They don't have to walk around like there's this chip on their shoulder. And this is voiced a lot to me by the kids, especially, it's like we can come here and be who we are.... I went to Albuquerque and Kateri groups down there.... They talk about Kateri with a lot of pride. They have it with the Kateri groups, now Kateri groups that are starting.... There is ... a movement out there to reach Kateri. More and more people are learning about her. And it's bringing more and more people together. And, to me ... because of that unity that Native American people are feeling at the conference ... it's carrying over to other areas in government ... and tribal schools. So ... to me that's part of the unity that she's bringing people together. And that of the Native American people, especially of the youth. They feel proud to be together and they're proud of who they are. At home and then the large group settings. And that's one of the things the kids told me a lot, was that they like being there because of all the different

Native American people. And one of my sons' words were, Mom, I didn't realize there was so many other Indians out there....

THIEL: What do you think about Kateri's non-Indian followers?

POIZNEE: ... I'm glad they're there. They help support her, they help pray for her, ... and that's all ... we're asking. That's what we need for her....

THIEL: You mentioned the Tekakwitha Conference and the Mini-Tek conferences?

POIZNEE: I've went to the Mini Tekakwitha Conference last year in Rapid, and one will be held here. And, I found them like ... little gatherings of family because, ... out of the people that went were people you knew from different communities that were involved in Tekakwitha. So it was really nice to get to them.... I think the Tekakwitha Conference that I've enjoyed the most was when we went to Washington, because we went to the different tribes, different places there and ... I went to the sacred fire and I was involved in the prayer services in the morning. And ... that was the attitude I went with is that I would enjoy every-thing. Because before it was like we took kids, the kids did a workshop one year. And the next year I did a workshop on racism, so it was like you're working and you don't get to enjoy as much. So, that one that we went to last year, ... I totally immersed myself in what I wanted to do, ... to pray and think about things. And I did. I just felt it through me. I came away with a spiritual high that lasted ... up until we start really getting busy. So it was really good....

Marquette University,
Kateri Tekakwitha Project Oral History Collection.
Printed by permission.

KATHRYN CLAIRMONT

IN MISSION, SOUTH DAKOTA, ON THE
ROSEBUD INDIAN RESERVATION, MAY 25, 1994

Born in 1927, Kathryn Clairmont was a 67-year-old bilingual member of the Rosebud Sioux Tribe who had graduated from the St. Francis Mission High School, studied nursing in Oklahoma, and then served as a nurse at the Rosebud (South Dakota) Indian Health Service Hospital from 1949 until she retired in 1980. A widow, she was married and raised seven children and has two granddaughters named Kateri. She had life-long involvement in the Catholic Church, including lay ministry in her parish, the St. Mary's Society, and the Catholic Sioux Congress; in 1984, she attended her first of several state and national Tekakwitha Conferences. Interviewed and edited by Mark G. Thiel.

THIEL: When did you first learn about Kateri Tekakwitha?

CLAIRMONT: I didn't go to school till I was nine years old. I don't know why they didn't take me to school right away. When I went to school I didn't know any English and I was nine years old. And it seemed like it was ... third grade so that would be eleven, maybe twelve years old. I learned about her and we used to pray, pray for her and all that. I always thought she was a saint already because we used to pray lots to her and they used to have programs, you know, like they act out Lily.... [T]hey used to call her ... Lily of the Mohawks and they used to have a little plays for her. So I learned that when I was twelve years old.

THIEL: What did you feel or think when she was beatified?

CLAIRMONT: Oh I was really happy, happy and grateful and as I said I thought she was a saint already. I always thought she was, I mean, always to me she was a saint already.

THIEL: When do you think she'll be declared a saint?

CLAIRMONT: Anytime. As I said I think ... to me she's a saint already. I just pray all the time that she will be a saint soon.

THIEL: So what do you think about having a Native American saint?

CLAIRMONT: I think we're really honored. We're really honored to have her for a saint. The Indian people need someone like that.

THIEL: How often do you feel her presence and think about her?

CLAIRMONT: Gee, I think about her every day. I think it's because I have a picture of her in my room and her statue is there and then I say that canonization prayer every morning and before I go to sleep; sometimes during the day while going driving someplace or doing something I just say it, say it and just plead and plead one day that she'll become a saint.

THIEL: How do you communicate with Kateri?

CLAIRMONT: I pray to her, and I have a real warm feeling, really good feeling when I pray to her, and I know that she's there or she's listening or something. And then back in 1986, I think, I was really sick and I had kidney problems and I went to the hospital and … they send me to Rapid City to see a urologist. So I went to see him and here he said that he found a cancer in my left kidney. And then he said it was as big as a golf ball and it was in my left kidney, so he told me that they'll have to remove it, remove my kidney—he said it was sitting right on top of my kidney—and so I went, Why don't you just take the tumor off, don't have to take my kidney. He said, No, that's a bad procedure. He said, We'll have to remove your whole kidney, he said. So, oh, I start crying and I really felt bad. I came home. And then I told my family. And then that next week I was supposed to go back and have surgery to have it removed. And here, I came home and told my kids, and they all start crying, and so one of my kids that's really faithful, she goes to church all the time. And she said, Mom, I thought we'd have a prayer for you, have a Mass for you right here in your house. So I said, All right. So she got hold of Father Jones…. And so my sister and all them came, and they had a mass in my house, and they offered it up to Kateri, and they ask for help and everything that I'll be able to—It won't be so bad. And so they had mass for me and we all received communion. Afterwards we had a luncheon. And then the next day I think I went to Rapid. I had the surgery and after it was over, the doctor came to see me and I asked him, I said, How bad was it? And he said, Oh, we took your left kidney out. He said, It wasn't embedded inside the kidney, it was sitting on top and it was just as big as a nickel, or something like that. He said, just small. So I said, and here you told me it was as big as a golf ball here. He said, No, when you got in there it was just as big as a nickel. So, … it didn't grow or nothing…. And so, he removed it. So, you don't have cancer anymore. And so I should of had it [documented] and everything but I didn't. So I came back. We had a Thanksgiving mass in honor of

Kateri, too. Said it didn't spread or anything. Came out of the surgery all right. Everything is all right. That was like a miracle to me....

THIEL: What does Kateri mean to your tribe?

CLAIRMONT: We try to have meetings and invite different ones but I think they all believe in her and they all favor her. Because when we go around and ask for help for fundraising and like that, they help us. They listen. They're glad that we're going to the conferences. They all wish they could go but they couldn't. But they all believe in her.

THIEL: And you mentioned you have a granddaughter.

CLAIRMONT: Yeah ... named Kateri.... She's named after [her].... I have another grandchild, her middle name's Kateri and they call her Kateri, just this little one. She's five years old now.... She talks about her all the time.

THIEL: Have you participated in the mini-Tekakwitha conferences?

CLAIRMONT: Yes. Ever since it started, I don't know how long it's been, but I've been there every year. And I've went to ten national Tekakwitha conferences, ten of them. I started going to Seattle, Washington and Syracuse, New York. That was 1984. Every year I've been going, this will be my tenth year. Same way with mini-Tekakwitha Conferences. I take part in it too. I do Eucharist ministry and some of the liturgy reading, present the gifts—we did that at Tucson, Arizona we brought up the gifts. Put them on the altar. And I'm really anxious and I'm looking forward to it.

Marquette University,
Kateri Tekakwitha Project Oral History Collection,
Printed by permission.

ROSALITA ROACH-AVERY

IN RED SCAFFOLD, SOUTH DAKOTA, ON THE CHEYENNE RIVER INDIAN RESERVATION, MAY 26, 1994

Born on the Cheyenne River Indian Reservation in 1947, Rosalita Roach-Avery was a 47-year-old bilingual English-Lakota speaking member of the Cheyenne River Sioux Tribe of mixed Cheyenne and Lakota ancestry. She attended Catholic and government boarding schools and public universities in several states and earned a bachelor's degree. She was a lifelong active Catholic who respected Lakota religious traditions and she attended some state and national Tekakwitha Conferences. Interviewed and edited by Mark G. Thiel.

THIEL: Do you have any religious articles in the home?

ROACH-AVERY: Yes I do. I have many religious items in my home: crucifixes, rosaries, Bibles, prayer books, holy water, palms, and also the Lakota sweet grass, sage, cedar, eagle feathers, medicine wheels, things that are sacred to our people. I have pictures, religious pictures, [all] very visible.

THIEL: When did you first learn about Kateri Tekakwitha?

ROACH-AVERY: I first learned about Kateri when I was growing up in Chamberlain I think it was more the story of the Mohawk girl, and … to me it was just a story then, … it wasn't [the] same as it is now. It was just a story of another person and her experience. I was probably ten years old when I heard the story. You know how when you're growing up you hear lot of stories of different saints. She kind of stood out because she's a Mohawk girl.

THIEL: What did you think when she was beatified?

ROACH-AVERY: I thought that was something really great. Because people had prayed for so long for it to happen, and it did happen. It seems, you know, that it was just a long time coming. And I suppose these things do take time. But I was really happy.

THIEL: When do you think she will be declared a saint?

ROACH-AVERY: Soon. And when I say soon, … you don't really know, but I think that it's gonna happen, maybe sooner than we really think.

THIEL: How often do you feel or think of her now?

ROACH-AVERY: I would say daily, since … the last six … years. She has really had an impact on my life. I try and say prayers daily for her, so that she will be canonized. Any time I need help, I pray to Kateri. My prayers are always answered. It has really helped me and my family.

THIEL: How do you communicate with Kateri?

ROACH-AVERY: I communicate with Kateri mainly through prayer. And also just talking to her, telling her why I need these prayers, and also, pray that she will be canonized, and that when this happens then it will really be a celebration. And, you know, lot of people will be happy and celebrate her canonization.

THIEL: When you pray to Kateri, what happens to you inside?

ROACH-AVERY: When I pray to Kateri, usually I feel really free after I've done my prayers, and the worries that I had are just not there anymore, you know, before I prayed to her and talked with her. Then after, I feel free and the worries are gone. When everything turns out right, my prayers are answered, then I always am really thankful and always remember to say thank you for all the help that I receive.

THIEL: Have you ever experienced favors or miracles?

ROACH-AVERY: I guess I receive both. Favors constantly. As far as miracles, I pray for family members. For instance, my dad was very sick and the doctors just gave him like a fifty-fifty chance. And so I prayed to Kateri and asked to heal him. And my father's still alive. And also during that time the doctors diagnosed him of having cancer, but … we took him back couple years later and the other doctor says well there's nothing there and everything's fine and all his major organs … are okay and he's still alive today. And he hasn't gotten sick since then. And, so I consider that a miracle because we had prayed for him. And also, my husband, I prayed for him and that was kind of over time, … it didn't happen right away, it took … anywhere from three to four years. I prayed that he would realize that he was sick because of alcohol. And that he would do something. Help himself. Even went to healing ceremonies and it has helped him…. It'll be two years he has been sober. And it's really nice. It's a whole different life to have a sober spouse. It's hard but … it's lot better than it was, because I didn't think that I could put up with his way of life for the rest of my life. And I just did a lot of praying because he was my husband I just didn't want to give up on him. I think that there is—it's a miracle, you know. Really thankful for that.

THIEL: What does Kateri mean to your tribe?

ROACH-AVERY: I think that Kateri means having a role model for members of our tribe. Having, I guess in the church way, a person that is recognized. And it gives ... kind of like having a sister in terms of like family. Having another person, a sister.... Somebody that they can go to for help, pray to, to look up to. That kind of thing.... [T]ribal members—many of them are different denominations. So I'm not sure if the other denominations know about Kateri, but I do know that the Catholics know about her. And they're very proud of her. And in our parish, we try and get involved with the Kateri circles. So it's really been a positive thing for our tribal members.

THIEL: How do children respond to Kateri?

ROACH-AVERY: I think different, depending on what age and where they're at with their own religious experience. Like, with my own children, the younger one, he's full of questions. And the older ones, they're more aware of her and I guess they kind of grew up knowing her because we have taken them to the Kateri conferences. So they know the story—her story. And they've been exposed to her. They think it's really something neat. And ... I always tell them in their prayers, to pray to her, and use her as a patron. But other children I'm not sure. I think our parish, they are aware of her. But I'm not sure of other children, like even here at school, I don't think very many children other than the Catholic children know about her.

Marquette University,
Kateri Tekakwitha Project Oral History Collection.
Printed by permission.

DEACON HAROLD E.
CONDON

IN RED SCAFFOLD, SOUTH DAKOTA,
CHEYENNE RIVER INDIAN RESERVATION,
JUNE 2, 1994

Born in 1950 on the Cheyenne River Reservation, Harold E. Condon was a 44-year-old bilingual member of the Cheyenne River Sioux Tribe. He attended Catholic boarding schools and earned a bachelor's degree in accounting and business management from Black Hills State College. He has served reservation schools and tribal government in various administrative capacities. He was married and raised three children. He became a member of Alcoholics Anonymous in 1976, when he became active again in the Church. He then studied for the permanent diaconate, became involved in healing ministries and the Tekakwitha Conference, and was ordained in 1985. He practiced both Catholicism and traditional Lakota religious traditions, and as a deacon, served parishes on both the Pine Ridge and Cheyenne River Indian reservations. Interviewed and edited by Mark G. Thiel.

THIEL: When did you first learn about Kateri Tekakwitha?
CONDON: … I heard about her through my lifetime. But … 1979 … was when I [first] went to a conference.… That's where I really heard about her cause, … why they were having the conferences, [and] why they were having in her name for intercession for ministry for Indian people.… So that's when … [my] interest [started].… [I began] attending these conferences and … coming home and promoting the cause.… [At] the Red Scaffold Parish, which I attended, we would get in a group … to raise money … [and] get scholarships from the Sacred Heart priests and brothers to attend conferences. So in 1979 was the first time I'd really heard of the fullness of what she stood for....
THIEL: What did you think when she was beatified?

CONDON: Well first of all, I wish I was there. I wasn't, but just knowing that a Native American is close to sainthood in the Church, made it all pretty excit[ing].... Wish I could be there. But as Indian people, throughout the land, we already consider her as a saint because she's helped us in many ways.

THIEL: When do you think they'll make it official?

CONDON: I really don't know, but I hope it's soon ... [that] I would get the word ... this year or next year.... We have our hopes that we will make it.

THIEL: How often do you feel her presence or think about her?

CONDON: I think about her every day. I carry a medal in my pocket and every morning I pray and ask her to be part of our day. [I] ask her to pray for us.... I carry it in my pocket ... because ... when I change my trousers every day [I] have to take it out to transfer it to my next trousers. So ... it reminds me to pray.... I've seen many miracles happen at the Tekakwitha Conference [when] I gave healing services there a number of years.... So ... since '79, [she's] been a very big part of my life.... I don't like to wear [jewelry] ... around my neck or anything ... but ... I carry it in my pocket. So she is very much a part of our lives every day.

THIEL: When you pray to Kateri, what happens to you inside?

CONDON: I know that when I pray to her, she [is] very much present in our life. She's at a place where she can make a difference.... She can intercede for us directly, to Our Lord and Savior, Jesus Christ. So I know that when I pray, that our prayers will be answered. It gives me confidence that whatever we ask for, will happen, because she is present. [I] get the feeling inside that she is present with us.

THIEL: Have you ever experienced favors or miracles due to her intercession?

CONDON: Yes. My son, when he was eleven years old ... [and] diagnosed with cancer.... He had surgery and they took a ... real big tumor out of his hand. Boy, it was really big... and it was malignant. So, right away they wanted to amputate his arm [above the elbow]. So we went to Sioux Falls and ... we asked for second opinion. So they took us to Rochester, Minnesota ... [and] after examining him, they recommended the same thing.... [So] we prayed. We prayed to Father, Son, [and] Holy Spirit, and we prayed to saints—Saint Peregrine [Laziosi], [patron] saint for cancer [patients]. We prayed to Saint Joseph, my patron saint, for intercession. [We] prayed to God. [We prayed to] Our Lady, [we prayed to Kateri] Tekakwitha for intercession, and I prayed the rosary a lot. And so I know [that] she [Kateri Tekakwitha] is a big part of my son being healed during that time. And when we had a room by ourselves for [a] half an hour before the doctor came to see us, all we did was pray that time. We called out to everybody. [We] called out to God—Father God, Son God, [and] the Holy Spirit. [We] called out to the saints for the whole half an hour, and when the doctors came in, [and] ask[ed] us about the surgery and so forth, something happened there that really was heart wrenching. It was like my heart was torn out of me, and as I talk about it right now, I can just feel it. My son began to cry. He said, "Dad! Don't take my arm off! I'll feel so helpless! Dad!"

[It was] 1985... [and] I felt so helpless. I reached for him and grabbed him. He cried.... The doctor ... said, "Harold" ..."We got a experimental thing we're doing right now. If you'd like to try it on your son." He said, "What might happen is when we do that treatment on his hand and arm, it might kill all—everything—and it might be just a dead limb hanging there." And we didn't even have to decide. My son says, "Yes! Let's do it!" So the next day they'd start treatment. But we asked if we could go in there and bless the machines. We did [and we] put oil, holy oil on that [arm]. [We] just anointed the whole arm of our son. [We] anointed and prayed over him and he went through 33 treatments from October 1985 to January of '86. And the doctors were amazed with his hand, because it was still working, even after taking lot of the muscles out.... And ... they caught everything.... The first year we went back every three months; second year, every six months' fourth year, once a year; fifth year, once a year.... He went back again just recently. Still get clean bill, the bill of health. He has to go back in 1996, and then he said, we'll forget about it. But the experimental treatment that they did on him is kind of a regular treatment today and he's had great success with it.... So I know that part of that was intercession—Blessed Kateri Tekakwitha had helped heal my son of cancer.

THIEL: What does Kateri mean to your tribe?

CONDON: It's growing. Her cause is growing on this reservation, and [the people] pushed it, and more and more people start to know her. And I would say as far as our churches, the Catholic Churches, they push up her cause. The tribal members who [have] come in contact with her, [have] really started devotion[s] to her. Though this is not a full-fledged devotion in the Catholic Church, [but for] the ones who [have] come in contact with her, [they have had] ... a lot of meaning in their lives and that's [been happening] every year [as] more and more [have] joined in her cause.

THIEL: How do the children respond to Kateri?

CONDON: I only can talk about Red Scaffold, because that's where I attend. During experiences of attending the conferences and especially the part of the youth, you have whole youth programs throughout the conference. Those who go there, I believe, always talk about it and want to go back to next year.… So the response to that has been tremendous. But I only can talk about [the] Red Scaffold [parish]; it's the only church … I attend.…

THIEL: What does Jesus Christ mean to you?

CONDON: He means all to me. He's the center of my life, my family's life. He's the one who died for me, to take away my sins once and for all. He made the supreme sacrifice, now he sits at the right hand of God, taking care of me and my family and allowing the saints that we pray to, Kateri Tekakwitha, Katherine Drexel, my patron saint—Saint Joseph, [and] Saint Ann. Saints like that … to intercede for us, to him [Jesus].…

THIEL: And what has your participation been like at the Mini-Tekakwitha and National Tekakwitha Conferences?

CONDON: It's very, been very active. After the 1983 conference, they really encouraged us to start reaching in regional type of conferences. And so when I came back, called Victor Bull Bear and asked him. I said, "We should [have] a regional one." "It's gonna be pretty hard," he said, "Why't we just start one for the state?" And of course, we's talking Lakota, the Lakota language. I translate that into English right now, speaking to the camera. And so he said to me, "Why't you take it first?" "I don't know, you're older than I am so you should start it." So in 1984, spring of 1984 had our first Mini-Tekakwitha Conference in South Dakota in Porcupine at Our Lady of Lourdes School. And 33 people showed up. We had a good time. And so after it was over Victor said, "It's your turn." I said, "Okay, I'll take it." So in 1985 we brought it to Cherry Creek. And that year was to be my ordination, and I haven't set a date, so Bishop Dimmerling asked when I'd like to have it. So I'd like to have it first day of the Conference on Friday, May 10 of 1985. I got ordained same time of Mini-Tekakwitha Conference. Over 500 people showed up for that. Course all 500 didn't stay for the whole thing, but that's how many registered that time. And from there it's really grown since then. And this year will be our tenth anniversary.

I've been going every year and very active in giving workshops and so forth. And I begin workshop this weekend the third and fourth of June 1994 with family at the Crow Creek High School. We're going to have it ... this coming weekend. So I think I'm very active at the local level, and also the national, part of that pretty much. I guess where it take off, 1979, went down to the Conference in Yankton, South Dakota. And there was a lot of people things in the ministry as far as Catholic Churches on the reservations. And so, Keith Swanson was from Minneapolis, and I'll remember always because he got up and told some things that were really true that wasn't happening on the reservation as far as human ministry. And we got riled up. So, we did away with the rest of the schedule for that conference and let all the Indian people get together. Circle 66, they called it. And we came up with twenty points that should we have. From there, with the meeting, the Lord used me to bring about reconciliation, and also healing. Felt good about that in 1979. And from there it has really grown. Things will go on for a long, long time. Especially after she gets [canonized] officially by the church, that ministry going to take off.

Marquette University,
Kateri Tekakwitha Project Oral History Collection.
Printed by permission.

SISTER ANTHONY DAVIS, O.S.B.S.

IN MARTY, SOUTH DAKOTA, ON THE YANKTON
INDIAN RESERVATION, JUNE 4, 1994

Born in 1915 near Belcourt, North Dakota, on the Turtle Mountain Indian Reservation, Sister Anthony Davis was a 78-year-old mixed-blood member of the Turtle Mountain Chippewa Tribe who was orphaned in 1918 at age three when her parents died of Spanish flu. She attended Catholic and government boarding schools in North and South Dakota, and in 1935 she became a founding religious sister in the all-Indian Oblate Sisters of the Blessed Sacrament. She was active in the South Dakota Catholic Sioux Congress. In 1948, she observed the missionaries' Tekakwitha Conference held in Marty, South Dakota, and since the 1980s, she attended the revitalized state and national Tekakwitha Conferences. She earned a bachelor's degree in education, and for many years she taught kindergarten and grade school in Marty, and Rapid City, South Dakota. Interviewed and edited by Mark G. Thiel.

THIEL: When did you first learn about Kateri Tekakwitha?

DAVIS: When they had the first meetings of Kateri, all the priests come to Marty and they had a conference. Every year the priests from all over the reservations, from North and South Dakota, came together. They met at Marty and they used to have no laypeople … just priests. We had these Kateri meetings in the rectory at St. Paul's Mission. That's when I learned of Kateri.

THIEL: What did you feel or think when Kateri was beatified?

DAVIS: Oh, I thought it was great. I didn't get to go that time, though, to the beatification. Some of … our sisters went. They went to Rome to it. Sister Inez [Jetty, an Oblate Sister of the Blessed Sacrament and Dakota Indian] was one of them, and Sister Christine [an Oblate Sister of the Blessed Sacrament and Dakota Indian].

THIEL: When do you think that she'll be declared a saint?

DAVIS: Hope soon. We're wishing towards this year. I've heard there's many miracles that she's doing and not all are reported.

THIEL: How often do you feel her presence or think about her?

DAVIS: Right now. And then we have meetings and we say her prayer every day, at Marty, for her canonization. And then we have our Kateri group that meet once a month.

THIEL: When you pray to Kateri, what happens to you inside?

DAVIS: There's a good feeling.

THIEL: Have you ever experienced favors or miracles from Kateri?

DAVIS: I think so. I didn't experience them myself, but I've heard other people say that so many things have happened. Especially when I was in Rapid City. Many things have happened by prayer to Kateri.

THIEL: Have you had any favors or prayers of your own answered by Kateri?

DAVIS: Prayed for a nice day today. It's beautiful.

THIEL: What does Kateri mean to your tribe, or the other Indian people that you know, that you work with?

DAVIS: It means very much, because, many of the people around Marty pray to Kateri every day. And then at home you have, in my tribe, you have a Kateri circle. And they're all going to that National Conference in Minnesota. There's about twenty of them in that group that are going to the Kateri circle, conference in Minnesota this year. It means very much to them.

THIEL: How do the children respond to Kateri?

DAVIS: Many of the children around Marty, there's very few that knew about Kateri in the past. But, some are named Kateri. They have the name of Kateri. So there's a lot of them, they know who Kateri is. Their parents tell them who she was, and why they're named after her.... Their parents tell the story. You know we have the stories of Kateri. And that's why they're named after, because they read the story of Kateri.

THIEL: What do you think about Kateri's non-Indian followers?

DAVIS: We have some—we have the priests that are the promoters of the cause. They're not Indians. I think it's great that they take such interest. Also I know some non-Indians that are really for Kateri in Rapid City. They belong to the Kateri group in Rapid City. But there's others that are named after her, some non-Indians.

THIEL: Have you met some children, who are non-Indians, whose name is Kateri?

DAVIS: One is from around Marty and they're about two from Rapid City, and one from Eagle Butte.

THIEL: What does Jesus Christ mean to you?

DAVIS: Well, he's my spouse, my everything. And I know that he died to save me. That's important.

The Kateri circle is more for the canonization of Kateri. Where we all get together and pray for her canonization and promote her cause. And get members to pray with us and spread her devotion. And we're praying for a young man right now that has cancer. Pray every day for him. We received a letter from New York. He was very in need of prayer so we been praying for this young man through the intercession of Kateri.

Marquette University,
Kateri Tekakwitha Project Oral History Collection.
Printed by permission.

DEACON FRANCIS HAIRY CHIN

IN RAPID CITY, SOUTH DAKOTA, JUNE 24, 1994

Born in 1916 in Solon, North Dakota, on the Standing Rock Indian Reservation, Francis Hairy Chin was a bilingual member of the Standing Rock Sioux Tribe who was a lifelong Catholic of Lakota and Irish ancestry. He attended Catholic boarding schools, and during the Second World War, he served in the U.S. Armed Forces. Thereafter he resided on the reservation and was employed by the federal government. In 1977-1978, he served on the national Tekakwitha Conference advisory board and then its newly established board of directors. In 1980, he attended the beatification of Kateri Tekakwitha in Rome, and later he was ordained a permanent deacon; he was a widower. Interviewed and edited by Mark G. Thiel.

THIEL: When did you first learn about Kateri Tekakwitha?

HAIRY CHIN: ...There were times when I heard about the Lily of the Mohawks [but] ... I never did investigate until they had a ... Tekakwitha Conference.... It [was] mostly priests and I was the first Indian layman to join, and this was at Blue Cloud [Benedictine Abbey, Marvin, South Dakota] [believed 1975 or 1976].... I came along—I used to come with a priest [to] every meeting—and then ... [I] began to read ... stories about her life, and ... that's how I came to know [the] Lily of the Mohawks.

She was a Mohawk [and] ... a full-fledged Christian.... She even broke tradition to become a Catholic because their tribal traditions were to get married, and she ... wanted remain a virgin.... She got her Catholic education from the Jesuits and she was persecuted and she ran away from the Mohawks into the Christian community....

Her mother was... an Algonquin and... a Christian ...[who] married this Mohawk chief.... She was captured by the Mohawks and Kateri was ... born part Algonquin and Mohawk. She was rescued from the Mohawks and stayed with the Christian communities ... and [that's] ... where she died.... Everything ... about her [was] ... strictly Catholic.

She was not one of these traditionalists that practice Indian religion.... She was strictly a Catholic, all the way....

I went to her beatification ceremonies in Rome [1980], and later ... I became one of the ... directors of the National Tekakwitha Conference [board of directors]. And it started right here. There's a little convent down here ... that's where they had the first Tekakwitha Conference and there was nothing but priests came up except maybe, maybe a couple Indians were there. But that's the first time Monsignor Lenz came to the conference. But nobody knew who he was, because he never told anybody. He just came as a priest, you know, he was sitting in....

At that time, the priests [were] about ready to give up the program [Tekakwitha Conference] completely and they were talking about that when all of a sudden a priest got up and he got on the podium and he started telling us, "Hey, what's going on here? You got a good thing going. Why are you throwing in the towel?" [It is believed that this priest was Monsignor Paul A. Lenz, then the new director of the Bureau of Catholic Indian Missions who made a surprise appearance at that meeting.] ... So that's when they start[ed to] revive it.... Before the closing, I went home, and I was back working.... Then Brother Martin drove by and stopped and said, "Hey, Francis, ... You're elected to be one of the board of directors, you and Sister Genevieve [Cuny, an Oglala Indian and sister of the Sisters of St. Francis of Penance and Christian Charity] and Father [Gil] Hemauer, [a Capuchin priest]." ... So that's how I come into the national conference....

We were very poor. We only had about maybe few dollars in the kitty. [But] Father Gil got around to it, got some money and little by little we were beginning to get funds.... The biggest conference we had was, in Yankton, South Dakota [1979].... Sixty people showed up—sixty Indian people showed up—and that turned out to be a very good conference, because Indian people were able to talk with the Bishops.... We had some Bishops there, including Bishop [Harold] Dimmerling [of Rapid City, South Dakota].... The Deacon program [of the Rapid City diocese] ... [hadn't started yet], but ... they had ... Deacon [John] Spears [an Ojibwa Indian from Minneapolis].... Father John Hatcher and Father Pat McCorkell were two young priests, Jesuit priests, who came on the scene then. They were hired by Bishop Dimmerling to start the deacon program for Indian people [in that diocese] and that's how come you have the Sioux Spiritual Center (Howe, South Dakota) today....

When I have to tell you the Tekakwitha Conference is now around 3,000 or more people coming every year. When there was only just a very, very few of us used to go. Just like this conference here. There's sort of a revival going on and revitalization and reorganization there. But Father Gil was an expert on reorganization. He knew who to contact or what to do. And whenever we meet, he has the agenda all ready for us to approve. So that's how come the board of directors—to me is what lasts a long time with me because I must have been in there about eight years before they start changing in new board of directors. So I know Monsignor Lenz real well. In fact, we used to go to Washington D.C. to meet with him. He's the one that's responsible for me to go to Rome to attend the beatification ceremonies. Later on, I saw the Pope again. This was at Des Moines [Iowa, Living History Farms, in October 1979]. He came there on a visit. I was selected to receive Holy Communion from him. And then again, a third time, when he met the Indian people at Phoenix, Arizona. I was an honor guard there. The Pope just went by me and I kind of reached out and touched him. So, the Holy Spirit has been moving me right along. Of course I didn't know these things. But it's not what I wanted to do; it just seems to fall in place. So I'll say, "Well, it's the Holy Spirit that's doing that." So I'm a great believer in the Holy Spirit movement. Is there any more?

THIEL: How often do you feel the presence of Kateri Tekakwitha?

HAIRY CHIN: … When we went to [the Tekakwitha Conference in] New York to visit her homeland, I went to a church [Saint Francis Xavier Church in Kahnawake, Québec] where they had her tomb and there [were] … all kinds of panel[s] lights up and people were all kneeling there, praying, and crying.

There was another time, too at Denver, Colorado, where they brought her statue, and people were to come and pray.… I could feel her presence that she was there. She's a great help to us. Only thing wrong with us is we never turn to her too much. I believe we should really honor her in all churches … [including] non-Indian churches. I think the country's in pretty bad shape right now and we need some saints to help us straighten this whole thing out.…

THIEL: When you pray to Kateri, what happens to you inside?

HAIRY CHIN: Well, I tell you, it's kind of hard to explain. Anyway, I know that her and I identify each other as Indians. She's an Indian and I'm an Indian. In this … I feel that I'm closely related to her, a sister. And so I used to pray in Indian, I used to call her sister. I'd ask her for something. I say, "Well, you're among the Saints in heaven. Among the Wakan [Holy] people in heaven. Please look down and help the poor Indian." That was usually my old prayer and it still is....

THIEL: Have you ever experienced favors or miracles due to Kateri's intercession?

HAIRY CHIN: Certainly. The Kateri [Tekakwitha] Conference wouldn't be what it is today, [without] ... all our prayers. It's ... the people who belong to the conference, who honor her.

In recent years they try to make a traditional thing out of it. But I don't think they can do it because it doesn't belong there. The pipe ceremony can be said outside. Mainly, the Table of the Lord is where God is, and let's keep it there, instead of interfering with the celebration of the Eucharist.... I see God as not a Jew or an Indian, but [as the] Son of God, he's God. That's the one I'm praying to. A lot of people say, ... "He's a wasicu, he's a white man." But that's not so. He is God!

Marquette University,
Kateri Tekakwitha Project Oral History Collection.
Printed by permission.

AMBROSE V. MCBRIDE

IN RAPID CITY, SOUTH DAKOTA, JUNE 25, 1994

Born in 1932 in Fort Thompson, he was a 62-year-old bilingual member of the Crow Creek Sioux Tribe and a lifelong active Catholic. He attended Catholic boarding schools and was active in the St. Joseph Society and the South Dakota Catholic Sioux Congress. He served in the U.S. Armed Forces in Korea during the Korean War. Interviewed and edited by Mark G. Thiel.

THIEL: When did you first learn about Kateri Tekakwitha?

McBRIDE: I learn that a long time ago in high school, I mean in grade school: Kateri Tekakwitha. But there was something, I thought she was a saint then, because I think we learned—we prayed to her just like we prayed to the Blessed Virgin Mary and to all the others, Saint Theresa and so, I learned that as a little boy. So, I thought she was a saint already. And so, we always just took it for granted, she was a saint so we always prayed to her.

THIEL: What did you think or feel when she was beatified?

McBRIDE: I think it's going to be the greatest thing for Indian people. That is what I wanted to name my high school, was Kateri Tekakwitha High School, the one that I envisioned to happen some time. And I think it's going to be a great day for Indian people throughout the world, the ones that believe in Jesus....So I think it's going to be great day for them.

THIEL: How often do you feel or think about her presence?

McBRIDE: Just when it's brought up, I will tell you the truth. Just when it's brought up like at a conference or when they would—It's brought up, then I would think of it. That's only natural, because there you have so much in your mind sometimes, and sometimes you don't think about Jesus either unless you go into the church. Then you think about—or you happen to have a Bible around and you start reading then you can start thinking. It really doesn't come up but I mean, when it does come up, where usually it's brought up by somebody else and then, or I bring it up then everybody gets all fired up, I guess you could say.

THIEL: How do you communicate with Kateri?

McBRIDE: By asking her just like I ask Jesus for something to be done, not for myself. I'm at that age where I am sick, like today I'm a diabetic and I've got heart trouble. But I do not ask for them to be cured, … but I pray for my other people, … the ones that have the problems, the drinking and the drugs, the elderly who are getting abused in the reservation. So, I'm always very active in that to bring it up all the time, to [the] upper authorities.

THIEL: When you pray to Kateri, what happens to you inside?

McBRIDE: Same thing that, I think that happened last night when we had the healing ceremony. I was thinking about her then…. I went through the process of healing [but] I didn't talk about my health but I said, "I hope Blessed Kateri Tekakwitha … can be canonized, to be a saint, you know." So, I was thinking about it….

THIEL: Have you ever experienced favors or miracles from Kateri?

McBRIDE: No, I tell you the truth, no, because I believe I didn't really ask for her help. I suppose because I wouldn't want nothing for myself but I have never asked her for my people, you know, anything. Maybe I will in the future….

THIEL: What does Kateri mean to your tribe?

McBRIDE: To really be honest with you, we have … over 400 tribes and I suppose to the Mohawks of the Eastern tribes, it would mean a lot to them. But as growing up I prayed to her…. I mean we used to in prayer, I think, ask her as a little boy, then it kind of died out till it come up again for her canonization. And always me, I been a congressman, I guess, the Catholic Sioux Congress. So, when this other organization come up, I was looking for it to bump heads with Congress, our Indian Catholic Sioux Congress…. So, and I suppose I had a decision to make which one do you want to keep, I'd have to say the Catholic Sioux Congress, because that's the organization that I've been with since I was a little boy. But she would probably have to come second. But I still think she should be canonized. I think maybe, there'll be awakening of Indian people then. It'll be something great for us, you know.

But right now we have so many frustrations as Indian people. They seem to put obstacles to, especially white-oriented … bureaucracy I guess it would be, going all the way up to the Pope, then. And we have the bureaucracies like that so much with the Bureau of Indian Affairs, Indian Health Service, that sometimes we need something and they turn us down. So, we're kind of tired of bureaucracies right there. We get frustrated and just do it, try and not have them not do it, I guess.

THIEL: How do your children respond to Kateri?

McBRIDE: My children? I suppose it would be my fault and my wife's fault. I think, I don't think my grandfather really heard too much of Kateri when they was growing up, because they were with the Catholic mission and most of it was by Jesus, you know, and the Bible. So I didn't hear too much of it when I was growing up, that's the reason....

Marquette University,
Kateri Tekakwitha Project Oral History Collection.
Printed by permission.

MARVIN CLIFFORD

IN RAPID CITY, SOUTH DAKOTA, JUNE 26, 1994

Marvin Clifford recalled his encounters with Kateri Tekakwitha while a student between the ages of nine and seventeen at St. Francis Mission School, Rosebud Reservation, St. Francis, South Dakota, ca. 1966-74. Interviewed and edited by Mark G. Thiel.

CLIFFORD: One day in catechism class they handed out these little booklets and here was a story about an Indian girl from the East coast somewhere—the story of Kateri Tekakwitha. This is the first time I ever saw that they actually gave me something on paper that said, "Jesus—God loves you!" I mean this woman, Kateri Tekakwitha, got touched. She was touched. There was a miracle performed on her because I believe she was sick and she got well and then she passed away, but she was touched by God. She prayed and was religious. She got to see God's work and I thought that was something that only happened to these people, not us.

I often sat and wondered, "How does God work?" "How do these miracles come?" And the Bible—I used to always see this light and the Virgin Mary would appear or all these glorious things. Yet they never happened to me or around me. To actually read about this Indian woman made such an impact on me that for the first time I seriously believed that God could touch my life.

They built a statue of Kateri Tekakwitha in St. Francis. We had a big commemorative ceremony and for the first time there was an Indian amongst those statues in church. Those other saints always seemed to be far-off people from a far-off land but I could identify with Kateri Tekakwitha. She was an Indian. I didn't know about the Iroquois or the Mohawk because I never met an Indian from another tribe and we weren't taught about other cultures and stuff about other tribes.

So all I knew was that she was Indian and it was good enough for me because I was assured there was a place in God's heart for Native people.

Marquette University,
Kateri Tekakwitha Project Oral History Collection.
Printed by permission.

DELORES J. SCHUMACHER, DORIS M. GILES, CECILIA MONTGOMERY, MABEL HAWKINS, GERALDINE SHERMAN, & GLORIA FIDDLER

IN RAPID CITY, SOUTH DAKOTA, JUNE 26, 1994

Delores J. Schumacher, Doris M. Giles, Cecilia Montgomery, Mabel Hawkins, Geraldine Sherman, and Gloria Fiddler, all bilingual Dakota or Lakota elders from South Dakota Indian reservations, attended government and/or Catholic boarding schools, married, and raised families: Delores Schumacher, age 67 and born 1927, was from the Cheyenne River Indian Reservation; Doris Giles, age 59 and born 1935, was from the Sisseton Wahpeton Indian Reservation; Cecilia Montgomery, age 84 and born 1910, was Oglala from the Pine Ridge Indian Reservation; Mabel Hawkins, age 84 and born 1910, was from the Standing Rock Indian Reservation; Geraldine Sherman, age 71 and born 1923, was Oglala from the Pine Ridge Indian Reservation; and Gloria Fiddler, age 63 and born 1931, was from the Standing Rock Indian Reservation. Cecilia Montgomery, whose father was a catechist, also actively attended the South Dakota Catholic Sioux Congress with her family as a child. All attended the Tekakwitha Conference in New York State in 1985. Interviewed and edited by Mark G. Thiel.

THIEL: When did you first learn about Kateri Tekakwitha? What was the situation, what was the event when you first learned about her?

HAWKINS [probable identity]: In our church it was always because we have a … big painting … of her....

MONTGOMERY: I learned about Kateri Tekakwitha when I was going to school in Holy Rosary already. And I was never one of the sisters [with] great devotion to her. So we used to have to say prayers. And gee, that was back in the '20s when I went to school. And when I get to thinking about it, it's been so many years since we heard about Kateri Tekakwitha. And … there's so many stories printed about her and of course, our Kateri Circle here sent Mabel and I to New York for the National Kateri Tekakwitha Conference and we got to visit the ground where she was born, the name, the theme of the Tekakwitha Conference, "Walking in the Footsteps of Kateri." That was the theme of the conference that time…. And they flew us over there, and everything was paid for for us. And I think we carried out our purpose by following in her footsteps. In her place we went to her birthplace, we visited her grave site and again we visit the place where they transferred her because the church was burned. And we experienced a lot [by] going to that place….

HAWKINS: Where we went to—that we were—where her body's laying in the tomb. [St. Francis-Xavier Church, Kahnawake, Québec.] Auriesville [site of Shrine of Jesuit Martyrs].

MONTGOMERY: … Anyway, I read the book about her but my memory's getting bad but it's been so many years, so many centuries. Seems to me like the time has come when she could be canonized a saint because there are so many stories about her where … she did perform a miracle. But I don't know what it takes to prove for her to become a saint because they say you have to have proof, you know. And this is what's prolonging it and is it because she's Indian saint? They're holding—she's supposed to be an Indian saint—rather holding her back. That's what I wonder, sometimes.

… We need an Indian saint regardless of what tribe she comes from and I still pray to her. And I believe she has performed many miracles for me. That's my way of thinking and I have told stories and stories about how I've prayed to her, and how she's helped me in many different ways. But that still don't help any. So, I wonder is it going to be another hundred years before she's canonized a saint?

THIEL: What are some of … your experiences where she has helped you?

MONTGOMERY: Maybe, what they're waiting for is for her to appear to one of us like the Blessed Mother does to … some of these children in Spain and different places or hear her voice. One of the biggest and saddest experiences that I had was with my little granddaughter.… Anyway, her mother was working, so her aunt took care of her. And that morning her aunt was giving her a bath and left her alone in the bath tub. I think she was a little over a year old because she left her in the bath tub to play and she went outside to take some clothes down from the line. And all of a sudden, she heard this terrible screaming, just shrilly screaming. So she came running back in and her little boy who was about two years old, he had gone into the bathroom and turned the hot water on full blast and this little girl was in there. And I guess when my granddaughter came running into the bathroom she's seen her standing up, just screaming and crying. And she put her little hands in the water and then pulled them up again. She just grabbed for her and that quick, she could feel her hands just sink into her scalded body. And I guess she just screamed and screamed and collapsed. I guess she screamed for help. And Dee over there lives just across the street from her so she heard her. So she went running over there and when she saw what happened, I guess Dee was the first one to see that terrible scene where she was … all raw. And so, Dee can tell the rest of the story before she had to call the ambulance.

Anyway, that story of it is they rushed her to the regional hospital. Regional hospital couldn't help her so they flew her to Denver that night. And she almost died. She was real bad off because they flew the mother over there with her and she called back and tell us what they were doing to her. She said they got her all wrapped up like a mummy. All you could see is her little eyes. Of course, it didn't affect her from the waist on, up, but she was all clear up to the elbows because the water went that far, clear up to her—above her stomach. And now, she's still suffering a lot from the burns. But that little girl almost died because we kept in close touch with the hospital. There was an open line for us where she could call and we could call. And that, I'll never forget the first night they took her, we all stayed at my house because I was the one with a phone. And they, we called back and forth. She'd call us and tell us what they were doing. And then one of the doctors would talk to us. They won't let the nurses talk to us. We had to directly talk to the doctor that was in charge of her and I think it was the second or third night when we talked to him. He said, "I don't want to scare you people but," he said "I don't think this baby's going to make it through the night because she was that bad off." And oh, we just cried and you know, that's all you can do, you're not over there. And right now we called Father ... and of course, we had mass for her the next morning. And one of the things we did was really pray to Kateri Tekakwitha.

I think, that's how our prayers were heard because of—a day or so later, while he kept calling, telling us how her temperature was up or pulse rate or ... that they didn't expect her [to] pull through that night. The next morning he called us and said that she was a lot better but that she was still in fear of losing her. And all we could do is pray, pray, pray. I don't think I ever said so many rosaries and prayed to Kateri with tears and cries. I tell you, it was something that we experienced the whole family. And that little girl did come out of it, And that's why, we to this day, think Blessed Kateri Tekakwitha was the one that touched her, that brought her healing to her and brought her out of it. Of course, she's still suffering because she's scarred up badly. She is now three years old, a little over three. But her little toes all glued together, you know and so did her little fingers. And wherever she was scalded like in her crotch and like that they had to relieve all that. She was over there, about two years a little over a year. She had to have special care but even now, she still has to have her little fingers separated because they [are] still glued together.... But I think the prayers is what's bringing her out of it slowly. So now in ... July, she goes back for some more surgery because all the tendons in the back of her leg, here in her knees, I guess they're getting stiff on her because they were so scalded. And her little between, her vagina, and so she has to have special care so she's going back for surgery. And we'll have to pray so that she'll come out of it again.

But Blessed Kateri is the patron saint, I think that is bringing her out of it. That's why I have complete devotion to her. And I tell this story all the time. I hope someday it will reach the Pope somehow, only because different priests have heard me. But they say it's got to be a miracle. Isn't that a miracle? When a baby that's dying comes out of it because of prayers. That's my belief. But I don't give up, I don't give up. There's times when I feel kind of angry. There's times when you get angry with God. You feel, "Why is He doing this to us? Why is He doing this to this little girl? Is it some kind of punishment?" You know, those are the thoughts that run through your mind but again if you have great faith, strong faith, you've got to forgive that and humble yourself to the Lord and keep it in prayer, that's my belief.

THIEL: Generally, how often do you feel the presence of Kateri and how often do you communicate with her?

SHERMAN [probable identity]: I communicate with her every day. I say the Kateri prayer after the rosary, I say. And I believe she's present and I ask help for all of the Native American Indians, you know, that she could help them. And we have our meetings twice a month here in this coffee room. And I do believe she is with us.

SCHUMACHER [probable identity]: Yeah, I pray to her everyday. And … most of the time when I am praying to Kateri, I keep my family in mind because I have so many young people, my grandchildren and my great-grandchildren. And I just sometimes feel like they need a young person to stand up for them or whatever. And she was young and she … had a loving heart and she cared for people and I just keep thinking maybe, my younger people she can, she can watch a little closer. And they are all aware of her and they know the story. And I [have] not been a Kateri Club member for that many years. I was only aware of it after I moved back here and start coming to see my sixth—and I think that was in what '82, '84, when Sister "Christine" made her aware to their bishop. And I have a lot of non-Indian friends and family that I have made her aware of. And I truly believe that she is with us.

HAWKINS [probable identity]: I was wondering if we members that we started our group here so that we could keep getting people to join. And it started to build fast and we had quite a few members till some of them just start falling away. Sister "Christine" was the one that started it, Sister Marty, too. She's dead now. But I was thinking that just think I was at her place where she was born and we even brought the soil back from there so that we can keep it in a little basket. And every time I think of her I can't help but think of all those places we went to where she lived, that maybe, we were in the same places. We went to about two different places where they have big meeting hall[s] and they sold a lot of their stuff that they make. Maybe Cecilia brought an instrument that they make, … some little flute that they make by hand. They were all carved but they work real good. And well, I bought a few medals. I still have some that had on chains and … we found it funny. We even saw all the different Jesuit priests that were treated so mean. And their statues are there on the ground, like that where you can see them. And they looked like they weren't—some of them looked like they weren't all there. Their heads were—can't describe them, how they look now.

MONTGOMERY: Isn't that the six Jesuits, that were tortured by the Mohawks and the Iroquois Indians. I remember that place.…

HAWKINS: We even went to see Auriesville, New York and from there we went in buses, like seventeen or twenty bus loads, big, big, long buses. They took us all over the place at the Mohawk Reservation. They were very poor that time when we were there. The way things looked to me.

THIEL: When you pray to Kateri, what happens to you inside?

HAWKINS: I just think what a wonderful saint she must be ... in that the whole world knows her and and there's always miracles that they ask for from her. So, she must be wonderful, a great person, miracle person.

MONTGOMERY: One of the things that I'm experiencing now is my vision. I'm going blind. I'm blind in one eye and the other one is slowly going. So, everything to me is a blur and that's one of the things I do is pray, pray to Blessed Kateri to bring her healing down so I won't be completely blind. And I think, I think that if I didn't pray to her everyday to how to keep my vision, I'll be completely blind.

So that's one of my prayers to her everyday, that she would help keep my vision of what little I have left.... I once played the organ. Ever since I [was] in music at Holy Rosary, I learned the organ. I was a church organist all these years. But my vision got so bad now I cannot play because I cannot read the notes. And that last time I played, I sat there and played and cried because I could hardly see the notes. They kept coming and going and that was the last time I played. I have a piano at home but I'm learning how to play by ear because I cannot read none of the notes. So that's one of the worst things that I'm experiencing now, to lose my eyesight. So I think all you people who have a good eye sight, praise the Lord because that's the most important thing.

THIEL: What does Kateri mean to your Kateri Circle?

HAWKINS [probable identity]: Well, I think in here, most of the tribes that have the Kateri Circles, I think they ... all ... know a lot about her.

FIDDLER [probable identity]: I don't think there's an awful lot of the tribes that have many circles because it just seems like there's one small group on each reservation, isn't there? Each one is kind of spreading the word, I mean just all the news the past few years.

GILES [probable identity]: I was kind of surprised because there was a lot of people who came from Bullhead, South Dakota, that's my reservation, Rosebud. I ... counted them and there was about fifteen that their knowledge really surprised me, ... as if they had their own circle there.

SCHUMACHER [probable identity]: Most of them distant, too.

GILES [probable identity]: And then at Fort Yates and Oglala, they had one ... and then ... we've had to go down to Pine Ridge, think we went to Kyle, ... to start teaching them how we got started so there they started their own....

THIEL: Isn't your circle one of the first circles, if not the original?

MONTGOMERY: Yes. I think the Kateri Circle here in Rapid City at the time Sister "Christine" started it, this was back in ... 1981. But anyway, she started that and of course, a few years later, she passed away. But we've had it going ever since. And to this date, we're known as the most active growing Kateri Circle in South Dakota. We're active, we participate in all the different activities where there's a Kateri conference meeting and we send our members to the National Kateri Conference. And we do a lot of fund-raising so that we can have enough money to send our representatives. This is what we have been doing for years.

HAWKINS: I can name a few where we all went to. Most of us went that time. We all went to Spokane and Minnesota and North Dakota and Rose, is it, Montana? And then Cel and I went to ... Syracuse, New York. There was several that I didn't get to go. Doctors' orders I couldn't travel....

Marquette University,
Kateri Tekakwitha Project Oral History Collection.
Printed by permission.

DEACON VICTOR BULL BEAR

IN KYLE, SOUTH DAKOTA, ON THE PINE RIDGE
INDIAN RESERVATION, JUNE 29, 1994

Born in 1939 in Kyle, South Dakota, on the Pine Ridge Reservation, Victor Bull Bear was a bilingual member of the Oglala Sioux Tribe, a lifelong reservation resident, and a lifelong active Catholic and Lakota religious traditionalist. He attended local government day schools, worked as a farm laborer, and was married and raised seven children. In 1980 he attended the beatification of Kateri Tekakwitha in Rome at St. Peter's Basilica, and his first Tekakwitha Conference. Later he was ordained a permanent deacon. Interviewed and edited by Mark G. Thiel.

THIEL: When did you first learn about Kateri Tekakwitha?

BULL BEAR: One of the missionar[ies] ask[ed] me to attend one of the [Tekakwitha] Conference[s] in 1972, and that's when I heard about the gathering was for this lady name of Kateri Tekakwitha. I never really [had an] understand[ing] until 1980 [as to] who she is and what she was about, and what the purpose of the gathering was. So the year of 1980 that we gathered for her purpose, for her occasion, that she was a saint. That's what ... [we] Lakota people received. I myself ... read ... stories about Kateri. The third thing is ... my difference between Kateri and our Lakota people.... She is [from] a different tribe and for us [Lakota] Indian people ... [we] know [that people from a] different tribe [are called by] the word ... "toka...." Toka is a translation of "enemy." But that's the regional translation ... [for] the word "different tribe." ... I think everyone's close to Kateri .... In general, when I learn about her, I hear people pray. I didn't know that I was helped through Kateri or she was helped through my tribe or the other tribes as well, to be recognized that she was a power. She has a power to help others. Today as I'm sitting here I still have a difference between recognize her as a real. What I've heard of her story and what I've learned from the people [is] that she was a young lady ... [and] she died a young lady.... My observation for Kateri is that she ... died supposedly [to] ... live with God, and hopefully that she helps people who ask of her.

THIEL: Have you ever experienced any favors or miracles from her?

BULL BEAR: No; never once and I never look for it to. Know why? Because we had our own miracles. We had our own favors among our own tribe. We got the most gifts then she ever probably had. To mainly … say part of my belief is that my Tunkaśila [Grandfather Spirit], … that would put him ahead of her in my [tribe], as a Sioux people, as a Lakota person. And we honor and praise to our Tunkaśila. So I believe that my Tunkaśila, our Tunkaśila is already a saint before she was recognized. Maybe her relatives in her society is whatever her tribe was can recognize our Tunkaśila too. To be recognized, I don't really expect that our Tunkaśila had never struggled like she struggled today. Our Tunkaśila is very common, well-received, without any hesitation. And that's why our ancestors had a faith, the true faith, believe in of what our spirit can lead us to, through our sacrament, signs as baptize, first communion, confession, and confirmation. That's all tied to Tunkaśila. The only thing that I like to inform, and to put my faith and trust, is that Tunkaśila is not a form of God. Tunkasila is a saint that lives with God and works with God. So, I so far support and believe what I heard from Kateri through the people in this country. I travel for her conference and gatherings because of my belief. My belief, the reason I support her, is because my Tunkaśila—our Tunkaśila—is already up amongst the saint world. He … became saint, and our values and rituals has upheld by our Tunkaśila the most. That's why we offer to Tunkaśila first, through him to the creator God.

THIEL: What does Jesus Christ mean to you?

BULL BEAR: If I answer that I'm gonna move back a little more to our ancient ancestors. When God, Creator God, create[d] the world, he create[d] the people. It happens he create[d] the Native Americans and that's why our ancestors have believe[d] in Tunkaśila because maybe Tunkaśila lived to be a hundred years old. And he died and received his spirit to be with God. To make the story short, there's lot of the honest spirituality, the truth has been lived in that society—our ancestors. Because they only knew the rules and regulations about the Creator God was the land of the law, the Ten Commandments. The only lie that they live was according to that commitment. Everything they do was according to that: deliver, abolish, abused. And … it takes me a long time, over twenty years, to recognize this is the traditional values. Our ancestors, they had medicine men, we called them holy men. They were received and honored by Grandfather because he was close with God.

And any card or gift that was given to them went through Tuŋkášila. And at that time the medicine men were called "yuwipi." They were tied to their ceremonies. So everything was justified, everything was truth. And then Jesus was to be born. And that's the creator's decision, that there would be a change of spirituality. So that the people will understand their values in equal way.

So when he sent his son Jesus on this earth, there was a pipe existing by a woman animal. Call her the White Buffalo Calf Woman, presented the pipe to the Plains Indians same time that Jesus Christ was born. Jesus Christ was born and I believe and I practice his rituals. Mainly his rituals were everything that was good. Everything that he did in his life as a young infant, child, teenager, as a grown-up, everything that he performed were the way of life. So that's kind of reset the value systems of our spirituality. We change from the yuwipi to the lowanpi. The church change to praising the wall, facing the people. The foreign language change to English version so everybody will be associated and shared by all.

Jesus is the man, is my breath, is the air that I breathe, my heartbeat, my system and my body is Jesus Christ. Because he control it when he was born. He gave me a life to live and he gave me a death to end my journey. But my journey will not end because I see him as a way of life. I too hope that someday when this life is over, I'll be in his world. So that's the way I see Jesus Christ.

THIEL: Is Mary … important to you?

BULL BEAR: Well, I believed that Mary supposedly is the one that we call her White Buffalo Calf Woman. So if I fail that gift of her present—the presenter to the Native Americans, especially Lakota people, then she's automatically the way it happened. She was a saint. She was a holy woman.

Marquette University,
Kateri Tekakwitha Project Oral History Collection.
Printed by permission.

REVEREND COLLINS P. JORDAN

IN ST. FRANCIS, SOUTH DAKOTA, ON THE
ROSEBUD INDIAN RESERVATION, JUNE 30, 1994

Father "C.P." was a member of the Oglala Sioux Tribe. He was a bi-
lingual mixed-race Indian of Oglala, Sicangu (Rosebud or Brulé), and
Scotch-Irish ancestry. During most of his life he resided on the adjacent
Pine Ridge and Rosebud reservations and he attended grade school and
high school at St. Francis Mission where he learned English and became
a nationally-recognized basketball player and coach. He never married,
and later in life he was ordained a priest who became an occasional
attendee at national Tekakwitha Conferences. Interviewed and edited
by Mark G. Thiel.

THIEL: When did you first learn about Kateri Tekakwitha?

JORDAN: ... I remember some Kateri plays, small religious plays
about her. And it was another one of those innovations ... an introduction by the dominant society ... by putting this Indian girl upon us.
My thinking on it is that we incorporate her into our culture, religious
culture as such, and it seems like it is an introduction where we are to
accept it and make some associations so that our religious fervor will
be strengthened, if there is such a thing.

... When we were growing up here we had a religious education and
we heard about Mary, we heard about different saints. And the fact that
she is Indian makes us proud of her, at the same time we don't know too
much about her.... She's a different tribe, and perhaps if ... we had some
prayers in Lakota about Tekakwitha, it might make some significance.
But even the language is being lost so we're just floating along.... Now
they're bringing in Juan Diego who is also Indian. And both of them
got as far as being beatified now.... I don't know too much about Juan
Diego, but I think that I identify with him a little bit, because he's a
man. And at the same time a very poor man, like the Indians.... Yet he
gives me hope because he's an Indian, poor, and he belongs in a lower
echelon of society. And I identify with him because it's my way of living.
I don't think anybody's any better than I am, because I've got a good

education and everything. But at the same time, I must remember that I, too, am Indian and Tekakwitha is also Indian. So then I identify with them in that regard.

THIEL: What did you think when she was beatified?

JORDAN: ... As far as beatification goes, what do the Indians know about beatification? There [are] no degrees of sanctity as what the church projects to the Indian culture. We always say that the Indian, when an Indian person has some kind of—might say virtue—we look upon virtue as something that's holy. "Wakán," we say. "Wakán," meaning "holy," and then, not too many prayers are not said in Lakota. So how [do] you identify? I was in here looking for that Indian prayer book ... the one the Jesuit put out, Father [Eugene] Buechel. So, our effort of introducing or maintaining this Tekakwitha in our religious ... pattern of thinking is not very strong. We know of people who are very virtuous in the Indian culture, and they're men who are wakán. That's the closest we can say it.... Wakán is what signifies a power, because once he becomes wakán, you have a power, you have a religious power.... At the same time, the Indian language tell[s] me that wakán also means a magic thing, something that works magic. And when you work something religious or spiritual-like, it's wakán. So it's pretty hard to identify.

We say some of the prayers. The prayers and petitions are very, very strong to me—"Ónśimala ye!" "Ómakiya ye!" "Have pity on me!" and "Help me!" have a very, very strong drawing significance. The very word seems to say that—"Have pity on me!" "Ónśimala ye!" and "Ómakiya ye!" "Help me!" And because of them, we are all educated here and right with us we ask for ... the ... Hail Mary or the Our Father. I think in order to make the Indian growing population conscious of Indian-ism, is to say the Our Father. That's the only one that they say now and then. [The] Hail Mary, [I] never hardly hear it. So how do you identify?

When we come to the religious part of our life, everything hinges on the religion, religious training that we got here at St. Francis.... I went here for twelve years and I know every inch of this place. And then it's still the religious, it's the prayers that we say. Some of it I used to be able to memorize it. But we can't do it in Lakota.... We have a mass in Lakota now, which I say, and it is good.... Some of the words in there are expressive, but at the same time, I don't have any hope in the Indian people. Just how many of us understand Indian? How many of us speak it? There's very few of us. I'm not a full-blood, and if you saw me out there walking and you go, "Who's that guy?" "That's Jordan."

Right away you conjure up in your mind a half-breed. Right away, he's
got a half-breed name, no Indian name. And yet I who have a half-breed
name can speak much better Sioux and can have a better command of
the Sioux then a lot of the people who have Native Indian names. As
a matter of fact, the people who are growing up now with an Indian
name like Crazy Horse or somebody, or Spotted Tail, Red Cloud, lot
of them can't talk Sioux, Lakota.

So our religious association with the Lakota culture is very, very, you
might say, not very strong, because, in order to have it strong, you have
to know prayers by memory.… How many Indians on the reservation
say the Our Father or Hail Mary in Lakota? None. The only one that
would ask for assistance, "Ónśimala ye", that's the one I like because it's
just a petition. Sometimes when I pray Lakota and I want something
real bad, "Lord have pity on me, "Ónśimala ye", those are the only ones,
and the Our Father, I don't know it by memory. Hail Mary, you rarely
hear it. Apostle's Creed, I've heard. I've heard the mass in Lakota. But
it isn't used enough so that it has the, you might say, strong attachment
… to the … Lakota culture because their religion is, you say, Wakán
Tánka, the Great Holy One, the Almighty One, the Great Spirit. We
translate the Great Spirit, Ónśimala, that's about the only … short prayer
that you can say. And once in a while I think you'll hear that once in a
while. I know I heard once in a Sundance. Wakán Tánka, ónśimala ye,
that's also divided. Wakán Tánka is the Great Spirit. Then "Savior" is
the "Wanikia," the "One who Raises Up," he rose up from the dead.…
"Woniya wakán," woniya, the breath, the breath-giving wakán. That's
the Holy Spirit, Woniya wakán. And there was a time when the Indians
wouldn't accept Jesus. Because when he assumed the full human [form]
… flesh and blood and all that, they thought that was the degradation.
Because once you fall away from the spirit and you become physical,
then you've lost it.… Woniya wakán … has a better acceptance because
that means his breath and everything about him is spiritual, holy, wakán,
and also has the power of producing things, come to your aid.… That's
what the Indian religion is more or less, the power to evoke strength, to
call in strength. It's a theology, in other words the Indians … would look
upon there as asking for help. Strength, which any religion would give,
calls to God for strength, and its here in Lakota culture, for strength
to help you in your daily struggle. In that, the Trinity, the strongest
persons are the First and Third; [the] Second one for a while was not
acceptable because he assumed … a human flesh.

So outside that, there is no other aspect that we can treat here with any significance. Her beatification, I can translate it, beatification, yu wakán, … made her holy. That's the concept that the Indian would get out of it, when you say beatification when you try to translate something. Yu wakán … means she's getting holy. But then when—and the only thing I could consider as being Catholic—is to be holy. And holiness gives power. That's all there is to it. As far as, well what difference, it says in one of these questions about beatification and go to Rome, What does it mean to us? How many of us go out of here and say, "I'm here because, for beatification." We just show a physical feature of it as American Indians. There's Tekakwitha picture of her. My big pride is that I'm glad that the church recognizes somebody.…

If she becomes a saint, what's the difference between beatification and a saint? The Indian language does not distinguish that. You reach a certain stage of wakán, holiness and does that have a degree? It seems like the White culture has, but the Indian culture, when you've reached that, you've reached it.… In White culture … you've got venerable, beatified, sainthood. But do you see the power? It's just a name, it's just a title. So with the Indians … that doesn't mean much. If you reach the wakán-hood, we'll make a word up, you've made it, and by your reaching it, you were a good man, or a good woman, virtuous and all that. That's it. So, … I don't know how the Mohawks measured that when she became, all they saw was in the measurement of White culture. It's all I can say about it. We've reached the, you might say, the classification of holiness, is when she was declared beatified. First she was venerable, beatified. Now, looking for sainthood, and when she becomes a saint, we say, "So what?" We can't see that holiness. And these "resurrectors" are out pleased with history to make her look real good so that it'll be a model for the girls.

THIEL: What other saints are special to you?

JORDAN: And now they're digging up Juan Diego so that he—what did he do? All I identify with him is he was poor.… I identify with him because the Indians are poor, but when he … opened up his serape or tilma or whatever you call it, and all those roses fell. To me I associate with him there because he had power. And where did he get that power? Not something out of his culture, but it was given to him from above. And that's all that can be said about the Indian-ness of Tekakwitha, about anything. It can't be brought up no more.

Well there isn't much we can say about Juan Diego.... I think ...,
again, they pulled him out of history as a ... male model. And he was
just a poor Indian. And if you can be selective enough, he performed
those miracles in front of those bishops and all that. So I gain strength
by acknowledging his power. In other words, as you believe like he did,
and then that guy up there is going to help you, and perform miracles
for you. So no matter what that story, you might say, Indian's strength
was to see this simple Indian perform these miracles in front of these
big shots and all that, bishops and all that. So, that means he had favor
with the Lord, and that is our strength. That is where I get my strength,
when I appeal to the Indian personalities in Catholic history. And we
only have two: Juan Diego and Kateri that I know of. There might be
someone else but then they passed on, so, we have hopes, a woman and
a man. And there isn't much about Juan Diego; it's just that the Blessed
Mother favored him. That's why I haven't read the most.... Favored him,
and picking up those roses in the middle of the winter somewhere,
giving them to the bishop, and it convinced the bishop. And that also
tells you that the Lord is very merciful, generous to the poor. Why?
Because he also was poor when he was on earth; Jesus, that's where we
are, then. So that's that.

Well sometimes ... they both help me when things are rough. Because
why? Because I feel that the Lord is kind to the poor and they are the
poorest.... When you measure it by Caucasian criteria.... First of all,
[she was a] simple Indian girl, very little education. Look at Juan Diego.
[They] didn't say anything about his having an education or anything.
He was just a simple peon.... And he went in front of those high church
people, the Blessed Mother favored him with those miracles. So that
gives us strength, it gives me strength. So, in other words, he has pity
on Indian people, the poor, specifically the poor. Well, only two examples: Juan Diego and Kateri, and all the other nationalities have some
saints. We don't have a saint here. Of course I thought those would
make Tekakwitha a saint when I became a priest, but it didn't happen.

I didn't pray to him until they brought him in. And then they didn't
play him up strong enough. I did. "Hey. Here's a poor Indian." And just
like us, I identify him. We're poor. And then the bishop listened to him
and performed those [miracles]—and the Mother ... then produced
those roses. If you have that kind of faith, you get all kinds of favors.
Because he was poor, and then they believed, and they built cathedrals,
those bishops, on the word of Juan Diego from the Blessed Mother, with

the strength of those powerful miracles that she performed through Juan Diego. That's the way it began.

THIEL: What do you think about the combination of Indian spirituality and the Catholic faith?

JORDAN: I think that when you ask for help, I talk Sioux. When I ask for help, the appeal vocabulary seems to be strong. And that that seems to have more appeal. Ónśimala ye seems to help me. Have pity on me.… And I think if we pray more to them, you can get things, because who thinks of them? You never hear much around here, anywhere. Once in a while I do, but it's rare. I say to myself, and not to the people. So in order to keep them, keep the people active is keep their mind on, hey, these are Indian people. Pray to them. They'll help. I think they're sitting up there in heaven with carloads of gifts. But who asks for them. There's all kind of help they're willing to give, you ask for it. An Indian to an Indian, more strength in Lakota means to help one another. And that you can get by praying to an Indian saint or she's beatified, because beatification also applies if you're in heaven. So that's all I can say. And I think that's enough. But my job is to keep reminding people to keep praying to them. Then we'll get some recognition. Right now there's hardly any recognition except the mothers that go on their day. And when their day comes, I think hers is on July 14 or somewhere— Tekakwitha. What about Juan Diego? Nothing. So, praying to ask for their help, amen.

Marquette University,
Kateri Tekakwitha Project Oral History Collection.
Printed by permission.

DEACON MARLIN LENEAUGH

IN ST. FRANCIS, SOUTH DAKOTA, ON THE
ROSEBUD INDIAN RESERVATION, JULY 1, 1994

Marlin Leneaugh was a 37-year-old member of the Rosebud Sioux Tribe and a lifelong resident of the Rosebud Indian Reservation, but not a Lakota speaker. He was married with three children and a convert to Catholicism who previously was active in first the Episcopalian and then Baptist faiths. He earned a bachelor's degree at the University of South Dakota and served as the Director of Adult Basic Education at Sinte Gleska University. Then he served first as Assistant Director and then Director of St. Francis Mission, St. Francis, South Dakota. Later he was ordained a Permanent Deacon. He attended his first Tekakwitha Conference in 1991 at the University of Oklahoma in Norman. Interviewed and edited by Mark G. Thiel.

LENEAUGH: ... My parish at St. Thomas in Mission ... is divided. We have about half and half, Indians and non-Indians, and that's kind of hard ... to minister in. I started going to Tekakwitha Conferences.... The first one I went to was in Oklahoma.... I really enjoyed it. I got a lot out of it and in spite of the turmoil that was going on ... I wanted to be a part of it. I really wanted to be [an] active part of the Conference.... Back at our local parish, we wanted to start a kind of a men's group because there was nothing for men.... We ... [had] three guys ... [who] got together ... and finally, we just joined the Kateri Circle ..., because there was no other organization.... It was good ... and we got together monthly and we prayed.... It was real nice and the big thing was raising money to go to the Conference.... The first time I experienced her was at the local circle and then at the National Conference. Until then I didn't know anything about her. But I was really amazed that there was such a person ... [who] was going to become a saint one day that was a Native American.... That really struck me as real important because ... we Indian people need to see ... that the church is respecting who ... and what we are.... Now, I pray for her canonization every day and I offer my mass intentions for her canonization, because ... I want it to happen in my lifetime. I think it would be neat to say that we have a Native American saint and that … she'll be the first one. I prayed to her before for intentions that I have and I know that she [intercedes] for us to God. I prayed … once that my little boy … [would] be all right … [when] he was really sick…. It was real weird because the next morning he was okay. It was real strange and I thank God … [because] that was … [what] happened to him.

It strengthened my belief in Kateri that if you pray to somebody … [and] ask them to help you ask God that your intentions [will] be answered. I think that's what … she's there for. It's kind of like what people say about the Native American practice…. They pray to the sun and they pray to different spirits but it's no different than to the Church, because in the church, you're praying to these saints to help you, to help you talk to God and that's what you're doing. In Native American rituals, too … you're asking spirits to intercede for you.

The one thing that I really like about Kateri is … at the [Tekakwitha] Conference … she brings together Indian people, [which] … is something that hasn't happened [before]. Usually it's … Native Americans … fighting … one tribe … toward another tribe…. In the Kateri movement … Indians are coming together. They're coming together in spirituality and I think that's … what needs to happen…. If people … [would] really become aware of their spirituality, a lot of the problems that we have on the reservation[s] would diminish.

I pray to Kateri … to intercede that our alcohol problem will diminish…. A real thing that I like about the Kateri movement is that people are coming together and they're becoming united through her. If anything … she's going to be counted as a saint … because she's bringing Indian people together … she's closing the division.

… I made a retreat on eight day[s], which … was an Ignatian retreat at [the] Sioux Spiritual Center…. During that time, I was praying to Kateri that I would have a good retreat and that was before I was ordained. So I was really praying hard that I would be given the answer if I … should … be ordained or … not…. I came away obviously with the answer … that I [was] needed. But during the retreat, one night, I went to bed and it was like all night, I don't know if you've ever experienced that but you dream all night, it was like a long night … just restless…. You know, you wake up and your sheets are all in a ball in the middle and you're sweating and your pillow's kind of sticky…. Every time I just closed my eyes, I would start dreaming again. But in my dreams, I …

was shown an Indian Jesus. I could see Him in the clouds and he had braids and he had feathers on and there [were] angels around Him. And I saw the church there and He was looking down at the church. And He went into the church, so I was really happy.... There [were] Indian things in this church.... There ... [were] feathers on the altar.... Indian blankets and sage and sweet grass were in there.... It was all one. I felt real comfortable ... because I saw both ... spiritualities were present there, the Catholic and the Native American.... I really felt at ease there. It felt good to me and ... I really wanted that for my people and for my community.... It was really inspirational to me because I ... [came] away from there, knowing that this is going to happen, that we are going to have a Lakota church in our reservation. It's going to be Catholic but yet, it's going to be Lakota. It's going to be rooted in our Lakota spirituality. Our culture is going to be the most important thing there, other than God, so it was really good....

So that was my vision ... and since I've come away from there, I've been to the sweat lodge and ... it means a lot to me to go there. You see people that you only see when you go there and you know they're real holy. They come there just to pray for their people; ... they come there, not being prejudiced or they come there being honest and wanting to talk to God; and accepting of others who come, wherever you're at. There's no judging if you're richer or poorer or different, anything; you're accepted there; and I think that's how our churches should be, accepting no matter if you come once a year or every Sunday, or if you're Indian or non-Indian or whatever. We need to be open to that. We need to be open to one another and accepting of one another.

Marquette University,
Kateri Tekakwitha Project Oral History Collection.
Printed by permission.

KATHLEEN LAWSON, LILY RICHARDS, AND SISTER GLORIA DAVIS, S.B.S.

IN FORT DEFIANCE, ARIZONA, ON THE NAVAJO INDIAN RESERVATION, JUNE 22, 1995

Kathleen Lawson, Lily Richards and Sister Gloria Davis, S.B.S. — three Navajo Catholics—were long-time parishioners at Our Lady of the Blessed Sacrament parish and members of the Navajo choir and the Kateri Circle. Sister Gloria Davis, also of Choctaw ancestry and a religious sister of the Sisters of the Blessed Sacrament, attended her first Tekakwitha Conference about 1980 and became a member of its Board of Directors; Lily Richards, married with several children, attended her first conference in 1984 in Phoenix; and Kathleen Lawton, married with several children, attended her first one in 1991 at the University of Oklahoma in Norman. Interviewed and edited by Mark G. Thiel.

LAWSON: ... I was reborn here after I attended mass here about ten years ago, and I've been active in the church here as ... part of the Navajo choir and also the Tekakwitha group here. I also help up with the music ministry.... I just became interested in Kateri about four, five years ago. My first conference was in Oklahoma ... and that's when I start[ed] to become active to Kateri.... I didn't know what it was all about at first. But as the years went by and we formed our [Kateri] Circle here, I became more interested in Kateri being a Native American.... It made me more interested in finding out who she really was. As a little girl in Fort Wingate ... we had a statue of Kateri there in our church, Saint Eleanor's.... I really didn't know who she was or what she did [and] I wasn't really interested in finding out.... Then I went to school at St. Michael's High School and outside our school ... [was] a statue of Kateri. Still then, I didn't find any interest. I just thought it was a statue until I came back to church here.... When I first went to the conferences, then I was ... introduced to Kateri, and since then, I've been praying to her....

RICHARDS: ... We sing our songs in Navajo and our hymns in Navajo, and the first time that I heard about Kateri Tekakwitha was way back from Ms. Ethel Yancy [possibly a non-Indian lay Catholic employed by the Bureau of Indian Affairs in Fort Defiance].... She ... told us ... this story about her and gave us a book as a gift about the life of Kateri.... I've read it, but it didn't mean too much to me until later on when we were going to the Southwest Conference in Albuquerque.... We met some people there who belonged to ... a circle in Albuquerque, ... the Kateri Tekakwitha circle, and they were telling us about her and got us interested.... Lawrencita Smith ... and I decided then, the next year, that instead of going to the Southwest conference, we would go to the Kateri Tekakwitha Conference that was being held in Phoenix.... So that was the first time ... we attended the conference and we got interested in it. We were inspired and we liked all the different nationalit[ies] or tribes of Indians that came from all over. From Canada, from Alaska, New York and Minnesota and the South, the middle states, the Plains people and South Dakota, [and] just from all over California....

We truly enjoyed visiting and knowing some other tribes of Indians and their culture, and we just decided every year we would attend because it was something ... that helped us in our spiritual way.... We don't know too much about our own people. So especially for myself, I was raised in a modern home, ... my mother and I didn't participate in our tribal traditional ways, and we didn't know anything about our culture.... I grew up not knowing anything ... except the language. We could talk the language, but we couldn't participate in any of the healing ceremonies that ... people used.... But after we got to going to the Tekakwitha Conferences we used to have healing ceremonies on ... Thursday evening.... Different tribes would tell us about how their people heal and how they use different types of herbs and medicines that they used ... before the hospitals came about.... We shared a lot with the other tribes of people.... I am 73 years old and I'm ... still learning about our Indian tribes, Indian ceremonies, and traditional ways and culture.

DAVIS: My interest in the Tekakwitha Conference was really the coming together of all Native Catholics, sharing their faith, our Catholic faith, as well as our different traditions, songs and prayers. We did focus on bringing about having several tribes participate in one liturgy [with] each tribe singing their songs and praying in their own language and sharing.... I felt ... a real coming together of Native American Catholics from all over the United States ... as well as Canada and Alaska.... Our people ... have been enriched by coming together and finding that we had a common bond when it came to the spirit world.... I really felt that maybe this is what Kateri really wanted, us to come together, pray[ing] together, and own[ing] our space in the Church, that we are Native American Catholics. When I was in Chicago, we had a [diverse] church—a German Catholic Church, ... an Irish Catholic Church, and then the Spanish had their own.... Different groups had their own liturgy, and here I felt that it was very unique that we've had say maybe, eleven tribes and one liturgy.... In the Eucharistic Congress we have 11-21 tribes and we use eleven languages. It was not quite that large in the Tekakwitha Conferences, but still we have at least ... nine or ten ... languages and one liturgy.

In this year, I'm looking forward again to be on Kateri's land [New York and Québec], Kateri Tekakwitha. It is beautiful to say it in her language, that we will be renewed walking on her land and be with her people. I remember when we had the Tekakwitha Conference in Albuquerque and [during] one of the liturgies, ... the women of the east and the south heard the drums of the Laguna people, they stood up, and they just start[ed] dancing at communion time, ... dancing with the drum and these tears just coming down! ... I felt, ... so many of our different tribes have lost so much of their own songs.... They've lost their languages, but they have not lost ceremonies, and it's been an affirmation for many of us Native Catholics. I think many of us had the wrong idea ... [that] we had to ... always [follow] ... the European mentality to become ... Catholic.... Now [in] this conference ... we are affirming one another [who] ... we are; I'm a Navajo Catholic. We are Native American Catholics and that we are equally affirmed in the Church even though we—at many times—are misunderstood. So, we ourselves have to affirm ourselves that we are fully Catholic and owners of a space of the Church with the liturgies and in the faith.... Now ... the liturgies—we have, you know, mass can be said in Navajo or my mother's Choctaw.... It means a lot to us.... We own our space in Church.... Another thing ... we really have to become more aware of is the canonization of Kateri. We ... would like to see her canonized, and as a sister of the Blessed Sacrament, we would like to have our own Mother Katharine Drexel canonized also.

LAWSON: ... I was re-born Catholic about ten years ago.... [Until then] I never knew what a Bible was.... I come on Wednesday mornings to our Bible sharing which ... gives me a strong feeling. I do a lot of my sharing there at the Bible sharing and we also have the prayer meeting on Tuesday night.... So in my daily life, ... prayer has become a part [and] ... in the past, ... it never was. I just took life for granted.... After ... I started praying, I [saw] a whole lot of change in my life, even in my attitudes.... At night, when I ... get off work after midnight, sometimes two, three o'clock in the morning and I'm tired, ... I take ... sometimes ten to fifteen minutes to [a] half an hour to say my prayer and just read a passage of the Bible ... whereas before, I ... just went to sleep and got up the next morning, never being thankful for anything. But now, I do take the time just to thank Jesus. Thank God and thank our higher power, you know, just being here on this earth. So ... I find it a lot easier of getting along with just finding peace within ... myself, accepting myself as who I am.

I also was taught at home to say the rosary at home. We did a little—every Wednesday night with our family prayer—when we got together and said the rosary.... My parents encourage[d] us to go to church and they sent us to a Catholic school, and after I graduated from high school, [I was] ... burned out [from] being pushed by the Sisters of the Blessed Sacrament, "Go to church, you get up, go to church," and sometimes we didn't have a choice. So that was my reason why I [left] ... the Church after I graduated.... But it was good to come back and [see] all the [post-Vatican II] changes in the Church.... We were able to bring our culture, ... to be seen in church ... to read the Bible, [the] Gospel, the interpretation of it which I thought was very good, and it was interesting for our elderly people.... I think that's what woke me up, and since then, I've been involved with ... this Navajo choir ... that just brings me good feeling and my prayer life is ... stronger that it was in the past.

[In my home] ... I have a crucifix ... a statue of Joseph and Mary, and also Kateri now. I have holy water ... medallions, the pins, the medals, [and] rosaries.... At first [when I prayed], I didn't see any images ... I just prayed. But ... within the last ... two or maybe a year and a half now, I have to really ... concentrate on what I'm going to be reading about or what I'm going to be praying about.... I pray in my room where I have Kateri's picture ... and I pray for her canonization. I also have a statue of the Blessed Mother in my room and, you know, those two images

[are] a model of a female.... I'm praying that I can carry myself as well
as they did and respect myself as well as they did. I pray in English.

RICHARDS: I've always gone to Catholic school. When I was a
little, I was taken to St. Michael's, and that was when I was about ...
four years old, maybe four and a half.... I lived most of my very early
days there.... My mother being a single parent had to find work, and
she used to work in Gallup as a maid to the people, the Catholic women
in families in Gallup.... So, I had to stay with the sisters and the sisters
practically raised me at St. Michael's.... I stayed there during the summer
a lot of times, and I didn't start school until I was six years old.... I just
more or less took them as my family, the sisters at St. Michael's, Blessed
Sacrament Sisters.... I learned quite a lot from each one of them and
Sister Edwards who used to teach me to say the Rosary. She's the one
that taught me to say the Rosary.... She's the one that taught me to
depend on ... our Blessed Mother as a mother and to pray to her for
guidance.... Even after I went back with my mother, my natural mother,
she used to always pray the Rosary. She was very devoted to the Blessed
Mother and she used to always tell me to pray to her.... But very little
was ever said about Jesus at that time. I didn't know too much about
Jesus. It seemed like it was always about the Blessed Virgin Mother....

After I was about in the third grade, when I was nine years old, I went
back to live with my mother. I left St. Michael's School and went ... to
live ... where she was working at that time [which was] ... at Lefton [near
Houck, Arizona].... There ... wasn't a Catholic church around there
... but there was a Good News Mission ... of another denomination.
It wasn't Catholic ... but I went there because my soul was starved....
I needed to go to church and I wanted to hear more about my religious
life.... So, I went to that church ... and there they taught me about Jesus
and about God and how Jesus died for me.... It seemed like they were
always asking me, "Are you saved by Jesus?" ... I thought gee, I guess I
haven't been saved. I don't know; I was all confused. But they taught
me a lot and I read a lot of the Scripture readings in the Bible.... In fact,
they used to have us memorize verses in the Bible and some of them
stuck. To this day, some of those come back to me and I'm beginning
to realize what they mean.... I truly enjoy that I learned to sing their
hymns, a lot of hymns ... about praising God and ... prayers in songs
to the Lord.... That's where I really learned to like singing, because it
was, it was like praying to God twice. You sing it and you pray it at the
same time, and you praise Him and glorify Him.... I even got baptized

over there. They baptized me because they didn't know if I was truly baptized. And I said, "Yes, I'm a Catholic." But they wanted to baptize me so they [did] … and I was faithful to going to church over there until I came to work here in Fort Defiance in 1951.

… One day Father Gail … came to the house.… He … introduced himself and … said he was from the Catholic Church and … says, "You were baptized Catholic" and I says, "Yes, I was baptized Catholic" and he says, "Once a Catholic always a Catholic." … He went on to talk to me and … invited me to come to church the next Sunday. And so I did, I went to church. I'm telling you, I felt like I had been away from home for so long, and when I came back, I really felt comfortable in church. I sat there, and of course, I had to sort out all my mixed feelings and wondered, … "Why did I ever break away?" But … we didn't have a [Catholic] Church … at Lefton … [and] I really needed to go to church. I wanted to pray to the Lord our God, and for a long time there, I didn't do much praying. I didn't even thank the Lord that I was alive or that he was helping me or anything.… I just didn't know that I should thank the Lord for giving me life.

… Since then, I've learned quite a bit and I got my family to come to church.… I have three children, two sons and a daughter, and [I] had them baptized Catholics.… My mother helped me quite a bit; she told me what I should do and we started in from there.… I learned quite a bit from that and it's a good thing that I did go break away from the … the Catholic Church for a while because I got to learn to read the Bible and the Scripture readings.… Of course, there's a lot of different ways of interpreting the readings. You might read, some—a verse and the next time you read it, you get a different picture. And you just go on and on and it depends, I guess on how you're feeling that day or in what situation you're in or something that causes you to see another way of—that meaning of that Scripture reading. And so, there's no end to what I can learn from the Bible. And since I've been here, the last few years I've gotten very interested in reading the Bible in Navajo. And I pray very hard to the Lord our God to help me to understand, to know how to read the Bible. And I pick it up every evening and I'll take an hour and I say a prayer and I ask Him—I ask the Lord to help me to know what those words are in Navajo. And I finally, I'm still not sure of some of the words that I read but I'm getting better. And I started reading in church, and the Gospel in church. And I even started having a group take turns reading the Bible, the Gospel in Church every Sunday.

And got the little children involved in it. And I had at one time seven readers to take their turns reading and it's been very, very good. And I got some tapes to help me out with those readings and the Navajo Bible that I bought and the tapes to go with it.… So we do … get involved quite a bit because about every second Sunday of the month, we have our, what we call the Navajo Indian mass.… Everything… our responses are all in Navajo. There are still some of them that we haven't sorted out yet but we're getting there.… The music, the … hymns that we sing in church, we have bought books … so we can learn more songs, and we got tapes to help us to sing those songs. So we sing all of our hymns in Navajo and it's been … a lot of fun. I decided that the people should come to my house to practice, so every Monday and Thursday evenings, we get together at my house and we practice our hymns there. It's very inspiring. We've truly enjoyed being together in singing of songs and being able to sing that in church so that the congregation can learn. And we've got books that we pass around and get everybody involved in the singing.

[My prayers have been] … mostly in English. Very recently about oh, I would say about seven years ago that I started in—since I've started reading in Navajo, I've been praying in Navajo also. And I found out that when I went to visit the patients in the hospital and to pray over them, I found out that if I prayed in my own language, the Navajo language, … it felt more comfortable.… The patients there truly enjoy it, because a lot of our patients … don't speak English. And I pray for them. I pray out loud so they can hear what I'm saying. And they thank me whenever, when we get through. They thank me for the prayers that I said for them.

… I still pray a lot in English. The only time that I do pray in Navajo's when I visit … the patients in the hospital. And then whenever there's a group gathering, when there—if there are more Navajos than there are English speaking Navajo, then I usually pray in Navajo. Like … for meals or whenever we get … together, if there's a lot of non-English speaking people then I pray in Navajo, say grace in Navajo.

[In my home] I have … pictures of the Holy Family, the Last Supper and I've got … little statues of the Holy Family. I've got [a] Kateri Tekakwitha statue and I've got Jesus, baby Jesus, and the Nativity. I usually put the Nativity scene out at Christmas time. I have them there blessed and so, I … pray whenever … we put them up at Christmas time. We gather together around the Nativity scene and we pray because we always feel that that's Jesus' birthday and we like to pray to Baby Jesus … at that time. Then we have Jesus of Prague, … the little green statue … holding the world. And … I have the Virgin Mary, … the Lady of Grace where she holds her arm out like that. I've got that…. I got that when I … belonged to the Legion of Mary. I used to … pray the prayers that went with the Legion of Mary whenever I belonged to that. And I light the candle and … pray to her. And then I have the rosaries, I've got rosaries that were given to me, all kinds of rosaries, even one that was given to me when I retired from the Bureau of Indian Affairs … and that rosary is one that was blessed by the Holy Father, Pope in … Rome…. So I've got rosaries and candles. I light candles when I pray certain prayers that I really want to spend quite a little time, an hour or so. I usually light the candle and close the bedroom door and say my prayers. I have a little altar in my bedroom where I do my praying.

[In my mind] … when I'm praying to Mary, I have pictures of her and as a mother. And then I have pictures of Saint Joseph and Jesus as a child. And … I think my mind just goes wild when … I'm praying. I see … the … Father the Lord God, too. I know they tell us that we don't know what he looks like but boy, in my mind, He sure is there. I can see Him like an older person of—a grandpa image. And I see Him like that and … when I see Him, He's always like a blessing, blessing me, … as I pray to Him.

DAVIS: When we're talking about prayer and devotion I guess, I didn't know about Kateri until I started reading about her and then, maybe the Mohawk people. I began to appreciate, appreciate her, her life. And I feel like as I do parish ministry today, I pray to her more often especially at bedsides. Many of the people when I visit them in the hospital and they're very sick. I know how a real friend of ours, of the family and we grew up with her. She had cancer. I really, really prayed to Kateri for her healing but it didn't happen. And I was very disappointed. I also prayed for another patient and I thought maybe, I didn't understand what a miracle of healing. And I felt oh, maybe the miracle was he went home to God. I don't know. It's awfully hard to see the young, the two young persons that I really prayed to Kateri for a change to come about. And I placed my own sister in her, her hands, too. Even though she passed away, I felt that she was blessed in a way. And Kateri helped us, I mean, her passage. So during the work that I'm doing, I feel like I call on her more often, to walk with me and help me with the patients to journey with them, knowing that many of our elders, especially those who are in their eighties right now, and there's a man ninety-seven and another woman eighty years old, I know God will be calling them home soon.... In getting to know the ... Mohawk Indians, I really appreciate her. And in praying, you talk about images I guess mostly, I really don't get images. It's like colors I guess. The colors of healing—Indian colors when I'm praying and I just felt that maybe that's, that I'm bringing the aura that I'm in, and images....

LAWSON: I don't have anything like that.... What I like to bring out again is—I have two sons and my youngest boy with the age of eighteen when he went into the Marine Corps which I was against. But in his high school youth, when he's a high school youth he indicate[d] to me that that's what he wanted to do when he graduated from St. Catherine's in Santa Fe that he was going to the Marine Corps. And I thought yes, you know, that's just a dream for him but not realizing that he really wanted to do that. So when he became a Senior in 1989, he graduated. And he enlisted into the Marine Corps. And after he told his recruiter in Santa Fe that he was interested in going to the Marine Corps, a day later a recruiter from Gallup came to see me at my office wanted me to sign papers at that time my son was still under-aged. And I was so angry at this guy, here I am signing the papers for my son to go to the Marine Corps and he's already at my front door ready to take him. So I was angry at the recruiter and ... we talked for a while and I calmed down and signed the papers and then he left. And then May came by, he graduated. And then on October he was ready to go. So I guess he psyched himself all up. And in the meantime, I was to go on surgery and my father was also ill. So the day that he was going to go to San Diego, he didn't pass the security test or there was something about it, clearance, security clearance. So he was all upset you know and that mainly, he couldn't go away. And they told him that he had to wait six weeks. So I thank God there, you know, to not letting him go. But he was so upset.... Just about that time, I think San Diego had an earthquake around the area. So maybe the Lord has something to talk with you like—it might have another earthquake or something. So after I went into this hospital, I said, "Well son, there is a reason behind that," I says. And I says, "I needed you here when I was in the hospital and also your grandpa." So, it wasn't until the following year of 1990 in January that he went. And he was one of the first ones to go to Saudi Arabia and it was this parish here that really helped me, that really strengthened me and that supported me here. And I ... got on my knees at that time and we started praying and started getting more of myself involved into the Bible. And … they also had some sharing here at the church and … I thought I suddenly found my peace there, too, and how I felt about my son being overseas.

But now he's home and I really thank the Lord. I thank everybody that prayed for him, for his safe return. And right now he's in Phoenix working. He's on honorable discharge and he supports me. Like this year, I'm going up to Potsdam and he keeps asking ,"Are you ready to go?" And I says, "Yes, I'm ready." And I tell him I'm all excited and he was waiting for me when I came back from Oklahoma. He picked me up here at the parish and then we drive. He asked me all about it. And I keep asking him or inviting him for some years, "When you want to take vacation, take it at the time when Kateri is having their conference." And take the time and go, go there. See what it's all about.

Marquette University,
Kateri Tekakwitha Project Oral History Collection.
Printed by permission.

ANNA MARIE SANDOVAL

IN LUKACHUKAI, ARIZONA, ON THE NAVAJO
INDIAN RESERVATION, JUNE 23, 1995

Born in 1939 in Fort Defiance, Arizona, Anna Marie Sandoval was a bilingual member of the Navajo Nation and lifelong reservation resident who grew up knowing both Catholic and Navajo religious traditions. She attended both government and Catholic boarding schools, where in 1952, she first learned about Kateri Tekakwitha from a religious sister who had taken that name. In the late 1970s, another sister invited her to join a Kateri Circle, and during the 1980s, she began to attend the national Tekakwitha Conferences. Interviewed and edited by Mark G. Thiel.

THIEL: When did you first learn about Kateri Tekakwitha?

SANDOVAL: When I was about twelve years old. I learned about her from St. Michael's [School], from the nuns…. And I may have heard about her earlier than that, maybe two years earlier than that. But … when it was … really presented to us was one of the sisters was a librarian and she was Sister Kateri. And then, so she would talk about … Kateri, "Lily of the Mohawks." … There was another nun that was my friend; she was the one that started going to the Tekakwitha [Conference].… She says, "Why don't you become a member?" … So … I paid my dues and I started receiving the literature from the National Tekakwitha [Conference]….

THIEL: What did you think when you heard about her being beatified?

SANDOVAL: Wow! I mean I had already thought she was beatified when I first heard about her in [19]52, and I thought, how come I already heard about her? I thought she was already beatified…. I didn't know; all that time it was just in the process. So all the time that she was in the process, I was already talking to her…. I just thought she was a pure person. I don't know how you would say that but I just thought that, and when the nun used to tell us about "Lily of the Mohawks," I just knew that she was a very prayerful person, and a very strong religious person…. A young girl to do that, wow! An Indian! … The other person that I always thought was just the greatest was Maria Goretti [Italian virgin-martyr].... So, I used to think those two were buddies together up there in heaven (Laughter). I don't know why but ... when I first heard of her, I was just becoming a teenager.... Maria Goretti was a real young girl when she died.... So, I figured, well these are just around my age, and to have two people around my age up there in heaven, ... it's just somebody you could talk to.... I say talk because at that time it wasn't prayer. It wasn't petition prayer. It was just talk.... How did the kids say? Your make-believe friend, ... my friends that I just talk[ed] to.... It was just somebody that I maybe told my secrets.... Later then, that's when I started praying different....

THIEL: Well, how do you pray to her now?

SANDOVAL: I think it's become different, very different about ... two years ago or a year ago.... My grandson was in the hospital. That's when ... I really petitioned to her.... He was just barely a month old. He landed in the hospital; he was allergic to his mother's milk. They couldn't find out why he was like that and he had all kinds of IVs on him.... So, when I would hold him and I would ... just press him ... and tell Kateri to make ... my grandson well. He's so little; he hasn't even experienced life. Just make him well! ... I believe she did because soon after, they started taking the IVs from him, one by one.... Then the next day he started getting well.... I don't know if she's the one that did it.... All I know is ... I would talk to you and I would say this is Kateri. She's who did it.... She knows you.... I would just, just sit there and hold him. And that's how my prayers have changed. And I know that ... she was orphaned [when] young and I have children that were orphaned that I ... raised.... I pray to her and I say, you know [what] these children are going through. You were an orphan yourself. Help them to cope.... Please ... look over them, help me like that. And so, that's my prayers.... I say, "You're up there with God." You know me; you know Indians; you know who we are. So that's how I pray now.

THIEL: How do you feel inside when you pray?

SANDOVAL: ... I really talk to her as an Indian, not as Saint Francis or another tribe or another whatever you call it like some Anglo or something. This was an Indian.... You know who we are. You know how we are. You know our clan system. This is how I talk to her.... I really feel ... she understands. She knows what I mean.... She was an Indian and of all her people, she's the one that really grasped ... Christianity like this, and when you grasp something like that, you know that these people are going to criticize you. But even in spite of that, she kept that. She wanted to believe in God. She wanted to believe that God was her maker, that Jesus was the one that died for her. And she kept it, in spite of all these people ... whatever they said to you.... But now when I pray to her I know that I'm talking to a strong person. Even though she was young I'm talking to a very strong person.... So when I think of the strong person that she is, it gives me strength. It ... gives me strength that ... I have somebody that I can look up to in heaven.... I can really talk to this person ... and put my petitions over there at the table (Laughter).

THIEL: Well, how often do you pray to her?

SANDOVAL: As often as I can. I have her picture right there on my wall in front of my bed and my kids tease me because I have Kateri, I have the crucifix, I have our Lady of Guadalupe. I have all kinds of stuff like that on my wall.... When they go by ... my wall, they say, "Boy, by gosh, you can't be [a] witch in this room." You know, because witching ... is probably an Indian thing. All bad things happen to you, so many people wish you bad or something like that. So then, they tease me about that.

THIEL: They say it can't happen there.

SANDOVAL: Yes, it can't happen there, uh-huh. So they say, "You better go in that room like this." [Laughter] Yes.

THIEL: Do you pray to Mary and the other saints, too? Or do you have some other saints that are favorites?

SANDOVAL: Maria Goretti is a favorite of mine; Saint Francis is a favorite of mine; of course Our Lady of Guadalupe is way up here ... too as ... she appeared to [us as an Indian] ... even though I knew Our Lady of Fatima first.... When I learned about Our Lady of Guadalupe, ... I felt like she would understand us Indians.... This is how she appeared to us, this is who she wants us to see her as she's our mother. That she wouldn't have to feel afraid that she is [a] mother person or something like that. She's really, truly our mother.... One of my chief things that I would like to do, I don't know if I should talk about it here but, it is to paint the outside of my house. I have a wall this big and I would like to put a mural of Our Lady of Guadalupe in honor of her. That's what I would like to do. But I don't know if I'll ever do it but I probably am sure going to try. I mean, she's just the greatest. I think in being myself and growing up by myself when the sisters told me about all these holy people or something like that, I was no longer by myself.

I'll always have these people to talk to. I'll always—I just always had. Even though my mother, the one that give me birth was not there. I always had these other there.

THIEL: How often have you participated in the Tekakwitha Conference?

SANDOVAL: Oh, I have been going for ten years now, I guess the conferences.

THIEL: Have you taken any of your children with you there...?

SANDOVAL: Yes, I've taken my oldest daughter, her children, her whole family. My youngest daughters have been going ... almost every year. I think ... when I really started doing this was after my husband died. I was in such a lonely state. And I didn't want to end up drinking or because I guess, when you're lonely that is the first thing people turn to is the bottle or something like that. And I didn't really want to do that. I've always been a Catholic. I've always tried to think of myself as a strong Catholic or a good Catholic. But there's always the temptation that you might fall off and you don't know where you're standing. You don't know if you're standing right at the edge or not.... The conference has probably saved me a lot and made me look forward to something with other people.... It makes me so happy that I can take my children that they can see what I'm experiencing, that ... makes me happy.

THIEL: What do you think that they get out of the [Tekakwitha] Conference?

SANDOVAL: Well, when I first went with them, they were just ... looking around; looking at all these different tribes of Indians, and then when it comes to the liturgy ... wherever we're visiting at wherever the conference may be ... they start doing their Indian prayers and their Indian thing. It's like, there's a deeper appreciation of being an Indian. There's a deeper appreciation of how we say our prayers and how we do our things at home, and lot of it is so similar to one another that it makes you ... feel like we are just one people.... My ... kids started to say, "Hey, I do appreciate being Indian, I do want to mix with all these different people." So they ... enjoy seeing different tribes ... and just being there with the ... people.

THIEL: When you pray, do you pray in English or Navajo?

SANDOVAL: It depends ... in the morning, "[In the] name of the Father, the Son, [and] the Holy Spirit."... Then ... I sing Navajo.... I've been praying in English and all of a sudden I'll be going in Navajo and then I'll come back say English....

THIEL: What do you see as how Navajo religious traditions and Catholic religious traditions … how do you see them as being alike or different? Or what do you think about bringing some Navajo traditions into the church, in using Navajo language?

SANDOVAL: I like to use some Navajo language in the church…. I wish we could get real strong and do the whole mass in Navajo—at least once a month. I have heard it and it's really beautiful because it's in your own language. The Navajo religion and the Catholic religion—a lot of it is similar. But as people, we don't practice enough of each. So that when some of the Navajo is brought into the church, little things we don't really know what we're doing because some of our … people that are my age some them were taught that Indian ways were bad or taboo or whatever. How do they say … sacrilegious? Maybe, or something like that.

We were taught that we—and so believe very strongly that—we picked up the Catholic ways, that that is the only ways…. We never learned enough over here … to know that there's good in both and it can be combined. So sometimes it gets kind of hard. Navajo religion is very complex, the ways of doing their different ceremonies. There's not just one ceremony. There are so many other different ceremonial[s] and sometimes some of these do not really fit in well over here. The only one that really fits well is the blessing way. That's the only one but there's other healing ceremonies, too. So, see if we don't know enough of these, if you'll just say, "Oh! That looks good." And you try to bring it in over here. Then, you're going to offend somebody over here that knows about this religion. So you better be careful what you use. That's how I see it. But it is good that people are beginning to open up and … kind of experiment with it. And I think the Tekakwitha Conference makes us see that, because the other people are bringing in their good, too. What they see good. And so when we go to the Conference we say, "Hey, we do that, too. That's good." And so it really helps us like that too, to accept and to use our good things of the Navajo religion.

Marquette University,
Kateri Tekakwitha Project Oral History Collection.
Printed by permission.

VICTORIA BLAIR

IN LUKACHUKAI, ARIZONA, ON THE NAVAJO
INDIAN RESERVATION, JUNE 23, 1995

Born in 1945, Victoria Blair was a bilingual and full-blooded member of the Navajo Nation and a lifelong active Catholic and Navajo traditionalist who was also familiar with peyote ceremonialism. She attended both government and Catholic boarding schools, as well as Arizona State College (now Northern Arizona University). She was married with four children and operated a rural general trading post. She first learned about Kateri Tekakwitha while in grade school, and since the 1980s, she attended several of the national Tekakwitha Conferences. Interviewed and edited by Mark G. Thiel.

THIEL: When did you first learn about Kateri Tekakwitha?

BLAIR: Probably in seventh grade, 1957. But ... [statues of saints] were just, I guess, like part of the furniture.... I remember hearing Kateri's name from the older girls.... Later I remember looking back at the annuals [school yearbooks], and ... her statue was right there all the time.... The statues were always there, and ... when I got older and had to do book reports or whatever, whichever saint that I picked, that's ... [the one] I got familiar with. But Kateri wasn't one of them till I got way older....

THIEL: When do you think that she's going to be declared a saint?

BLAIR: When I'm gone, when I'm gone! I've been a Catholic for a long time, so I know it takes a lot of time. It took thirty plus years for that part [to reach the beatification]. I know it's going to take a long time.

THIEL: How often do you pray to her?

BLAIR: Every Sunday in Mass and once a week ... when our Kateri Circle gets together and prays, and at times that, that I need specific help, I pray.

THIEL: How do you feel inside when you pray to her?

BLAIR: Real calm, real calm.... I don't know how to say it. When ... you have a life that I've got to get up and I've got to go and I've got to do lots of things not just a few things, a lot of things. And I'm busy quite often. I need this calming down a lot. So it's real helpful.

THIEL: How do you communicate with her?

BLAIR: Just talk. Just talk. On your drive from Fort Defiance today, you came through beautiful country, and that's why I pray a lot, driving down the road to the bank. We go to the bank, if I go to the bank, once a week, twice a week, three times a week. This is the time that I turn off the radio and just start with my morning prayers….

THIEL: When you pray to her, what happens to you inside?

BLAIR: Real peaceful. Depends on how I am at that time. If I feel like I'm going through a hardship, there being—like persecuted, then … I think about her and how she was during her lifetime. So it's a connective type thing….

THIEL: Have you ever experienced favors or miracles from Kateri?

BLAIR: Lots of favors, asking for … help, and when we do go to the conference every year, it takes a lot of money. It takes a lot of work, and it takes a lot of different personalities, and women that don't see their own gifts. If someone's an artist, they don't consider themselves an artist. And this is what's wrong…. Everyone's [got] gifts … the talents and working, working together to get five ladies to agree on something is quite a deal. So Kateri's been a real big influence on our lives, and there's been more than five, but I'm just saying five to get to agree, you know, and to pray with each other, to work together, to acknowledge each others' talents. I don't think we would have that. I don't think we'll have it.

THIEL: How do your children respond to Kateri?

BLAIR: They're aware that there are saints…. [They've been] baptized and go … to mass…. They know that when I pray, I ask through the intercession of Kateri [and] all of the other saint[s] that I need that day to help me. But they're not sure. They know that I pray to someone and they are very aware of Kateri, … the church wanting to let her become a saint, become canonized. But as far as their working on it, they know when they work with me that they're doing this for someone named Kateri….

They've been to the conference, and so I know as they get older and they get more familiar with her works and what we want, you know, then I think they [will have] better understanding…. I want to keep it positive for them and a place for them to go…. All of my children had been with me to the conferences…. I like the involvement that they have as far as with other Native children and travelling to different parts of the United States. It's been real good for them....

Marquette University,
Kateri Tekakwitha Project Oral History Collection.
Printed by permission.

DEACON DANIEL NEZ MARTIN

IN WINDOW ROCK, ARIZONA, ON THE NAVAJO
INDIAN RESERVATION, JUNE 23, 1995

Born in 1945, Daniel Nez Martin was a 50-year-old bilingual member of the Navajo Nation who attended Catholic and public schools in Arizona and California. For most of his life he has lived on the Navajo Indian Reservation. For several years he served as a Franciscan religious brother and later he married. In 1988 he was ordained a permanent deacon, and in that capacity, he has since ministered to Our Lady of Blessed Sacrament Church in Fort Defiance. For several years he taught high school and college level courses in Navajo language. He first learned about Kateri Tekakwitha about the time of her beautification, and since then, he attended some of the national Tekakwitha Conferences. Interviewed and edited by Mark G. Thiel.

THIEL: What sort of religious objects do you have in your home today?

MARTIN: We've got the crucifix there. We have this house blessed for us.… We asked the local priest to come over. We feel very strong about having our homes blessed.… This is our first real home. So it was quite understandable that we would … have someone … really bless this house the way we would like—the words to sink into our hearts, to our minds and hearts about what's holy or sacred about living in this home. We have a sign there at the door that says love stands tallest when it suffers. And we live by that.

We had a picture of the Blessed Mother, which my wife made, and … besides the crucifix, I think we have like Kateri Tekakwitha on top with a lot of the Blessed Mother. Her head was broken and for some reason or another, we felt very strongly about putting her back together again. We really wanted to make her a part of our home, totally.… So these statues mean a lot to us.… The main symbols that we have [are] the crucifix symbolizing that the house has been blessed, and Kateri Tekakwitha, honoring her and welcoming her to our home.

THIEL: When did you first learn about Kateri?

MARTIN: When they started opening up the conference to the lay people. I forget the year but anyway, it was at that time that we were exposed to this young lady and all of us she represented. And at that time I was thinking, "This is great!" ... Now we have one of our own. We have someone who can really help us in our time of need, and yet we can feel very comfortable to know that for once this person is more than understanding, but we can also identify with her.... That's what caught my eye back then, and eventually, my love for her grew the more the Mohawks talked about her and the more the other tribes presented plays or story books.

Even today, this new Disney film Pocahontas is coming out. And I swear there must be a hunger for Kateri. If they really want the real thing, they're on the right track but they didn't go deeper than that. I think they can—we have something in our grasps as Native Americans that we can share with the American people. And this is just the taste, it's like Walt Disney or the Disney Company is playing right into the hands of God, so to speak. It is kind of giving the people now and the Native people or everybody a taste of Kateri Tekakwitha's spirituality, true. This can be called Pocahontas....

THIEL: Well, what did you feel when she was beatified?

MARTIN: I felt very strongly that we were on a big high. I had mixed emotions. On one hand I was thinking, we're on the right road. She's going to be a saint one of these years. On the other hand, it's not only having another miracle presented to Rome in order for her to be canonized, but all those other obstacles ... [which] are nothing compared to what she went through in the 17th century....

Obstacles that are, well you look at the conference today. There's a lot of squabbling, and there's a lot of people wanting to know who Kateri is today, and we have the hierarchy trying to shepherd the people to meet [their] objective ... to bring Kateri to canonization.... Maybe it's kind of like a period of trial ... not for Kateri, but for us as Native Americans. We need to go through that now just like the Aryan people, the Jewish people. What's forty years in the desert? I've only heard about Kateri the last fifteen years.... We're going [through] ... a purification period ... [and] the ... good news ... is that we are going to be having her canonized one of these days. That's the good news.

THIEL: Do you know anyone that went to Rome [in 1980] for the beatification?

MARTIN: Oh, yes. [Sister] Genevieve Cuny, Francis Hairy Chin, [Sister Kateri] Mitchell.... I was asked to go, but ... that particular summer I was right in the middle of running a summer camp for a hundred Navajo kids.... I just couldn't just take off.... I would've liked to have seen Rome, but I was really committed to the kids....

THIEL: It was like kind of a test for you, too.

MARTIN: Yes, it was a test for me, but I knew where I had to go.... Rome will always be there till the end of the world, but maybe I'd get a chance when she's canonized. [But] how did I feel when she was beatified? I felt very warm. I felt very happy that she was beatified. It's like jumping on the bandwagon and it's like, I can't imagine the trials and tribulations that she went through to bring her to where she's at today. In other words, this woman was born in the ... 17th century.... It seems like she went through quite a bit in her lifetime even though it was so short.... Yet the repercussions and the ripple-effect ... caught us and we're just barely getting to know who she really is, spiritual-wise. We've got a long ways to go.... I'm talking about us as Native Americans all over, not just individually. But we're all growing at different rates, and highs and lows, but we're all going towards honoring her.... To me, it just seems like ... there was a lot that went on before I came along. So, I'm just trying to appreciate all of what other people went through and together to be recognized....

THIEL: How often do you feel her presence?

MARTIN: Just as much as I feel God's presence Himself. And every time I used to sit in my office, there's a prayer to Kateri Tekakwitha I had inserted it in a book as a bookmark. It's a prayer to have her canonized. And ... every once in a while I try to think about what she means to me, personal.... It's not only Kateri but God Himself, the Church sometimes. Sometimes I feel like isolating [me] from the Church because ... the secular world has a lot of demands.... So that's the way it goes. It just seems like I'm trying ... not to force her to be here but it's like, I'm sure she's already here. And the times and moments like, when I'm not aware of it that's when she's present. Like, for example, last week ... I was giving a homily and I told the people ... this Pocahontas Disney film has really gotten me all stirred up.... It hasn't even come out yet, and yet, I already know that it's going to be a big hit for a lot of people. But I also know that her presence has been made, not Pocahontas, but Kateri Tekakwitha. Her presence has awakened me again to say that somebody is—just like John the Baptist. He came into the world to let people know that Christ is coming. And Confucius, Aristotle and all these other people, Mohammed, nobody came into the world to tell people that they were coming. In fact, all these other people ... whoever, they all came into the world to live. Christ came into the world to die. Here we have Kateri Tekakwitha and we have Pocahontas kind of giving us a taste. For some reason or another ... God is using the Disney World Company to tell the people, get ready because maybe Kateri Tekakwitha, the real Pocahontas is coming to you, to be one with us. So that's ... one time when I felt Kateri's presence. At other times, like when I go, when I used to go to the [Tekakwitha] Conference, I used to feel her presence there. But being here, there's no difference, it's like I try ... not to forget her because I knew she hasn't forgotten me. And so I think it's mutual here. She's very much aware that we all need God and ... she knows her place as far as being ... in the whole Catholic Church movement. And both my wife and I, we think about her often because we've been in situations where we've been close to death or in danger of death. And for some reason or the other, we always think ... our guardian angel pulled us out of this mess.... But sometimes I think it's Kateri. Yes, sometimes it's her....

THIEL: When you pray to her, what happens to you inside?

MARTIN: I pray for the Native peoples, all Indian peoples. But what happens to me inside is that I have warm feelings of she's like a little sister to the Blessed Mother. It's like we have another person that we can go to pray to, or a person who can intercede for us, Kateri that is. And when I pray to her, it's mainly just trying to ask for whatever she had going for her ... holiness. And pray to her that I would be a better person, or a better deacon or a better teacher, whatever, a better husband. But for the most part, what really happens is that I have the satisfaction. I have an easy-going nature ... except where I'm at right now and what I'm doing. And if she moves to present herself to other people, so be it. What I'm trying to say, I'm trying to say that she needs one more miracle to be canonized. If she ... cured someone, and I'll be happy to know that once she does that, and everybody else will obviously be happy that she'll be canonized. Because me, it's just like having another older sister which I never had. So to me that's when I pray, that's what I pray to, an older sister.

THIEL: Have you ever experienced favors or miracles from Kateri?

MARTIN: Miracles? Have I experienced miracles? Some years ago my wife and I went over to Denver. And we crossed these mountains and down at the base of the mountain was a rushing river. And we stopped by there just to take a few minutes to relax, just to watch the water. We didn't realize that, well, my wife was close to the edge and the plank gave way.... She could've been swept to her death.... I was down the stream and ... she was calling for me when that happened. For some phenomenal miracle, somebody pulled her back to the bank, you know, to a dry spot.... We didn't talk for quite a while. We travelled on and we didn't say anything. Anyway, we began to think ... somebody had pulled you away from danger.... We went to the obvious, her guardian angel, but it could have been Kateri herself. That is one incident where we really feel that she came to our aid.

Some years ago, right before I left the Franciscans, there was a shooting at Lukachukai . There was a priest there that was shot; he is paralyzed today. But that whole incident of somebody shooting a priest, of course, nobody really knew who they were really shooting at. So it could have been me or another priest. But it was like we were being protected or shielded from harm. Then when the Navajo police came up the next day, you know, you walk in that house, you could almost detect the sense of evil being there. Taking life's lessons ... you know just know there was something there that shouldn't be there. So I think that miracle of keeping us from harm was probably her, and we're not even aware about her at that time. So those were the two incidents where I ... felt that she made her mark. It could've been as I said, anybody else but the more I think of it, it really was her....

THIEL: Is there any evidence that makes you think that it was her rather than your guardian angel?

MARTIN: Well, if you look at nature in itself, it was out in the woods. We had the elements, all the four elements that Indian people thrive in, water, air, Mother Earth, sunshine. You're going to say fire but sunshine, all the elements were there that she also identifies with. And I'm sure she spent a lot of time meditating and praying near the river. And she respected the river herself. So it was like, we were in touch with nature. It's a commonality.... We could identify with her. But as far as having been put to the test over Lukachukai when that priest was shot, I went through a ritual of healing, healing of memories with my spiritual director. It was like, we went through each frame. Afterwards we went back in time and tried to reconstruct what happened at each moment in time, and the spiritual director asked me to simply, simply say where Christ was. And in each frame, Christ was there, even when the priest was lying in the pool of blood. He was there. But a lot of times, maybe it's just me. I just try to shield Kateri from anything … bad that happens to us. It's like, well, I try to deny that she [was] there, whereas in fact, maybe she wasn't in there. In other words … what is the resurrection without the crucifixion? So, she probably was there and again fighting the evil one for us and protecting us from harm…. These two places where we could identify with her, we can call it miracles.

THIEL: How do you see children responding to Kateri?

MARTIN: I think children have … greater insight into the things of the spirit. Children have a sense of knowing who really loves them. Indian children … really … know the score. When somebody's drinking or when somebody's cheating on somebody else like their mom and dad, when there's discord or when there's anything that happens in the house, the kids know about it. So I don't have any doubt that the kids pretty well … know Kateri and her life, especially those that have been to the [Tekekwitha] Conference and ask questions about her. I think those people have never really forgotten her. And so I see the same thing happening over again with younger kids. For example, my niece, we took our niece when she was really small. We took her to the Conference and she fell in love with Kateri Tekakwitha. I look at her life today and I'm sure that she's in good hands. She's struggled and she went through a lot of obstacles herself. But I'm sure that Kateri is continually with her. So I would say … to the kids, "You all know more about Kateri than we do." And I said that insofar as sensing her presence, and sensing her love, sensing her greatness and sensing her charismatic movement in 1995.

THIEL: You said that you've gone to the Tekekwitha Conference now for several years since the 1970s. Could you tell us more about your involvement in the Conference over the years, I mean, what have you contributed to it?

MARTIN: Back in 1971, we had this Association of Native Religious and Priests, and they were involved with the Conference insofar as helping the conference or our part … as Native religious and priests. Coming up either with speakers or actually helping with registration and helping personnel coordinate the whole conference. And our involvement every year was, it was separate…. They have their meeting right before the conference [but] they go hand in hand [with it]. Some of the issues are pretty much relevant and pertinent. Other times—of course, it's about liturgy, native-ness, what would you do in the Catholic Church….

THIEL: Can you give some examples?

MARTIN: Yes. Right now we're trying to ask the question, "Where are the vocations from the native communities?" As far as liturgy goes, there are a lot of aspects of worship from so many different tribes. How do you address the issue of each tribe wanting to do something? And yet, they accepted fully into the liturgy. For example, South Dakota, we have the pipe ceremony. What response has the church given to the Oglala Sioux or all the Sioux in terms of accepting the pipe ceremony into the liturgy? To us, as Navajo people, we have a totally different issue. We don't have the pipe but we have corn pollen and we have the medicine man, and we're trying to put all these together to be as one people. We're in transition, and I'm sure the hierarchy, the bishops and the priests, are still going through a lot of disturbance as far as the liturgy is concerned.... And that's what it really comes down to, really the whole issue of the liturgical ... functions within the Kateri Tekakwitha Conference. Why is it that the very thing we want to do is worship God in our own way is also the very thing that separates a lot of people? Again, we can't have the resurrection without the crucifixion. There's a lot that people have contributed to the Conference by their talks, by their traditions and the Church has been willing to listen at times. But then again, they have strict rules to go by when they're listening, and it becomes difficult for them, too. So it's not a pretty sight. It hasn't been for the last fifteen years.

Native people are crying out for expressions to worship, and the bishops are trying to come up with their own guidelines, which is very hard to do in this day and age. And that's where we need Kateri, and that's where we really need her to help us out.... I see the whole area of liturgy as the center of ... confusion and ... enjoyment. Because we—you look at the liturgy, you look at the mass—that's the essence of worship in the Catholic Church. But you look at the Native peoples, they want part of that, either in their own language or else on their own way of dancing. So in the Catholic Church, you see things that you don't normally see in other cultures. So they have to kind of get together on that. It's very hard. I just say that we're just going through a transition until we come up with an acceptable Gospel approach by using the Gospels in order to get to liturgy. And then they'll all be pretty much the criterion for worship, I think.

THIEL: Take corn pollen, for example. Are there other certain uses or practices in the context of the mass that are generally acceptable?

MARTIN: Yes, the readings in the Navajo language, the traditional dress, ... I think just the whole idea of looking at God as a Navajo, as a Native American. I mean, we look at the Blessed Mother, and you know, she's appearing all over the world. And when she appears all over the world, she appears in their native costume. And the way she dresses and the way she speaks and the way she carries herself. So it's like God's ambassador doing that, showing us as them can do that just as well. And I really think that Kateri Tekakwitha can do just as much through us. But ... we still have people who don't know anything about Kateri Tekakwitha today.... So, it's to get people to know more about her first. And that takes quite a few years, yes. But for the people who are trying to do something within the liturgy, like the mass by way of bringing the gifts, that they feel that are very much Indian. By processing or dancing to languages.... All these have been pretty much coordinated and pretty much accepted within the local of each tribe or reservation or preserve. So that's where it comes down to. We talked years ago about regional conferences. We had none.... Other parts of the country are having theirs. That seems to be pretty much acceptable because they are addressed to those issues that are on the regional level.

THIEL: You mentioned about Blessed Mother taking different forms in different cultures. It's like as Our Lady of Guadalupe, is she important to you?

MARTIN: Well, they're all important. I think before Kateri was known we latched onto Our Lady of Guadalupe because she appeared to Juan Diego who was of Indian descent. And so we could identify with both, Juan Diego and the Blessed Mother. And you look at Our Lady of Guadalupe—she epitomizes the very fact that she's carrying a lot of symbolisms like the moon, the stars, [and] the snake. There's a lot of symbolism, colors, and the way ... she has presented herself as a mother. So obviously, Kateri is not married or is not Our Blessed Mother. Yet, it's like, Kateri is getting stronger, and yet Our Blessed Mother is getting stronger, too. So it's not like what Saint John the Baptist said, "I must decrease and He must increase," speaking of God himself. In this case, they're both increasing, one is the Blessed Mother, and one is a young maiden about to be canonized. Yet, they are both religious models for today, and for our Native Indian people. So the more, the better, if we can get more saints our Indian people can identify with. You see, there's restlessness in the United States among Native Americans.... On [the Navajo] reservation we have teepees, we have powwows. And I always look at them as a form of expression of wishing, wishing for what? Wishing for the real thing! That's the way I look at Pocahontas, wishing for the real Kateri Tekakwitha to come up. So that's the way I look at a lot of our wanna-be Native Americans and their expressions. They want something deeper and I think sometimes myself, "Gee, if only they knew what we have, it's right in their grasp to achieve. Let's say Kateri's spirituality, Kateri's outlook on life together. It's very much just like Saint Francis of Assisi where the sun and the moon—she [Kateri] had all that. And it's very much like—Kateri Tekakwitha for 1996 if you will. So she is going to make her mark. But the Blessed Mother will always increase so far as her stature to reach out to hers. So I think they're both going to be increasing. We just have to be willing to respond. That's the way I look at it. She's very much here and we have to ... not try ... to put her in a little cubby hole, in a little cubicle.

THIEL: What is the role of the Tekakwitha Conference?

MARTIN: The role of the conference is really to focus on Kateri Tekakwitha and having her canonized. But it's also to meet the needs of the Native Americans in their journey to get them to heaven. At least, that's how I see it. And Kateri can really help us in our lives.... We need a lot more miracles; we need a lot more.... And there's a lot of energy out there that's being blocked for some reason or the other. I can just see it, it's just building up. And when ... the dam breaks or as I talked about this sleeping giant, I think that's what Kateri Tekakwitha is—sleeping giant.

Marquette University,
Kateri Tekakwitha Project Oral History Collection.
Printed by permission.

JOE AND JUANA PECOS

IN JEMEZ PUEBLO, NEW MEXICO, JULY 11, 1995

Mr. and Mrs. Joe and Juana Marie Pecos of Jemez Pueblo discussed their Keresan Pueblo and Catholic prayer traditions and the events pertaining to the 1989 enshrinement of Blessed Kateri Tekakwitha at San Diego Mission, Jemez, New Mexico. During August 7- 11, 1985, Mr. and Mrs. Pecos participated in the 45th Annual Tekakwitha Conference: "Walking in the Footsteps of Blessed Kateri," LeMoyne College, Syracuse, New York, with tours of the birthplace of Blessed Kateri Tekakwitha (National Tekakwitha Shrine, Fonda, New York) and her tomb (St. Francis Xavier Church, Kahnawake Mohawk Reserve, Kahnawake, Québec, Canada). Interviewed and edited by Mark G. Thiel.

THIEL: When you close your eyes when you pray, what sort of religious images do you see?

JUANA PECOS: ... I see this beautiful Indian girl, and you know who that is, that's Kateri! And way back there, it's a light.... [T]he light is the Father Spirit ... a bright light. That's what I see when I ... close my eyes and pray.

And Kateri is the one that's praying for me. She's the one that's laying her hands on me. And I am praying for the well-being of my family, my children, my grand-children, my people in the pueblo, all my friends and everybody ... [who] asked me to pray for them, especially the National Kateri Tekakwitha group ... [and] our new chief, King. Sometimes I mention all [of] their names ... so ... this Kateri Tekakwitha Conference will continue on because it's doing a great job for everyone.

I'm very grateful that we have ... Kateri Tekakwitha. And in the pueblos, we have ... formed our own "Kateri Circles." Our ... Circle here is ... named ... "Awaladuwa Kateri Tekakwitha Circle" [and] what I am trying to do now is form a new group because those of us that have been members ... are kind of getting old and we can't keep up with ... our meetings and everything anymore. So, I'm trying to form a new group—[a] younger group ... of boys and girls, ... so that this Kateri

Circle in Jemez will keep going. That's what ... Joe and I are doing right now ... [organizing the] new group, ... [with] young people as officers....

Everybody ... even the non-members are very dedicated to Kateri now that we have her enshrined in the church.... [There] ... are ... a lot of times I just sit there after mass and ... watch the ladies and the different people come up to her statue and just embrace her and they'd be praying.... I love that and I know Kateri loves that, too. And I would just sit back there and I would say, ... "Lay your hands on her," or "Lay your hands on him," or "Pray for their patients, take them to the Lord, your holy spouse." I always tell her, "Take them to your holy spouse, please send them to Him." Because I believe that's what she told us to do.

THIEL: ... [H]ow ... [was] ... her statue ... enshrined here in Jemez?

JUANA PECOS: ... [W]hen Joe and I went to the sacred walk ... at the [Tekakwitha] Conference ... in Syracuse, New York, [1985] ... [w]e saw all the places] where she lived and ... the Mohawk Indian people put on a beautiful program to show ... and tell us about her.... [W]e were all taken to her birthplace [near Fonda, New York] ... [and] then we ... [went] to her tomb [Kahnawake, Québec, Canada]. We prayed there, ... and ... it seems to me like I was really touched and Joe was, too.... [As] we stood there in front of her tomb ... it seemed like you could feel her.... She was there for us, she met us, and I asked her ... "Please Kateri Tekakwitha, show me how to take you back ... [to] Jemez." That's when Joe and I felt the idea to bring the statue.... [W]e got the idea to bring her to our Indian people, and we did. We ordered it, and it was sent to us, and then we set up a day. The group that went with ... Joe and me], ... Bernice Kachupi, ... Francis Toledo, ... Leonard Toledo, ... [and] Mary Dodge and her son, ... we [all] wanted to do ... [this] ... so, ... [at] our next meeting ... we [planned on how] to enshrine ... it here. We ... talked to Father Bob [Robert Mathieu, O.F.M., our pastor], and he arranged a beautiful ... (time] when to do ... [this,] and in the meantime, Joe and I went and told our caciques, our governors....

JOE PECOS: Candido Armijo.

JUANA PECOS: Candido Armijo, he was ... governor that year.... [W]e talked to him and he told his officials ... and everybody was real happy ... and they all looked forward to that [meeting].... We usually have once a month [a] meeting of all the different tribes and ... we ... invited ... [a] big group from the different pueblos and ... they were all real happy to come.... (I]n the meantime, my relatives and everybody [in the pueblo] got busy and cooked. They cooked, ... baked bread, ...

all kinds of goodies, ... cakes and pies, and everything.... [On the day of
the enshrinement] the cacique came here to the door [of our home].
... [He] got his pollen [out of a pouch] and [referring to the statue] ...
said, "Lady, I am so glad you are here. I am so happy that you have come
to Jemez Pueblo. We have always heard so much about you and now
you are really here.... I want you to follow me. I want you...." [T]hen
he went with his corn meal [sprinkling it on the statue this way] and
that way and ... says, "Come with me, I'm going to show you where you
are going to stand, taking care of you[r] Indian people in this pueblo."
So we went.... [W]e had a procession from here to the church.... I saw
all that group behind me.... [T]hey were singing, some were carrying
flowers.... Some were singing Indian and some were singing, ... "This
is the Day the Lord has Made." [W]e were in the procession carrying
our statue and our pictures of her .... And oh, it was just beautiful—the
whole procession to the church.... [A]nd on the way down there, I was
thinking, "Oh dear! I forgot to tell Father Melvin! I've got [to get] hold
of him" because ... he was my favorite [priest]. And mind you, when
I got to the front of the church, I looked up there, there was Father
Melvin, all dressed ready! I said, "Oh Lord, you did it!" There he was!
    ... We all walked into the church and we're placed [seated] and they
were blessed [by] Father Melvin and Father Bob.... [T]hen the churchman
came up and talked to the cacique and the cacique said, "You [put a]
place up there ... for her to stand ... [with a bag of] ... corn meal.... "And
they did.... Father Melvin and Father Bob did the mass. It was beautiful
and my brother Mike ... was the sacristan.... (He's [now] passed away
[but] he had been sacristan till he died.) ... The mass went on ... [with]
the blessing of each statue and each picture.... [W]e stood with Kateri,
the statue and then there's ... [the] one ... made [by] ... my daughter ...
Esther, ... [which] was blessed and ... given a place ... [in] her house.
    ... [A]fter mass, we all made a procession around the pueblo and that
cacique [referring to the statue, said] ... I've been ... told, "Come Mother,
see your children. See the Pueblo." ... Then he walked ahead of us and
everywhere he said, "This is [someone's family] house, bless it and renew
the members." And over here's the cacique's house, "Renew the place." ...
[T]hen we went on...."Here's our Pumpkin Kiva." ... [T]hen we went on
and he just prayed for all the different [people]. ... [Y]ou should [have]
see[n] all the people that heard us coming. They all start[ed] coming to
greet her. It was just beautiful and all the men came out to greet her and
to pray with their corn meal and welcome her.... We went all the way

down to the missions ... where we had our meeting ... our celebration.... It was a big, big celebration and that's how we honor[ed] Blessed Kateri Tekakwitha ... [in 19]89, I think. And ... the San Juans, ... the Cochitis, ... and the Lagunas [people of other Pueblo tribes] were so impressed ... they said, "Let's enshrine her in our pueblos." And they have. We ... had a celebration in Laguna, ... San Juan, ... Cochiti, and all the different places.... So [now] Blessed Kateri is ... a big part in the Southwest, ... [but] she was enshrined ... first ... in Jemez Pueblo....

Marquette University,
Kateri Tekakwitha Project Oral History Collection.
Printed by permission.

MARK J. CHERESPOSEY

IN LAGUNA PUEBLO, NEW MEXICO, JULY 12, 1995

Mark J. Cheresposey (Laguna) of Laguna, New Mexico, recalled his son's life-threatening accident in 1984 and subsequent recovery amid prayers by many for Tekakwitha's intercession. Included were references to the 46th Annual Tekakwitha Conference: "A Journey of Hope," August 1-5, 1984, Phoenix Plaza Civic Center, Phoenix, Arizona. Interviewed and edited by Mark G. Thiel.

THIEL: When did you first hear about Kateri Tekakwitha?

CHERESPOSEY: Oh, ... when I went back East [as a boy]. I ... [had] visit[ed] her homeland because we used to collect [solicit donations], like I said, [for] the missions.... [A]lready then I knew that she was being considered for beatification.... I read a short article on her and I knew that she was a great lady.

... [But I think the most impressive thing that ever happened was when my son got hit by a semi [trailer truck].... [M]y brother—one of my brothers and one of my adopted sisters—were on call that night with the ambulance and they couldn't recognize who it was even though they [knew] him.... [T]hey took him into Albuquerque and gave him the name John Doe.... [W]e weren't too worried [when my son didn't call home] that night because generally they['d] call and say they're gonna stay at ... grandma's house ... [as] we used to live down in Mesita where I work. So in early morning we found out that there was an accident. Somebody was taken into the hospital so we went in. We identified him and in the meantime they['d] given him the name of John Doe ... and when ... the doctors ... operated on him they told us that, "I don't think your son's going to make it. If anything, we'll give him a so-so chance." ... I think being kind to people, ... knowing a lot of people, always having a kind word was repaid to us almost instantly.... [Within the next week we had over 500 people [had] come in and encourage[d] us and tell us they're praying for us ... [and] he was in there four months.... [A]bout a week ... [before] that it happened ... my mother had already made plans to go to Phoenix for the [1984 national] Tekakwitha Conference. And she was worried about it. She came down there and she says, "I don't think I should go. I think I should stay." I said, "No, Mom." I said, "I think you're doing more good down at the Tekakwitha Conference. Ask Kateri to help, help us." There's a lot of people who come by here and said that, further, to encourage them. Ask them to ask Kateri to intercede.

And so she left while my boy was still unconscious. He was unconscious for almost a month and a half. And he was unconscious there then. So, she left and she had arthritis and all kind of medical problems, barely got around. But she said, "I'm going to offer this to Kateri. Let's see what I can—what we can do." And it was during the conference that we were in the hospital—but I stayed with my son for two straight months. I just forgot about my job, just stayed there. And it was during the conference that we found out that he was—he actually responded. He opened his eyes and looking at us and he said, "Hi, Mom. Hi, Dad." It was—you couldn't understand quite what it was but we knew what he was talking about. And then we reminded, we said, "Grandma's down. She's in Phoenix praying for you. And she's praying to Kateri to help you up." He said, "I know, I know." And then when she came up, she—one of her first stops was going down to check. And she brought him a T-shirt, Kateri at the front. And by that time, he would say, put about three or four words together. And he put the T-shirt on. And he said, "Grandma gave me this T-shirt." "Yeah, you know who that is?" "Yeah, she made me well." Just looking at Kateri. "She made me well." And this was, you know, just the doctors even them they said, "He's going to be a vegetable. I don't know. I don't know if he'll ever be able to walk. He's lost about three or four cells out of the eight in his head. I don't know." They were giving us the—we told them to be honest with us. They said, "I don't know what else we can do." And we told them, "Well, we have faith. We have a lot of people, a lot of our friends, a lot of our relatives are praying for us. He'll pull through," I said. "Well, I sure hope your faith does something," he said, "Because I think your son's going to be a vegetable." But ever since after that somehow, he really improved. And we kept the faith.

There was another boy, a Spanish boy that was in there before him with [the] same situation, injuries and everything. And they were so surprised at how our boy started improving so quick. And they said, "You know, it just makes you wonder, it just makes you, maybe see the way the Indians are in their faith." It's so much more sincere when they come and tell you, they visit you. They tell you they're going to pray for you and all this and that. And your boy is just improving so much quicker. And I naturally had problems at work. My boss said, "Well, when are you coming back?" I said, "Well," I said, "I have sick leave and my boy comes first, my family comes first." I said, "You do what you want to but I'm going to stay here." But his other boss, the one that's higher up understood. I said, "You know that's family." He said, "You take all the time you want. It can help." They were very good about it but personalities are different in certain areas. But our arguing, I try to do what I could anyway.

So my boy was—he increased so rapidly. In fact, let's see that was July, August, September, October he went back to school four months later. And the doctors couldn't believe it. They said, "You mean you're going actually to send him back to high school?" We had a conference with the doctors, just about school and everything else. And his memory is not that great, but somehow he was ready, I don't know how he did it. He graduated from high school then in the fall, oh no, in May. But he went through the whole school year and I just can't understand it but he's very much back to normal now. And he has [married], in fact this is his … oldest daughter and his little one [referring to photograph], another little one that—he's in the hospital with right now. But to this day he still remembers Kateri. He remembers who helped him ... [with] power of prayer. And although he gets discouraged a lot of times, he—he's [God?] reminding us, you're not only—you're going to hurt yourself.... All these people ... prayed ... [and] their prayers brought you this far. Everybody else sacrificed and that reach of spirit ... helped us out.

THIEL: How often do you feel the presence of Blessed Kateri?

CHERESPOSEY: I think it's not really that frequent. Like I said we don't—we have, I think we have—yes, we do have a statue but the presence I feel is when we participate in mass, when we have our Indian mass. When I see the older people participating, getting ready for the convention or the area meetings it's just the—I don't know. It's a—looking at them, they seem weak but their spirit is so high. And they don't complain about not being able to walk. Right there they're preparing what they want to do. In fact the songs that are composed of her over in our language, it really—I think every time I hear them, I feel like a lump in my throat. And I want, I hope and I pray that she would be canonized where we could have a satisfaction of the Christian part of our upbringing-ness to see her as a saint. But in our heart as Indians, we know she's a saint. We know because we feel it and we've experienced the gifts. I think especially at Laguna. We've experienced the ministry has increased because of the lack of priests. But also because I think Kateri, she wants us to—I hate to sound like I'm bragging of the Laguna people, but I think she wants us to be an example of what faith can do. Indian, with an Indian in the Christian faith. And it's really our music has been great, music ministry, our Indian music ministry and then our, our RCIA [Rite of Christian Initiation for Adults] instructions. Oh, I saw many ministries down there that its faith has brought the people together. And somehow we don't maybe segregate and say, "Well, this is only our thing."

Somehow, I think a miracle in itself is all the people realizing that we're working for a common goal. And I think it's brought on by, I would say, Kateri. Its strength, you hear at mass or we pray for the people and pray for all the saint[s] or ask her to intercede, intercession. And she's always included along with Mother Katherine Drexel who is also one of our big contributors to our faith. And I think, you know, there would be a great—I guess you might say, a great feeling to see both of those two that have influence. The Indian people hope so much to have them become saints. I think it would just, let's say, maybe being the pinnacle of what we would like to see.

Marquette University,
Kateri Tekakwitha Project Oral History Collection.
Printed by permission.

REVEREND DIEGO MAZON, O.F.M.

IN GALLUP, NEW MEXICO, JULY 17, 1995

*Born in 1929 in Zuni Pueblo, New Mexico, Father Mazon was a
66-year-old mixed-blood Indian of Apache, Zuni, and Mexican heritage.
He grew up in and graduated from high school in Gallup, and then attended a Franciscan seminary in Dayton, Ohio, where he was ordained
a priest in 1960. During the 1970s he served in parish ministry in New
Mexico. In 1980, he attended his first Tekakwitha Conference and then
became a regular attendee in both that movement and the Association of
Native Religious and Clergy. Interviewed and edited by Mark G. Thiel.*

THIEL: ... When you pray to Juan Diego, what happens to you inside?

MAZON: I feel like I'm talking to somebody that's really like my own
brother, like we are equals, very comforting close relationship, intimacy.
Nothing spectacular, nothing special, it's just more of conversation
type of thing. And from what I've read, of the things that happened to
him and the Blessed Mother and his relationship with the bishop and
the way he talked to the bishop, his talk was always very simple, very
open, very honest. And so that's how I kind of deal with him in terms
of asking him for help for whatever the situation might be. Telling ...
Mary ... what I'm telling him, ... whatever it is that we're talking about.
Let her know what it is that we've said together to each other. Then I
always ... remind him that he has a sister with the name of Katarina,
that's the Spanish name for Kateri. And that we would like to have
her canonized and along with him. But that's not a real big priority in
general. You know, we know you are saints, and that you're holy people.
But we'd like the world to know that you're here and what has happened
to all of us because of you. So those are the kinds of thoughts that I
express to him all the time.

THIEL: Then, I would assume you're mostly English-speaking, so
you pray in English?

MAZON: Sometimes, and then I would break off in Spanish, ... more
so now than I did before I'm more into the Spanish culture right now
because of the people around me. But I haven't spoken Spanish since

1972, no '75. And so, it's kind of hard to get back into it. So up until recently, most of my thinking has been done in English. And so now, I'm getting back into, beginning to think again in Spanish and to express myself more in Spanish, maybe. But I figure, Juan Diego is a saint so he knows English and he knows Spanish. But recently, I've been praying to him more in Spanish, expressing myself in that language. Sometimes I joke and [say] I wish I knew your language so that we'd speak to you in your language. But I haven't had the privilege of knowing that.

The same thing with Blessed Kateri and I pray to her pretty often. I tell her I wish I could speak to you in your language but since you're with God, you know what English is like and you could understand that. So I hope you could answer my prayers. I've asked her to help a lot of people that are sick, that have asked me for prayers. So I always direct them to Blessed Kateri and Blessed Juan Diego. So I don't know whether there's been real healing as far as I'm concerned, as far as I know. Just recently this one lady was in the hospital.... [S]he was pretty sick … and she didn't think she was going to make it. So they took her to Albuquerque to the hospital and they found out that it wasn't her heart that was bothering her. They … never did really find out what it was but just last Sunday I saw her in mass. And she looked real good, she looked real healthy. So I told Blessed Kateri, Blessed Juan Diego to help her if it's God's will to put her back on her feet again. So I was really surprised to see her last Sunday night at mass. She thanked us for the prayers. That's good. A lot of times I never hear any word on whether these people get well or not, or what happens to them. And I just leave it all in charge to Blessed Kateri or Blessed Juan Diego.

THIEL: When you pray, do you ever visualize any images?

MAZON: Yes, I do kind of like, I like to picture Blessed Kateri up in the woods, walking around in the woods and just singing. I like to visualize Juan Diego in the desert. And sometimes I joke him, I ask him to give me some roses from the bushes. Well, I think he was mostly in a rocky, almost just like what we have out here, you know, rocky, sandy area. Just walking around and a very joyful person…. When I was in Roswell for the five years that I was there and every morning when I get up, I get my coffee, go outside in a little patio that we had there. And there was this little niche where there was an image of Our Lady of Guadalupe. So I would talk to her and then talk to Juan Diego also. That's before I really became aware of the fact that there was such a thing as Blessed Kateri Tekakwitha. But I very definitely would speak to Our Lady of Guadalupe and to Juan Diego whenever. Very simple prayers, you know, thanking them for the morning and, for the beautiful morning and asking them for help during … the day, to help those who would come to the door, who would call, those sorts of things.

THIEL: When do you think that they will be declared saints?

MAZON: Gee, I don't know. My hope is they would do this either this year or next year. I don't know what the delay is. I think Blessed Kateri has got a better chance than Juan Diego does, at least in this country, more publicity and more activity. I don't know what all is going on in Mexico in terms of Juan Diego. It doesn't seem to be that much of a devotion up here in the United States with Juan Diego. It's … sort of in its initial stages. I think everybody just kind of assumes what you know, the Blessed Mother appeared to him so he's a saint, type of thing. But the official recognition of that by the Church has not happened. And I find among a lot of Native peoples their whole thing is Blessed Kateri is already a saint as far as they're concerned. So we're just waiting for official recognition of the fact. I hope it comes soon, I think it will help a lot of people in the church. I had hoped that maybe it would be happening, it was last year or before. But it just wouldn't materialize.

And like most people, you know, I'm not aware of all the steps and everything else that has to take place. I guess that's part of the process. Maybe, I keep hearing that they're waiting for another big miracle or something to happen in terms of Kateri Tekakwitha. But I really haven't heard a whole lot about Blessed Juan Diego or as to where his process is, in terms of his canonization. But I know we get our hopes up. Probably this year, they're going to do it this year. It never materializes.

THIEL: You've been a pastor now in more than one Native American parish amongst the Navajos and Cochiti?

MAZON: Well, that is Peña Blanca … from that Hispanic community.… We've ministered to three different pueblos. I was there for five years, and then from there I went to Fort Defiance [Arizona]. I was there for four years and then I came over here.

THIEL: How would you characterize their devotions to the saints and particularly Blessed Kateri and Juan Diego?

MAZON: Well, with the Cochiti people, there is a very, very strong devotion to Blessed Kateri. Among the Santo Domingos in San Felipe, they know of her, but there's not that external show at all, not that much. It's mostly with Cochiti Pueblo that I ministered to. With the Navajo people, they're pretty much aware that there is such a one as Blessed

Kateri. But I don't see that external expression so much. It's there, but they have a whole different approach to the spirituality than the Pueblos. But you know, I've noticed among the people of Cochiti, that there is a big, large group ... that really has the devotion to Blessed Kateri.

THIEL: Would you characterize their relationship towards Blessed Kateri as being more of a personal relationship generally?

MAZON: Yes. That's the kind of the way that they deal with all of the saints. It's more of a personal relationship. There's not that external show except for once a year like, well the Cochiti—there is sort of a conflict because the day of the feast for Blessed Kateri is the same as their patron feast of St. Bonaventure. So I see a merging of the two. And their celebrations ... on that day, they have ... preparation for the dancers and everything else. And kind of an inclusion of Blessed Kateri as part of that patronage.... That's about the only external expression of their devotion to Blessed Kateri. But the Navajo people don't have that kind of an external thing with the saints and so on. It's more of a personal tie-in.

THIEL: I'm not quite sure I understand what you mean by personal tie-in.

MAZON: Well, you see the Navajo ... mostly their spirituality is around healing. So they see her more as being the kind of a person that they can appeal to, someone that they can go to for bringing about healing and peace. And ... so that's being the kind of a tie-in that they have with the saint. It's more of a personal approach, individualistic approach.

THIEL: Okay, an individual approach rather than a community approach. Might an individual, say Navajo then have as close a relationship to Blessed Kateri as say, someone at Cochiti, on the individual basis?

MAZON: On the individual basis, yes. But ... we tried to get ... a move together there in Fort Defiance, ... for these people to come together to form some kind of a group around Blessed Kateri. And it's very difficult to do that. Whereas with the Pueblos, yes they come together. And they form a band you know, where they can come together and pray and talk about Blessed Kateri and those things of that nature. Whereas with the Navajos it's very difficult to do that.

THIEL: So clearly, in both cases then their relationship to spirituality, it comes from their respective traditions.

MAZON: So I mean with ... a lot of the other saints, you know, that you have a Society of St. Anthony or something like that. With American people, the English speaking people, ... they don't have any problem coming together as a society, especially devotion for the Sacred Heart, for St. Anthony or those types of things. With some of the Native Americans, it's not the case. Some of them do, ... a lot of the groups ... from the Plains Indians and so forth. They do have the societies for Kateri and so on, ... a lot of the Pueblo people have that but among the Navajos, it's very difficult to get together....

Marquette University,
Kateri Tekakwitha Project Oral History Collection.
Printed by permission.

JOSEPH W. THOMAS

IN SACATON, ARIZONA, ON THE SALT RIVER
INDIAN RESERVATION, JULY 22, 1995

Born in 1933, Joseph W. Thomas was a 62-year-old mixed-blood Indian of Pima and Apache heritage, a lifelong active Catholic and Pima religious traditionalist. He attended St. John's School near Phoenix. His father was a Catholic catechist and his older sister was named Kateri. Previously he resided at Laguna Pueblo, his wife's home reservation. He had four children and eleven grandchildren. Interviewed and edited by Mark G. Thiel.

THIEL: When did you first hear about Kateri Tekakwitha?

THOMAS: When I attended school at St. John's [near Phoenix, Arizona], we sang a song. I can't even remember how it goes, [but] I knew it says Kateri Tekakwitha ... that's all it was. It was just a song, but ... not really connected ... to her or anything until I guess just prior to the 1980 [Tekakwitha Conference] I heard ... they were having conferences and stuff in regards to Kateri Tekakwitha.

I have a sister, the youngest sister in our family [whose] name is Kateri. But [growing up] I never connected her name to anything.... I just knew her name was Kateri. So, when I started hearing about the conference and ... [my mom told me how she] got the name Kateri [for my sister]....When she was born [in 1932 in the Phoenix Indian Health Service Hospital], she got pneumonia and ... the doctors told [my parents] that ... she would probably die. So some nurse [told] my mom ... about Kateri and said why don't you pray to her. Maybe she'll help you.... Mom never knew about Kateri ... [but] she prayed to Kateri and she saw a picture where she had that wigwam.... So she said if you let my daughter live, I'll name her Kateri and then I will not cut her hair ... until she becomes of age as an adult, which would be eighteen years. So she lived, and from that day, my mom never cut her hair except for the bud on the tips of them.... I [had] often wondered when I was young and I [had] seen ... she ... had this long hair. It just grew, it just grew, it just grew, and it just grew and grew, until it gone down, down to her ankles.... My mom would ... always braid it and it got so long for her, the braids got so long where they had to go back up and at that time I never questioned why.... I just thought maybe, because her hair was real, real dark and it looked really good, I thought that was the only reason.... So finally, when she was eighteen, and she just was about to graduate that year, I was in New Mexico then and I came back and I saw her, her hair was cut for graduation and to this day I think it's [the "horse" tail] still at my mom's house.... So that was the promise she made and she kept it, to this day. That's how I learned ... with regards to Kateri.

So ... after hearing about her, [I started to get interested] ... and that's the reason why in the 1985 conference they had here in Phoenix, I noticed there was no song.... [Since] I can't remember how it went or anything and I couldn't find it any place... that caused [me] to go ahead and write a song. So I wrote a song, and I remembered they called her "Lily of the Mohawks," so I just named the song "Lily of the Mohawks...." When I began to write it ... I prayed to her and I ... [asked] her to guide me ... because I'm going to write a song about her. So one day I went to work and ... I was loading big rough trucks in the pit.... I started out, and every time I would think of something I would write it down and ... all day it just kept getting bigger, and just got long[er] and long[er] and ... the words just came....

THIEL: Did it come to you in English or Pima?

THOMAS: In English. So by the time I finished, I got off work and went home I told my wife—I got the words for Kateri's song. So after supper I went, I went and picked up my guitar.... I started to strum and try to get a tune to it and in less than an hour I had the tune. And in writing a song, you can't put the notes to a song because of the words. It's hard. You have to either cut your words or cut your notes, or make something. But it wasn't that way, it just came, and in one day, I had Kateri's song.... I sang it to her and she said, "That's good. That's beautiful." So I told her, "It still must have something to do with her giving me this thing, because I couldn't do it. I've tried to write before and I'm all so troubled with the words.... The tune ... everything just came off. So that's how that came about.... I think that was really what she gave me. I still feel today that she was the one that inspired me to write this song.

THIEL: Can you think of some reason, specifically, why she inspired you?

THOMAS: I think because there was no song at the time … no song … written [for] Kateri except … the one … way back. So … I wanted to write a song for her … as my gift [to the Tekakwitha Conference] … to do something for Kateri.… We did present it to the 1985 conference in Phoenix and it was well-taken. Everybody liked it, and so as of today, most of the [Pima] on the Gila, Salt, and all the people [in the local Native communities] are singing this song.… They've learned it as their [song], and that's the song they sing in regards to Kateri.

The … [second] song that I wrote … five years ago is more of a prayer song, a song asking God to … canonize her.… I call it a prayer song, and it's called "Why Not an Indian, Lord." But that took me a little bit longer.… I worked on that … about a week or so before I could get it together.… [It's a] … song that just tells about her life … from the time she was born till … when she died.… It's asking God to make her … a saint. …that's the song … I thought [about] after all these years from [19]85 to five years ago when the … [Tekakwitha] Conference was in Tucson.… So I thought … maybe this would help, to … try to pray to God to make her a saint.… Tapes [of this song] are out now … [which] I've given to the people … to have them sing fresh at their circle instead of singing …"Lily of the Mohawk."

THIEL: How often do you pray to Kateri?

THOMAS: Well, we have a big picture of her that I got … when I was on the pastoral council. A lady who's an artist … asked me about Kateri and I told her, I was … trying to spread the word for her.… She [asked] … if we had anything of what she looked like.… So I … [showed her a small prayer card with a picture] and she asked me, "Can I paint this? I would like to try to paint it and reproduce this in a regular painting.… She drew a real beautiful picture and I have it at the house and so we pray to her.… Right now, with the [Kateri] circle that we have, we have a … a nine-day novena [that we do], the first of the month.… We used to do it at home with ourselves just to do the novena myself.… Sometimes I get frustrated.… Then I'll ask her to intercede for me to either have God send the Holy Spirit to help me or whatever I need.… I think she's helped me quite a bit.… I haven't really asked for anything where it would say it's a miracle or anything like that, like my mom did. I feel … she's watching over us, and watching over the household, because of the presence that she has with her picture.

THIEL: You've been involved with spreading the message about Kateri. Is there anyone else you know [who received] some favors?

THOMAS: There was a lady [from the Gila River Indian Reservation] at our last meeting at St. John's about three years ago.... She was talking to me, talking to me about the song and ... [she told me] she had been in a car accident [in 1988 or '89].... [She] was pretty well crippled up. Her arms were all [injured and] she couldn't ... move her legs.... The doctors [at the Phoenix Indian Health Service Hospital] ... said ... she would never walk again. In other words, she had the use of one leg, but she couldn't walk. It was paralyzed.... She told me ... she did pray to Kateri, asking her to help her, because she wanted to walk and she said that gradually her feelings started to come into her legs.... Pretty soon she could move her legs. So she went back to the doctor.... [He] was astonished because ... she had movement ... and pretty soon ... she was walking. She was able to get here and there, but her arm was still paralyzed and she couldn't do other things ... and she claims truthfully, that to her, it was a miracle....

THIEL: How do you feel inside when you pray to Kateri?

THOMAS: I feel great. I feel good and it gives me a great sense of ... courage.... I just feel joyful ... and when I sing the song, the Kateri song especially ... my emotions get carried away....

THIEL: How do you visualize the relationship between Kateri, the other saints, our Blessed Mother, and Jesus?

THOMAS: From my teaching in regards to the saints ... certain saints are ... closer to God because of what they did.... Now certain saints are here ... some saints out here, sort of down the line as to what they did, and how much they did. I kind of focus it like that. Because I feel that all saints are not all on the same level.... I kind of picture [Kateri] just like in any job situation, that when you first get a job, you're at this level, and then you work your way [up]. I guess I kind of focus that ... she [is] down here right now, being beatified. I still think that she has much favor with God.... You might say, if you want to, call it "pull." But I think when she becomes a saint she'll be elevated quite up there....

THIEL: What do you see as the relationship between being Catholic and your Pima spirituality?

THOMAS: There's not very much difference. The only difference ... I feel, is that the way it was taught in the pre-Vatican until now. With Vatican II it has come, the church has come out of its ... cocoon, I think I'll say because—I say cocoon because in the past the Church seemed to be, everything was just inside. You weren't allowed to even participate or even mingle with other religions. You were cocooned..., say, you're a

Catholic, this is what you do, it was strict. And once you left, if you did something from outside of that you were … excommunicated. That was the big scare, and I think to me being a Catholic in the past has been the main instrument that the Church used to keep its family together, keep the Catholics together, was scaring people. And then when they said O.K. excommunication if you don't do this.

… Our religion, we have a religion which has to do with nature and has to do with God. We knew about God. We knew what God wanted, our creator of life, which is God to us, and like I said, we had all the things the same as the Church in regards to commandments, which is really what the Church is about. You have the commandments, the other commandments in regards to the Church commandments, the six of those. And we had all those, so there was really nothing different. It was just the idea that the Church told us that our religion was heathen, we were heathens because we didn't believe in what they wanted us to believe in, yet if they would have only looked and asked questions they would have found out that all our religion was the same, except for one item, which Jesus Christ. And so when Jesus Christ was brought into the picture, we were baptized. O.K., so, all they did was made is Christians. But before that we weren't called Christians but we had a religion….

And our spirituality was always there because we lived to the way we felt about our religion, how we felt about one another and how we felt about our Creator, that we were one with our neighbors. In order to do that, we had to be one with ourselves and one with our neighbors, before we can be one with our Creator. And that's our thing. If you don't feel that you're one with yourself, and not one with your neighbor, and the say I'm one with my Creator, then you're a hypocrite because you're not, you cannot be one. If you disregard your neighbor and not love your neighbor and try to say I love God, you can't do it, because it's through God that love comes. But that's the way were we … we all treated each other as equals. Our community lived together happily because of that religion. That's how it worked out….

Marquette University,
Kateri Tekakwitha Project Oral History Collection.
Printed by permission.

MASELINE ALBRING

IN MILWAUKEE, WISCONSIN, JUNE 6, 2012

Maseline Albring is an Ottawa Indian of the Michigan-based Little River Band and a life-long Catholic. She was born in 1932 in Eagle River, Wisconsin, where she was raised by her parents on a nearby farm, and her grandmother, who lived in town. She married in 1949, and raised three daughters and a son. In 1958 she moved to Milwaukee. Later during the 1960s and 1970s, she joined the outreach programs and the Siggenauk Center of the Milwaukee Archdiocese, and its successor in 1988, the Congregation of the Great Spirit. Interviewed and edited by Mark G. Thiel.

THIEL: When did you first learn about Kateri Tekakwitha?

ALBRING: I [first] learned about her around 1977. I think it would be wonderful to have our own Saint Kateri Tekakwitha.

THIEL: How often do you think of her?

ALBRING: Every Sunday at the Congregation [of the Great Spirit], we say the Kateri prayer before Mass. That is when I seek her.

THIEL: When you pray to Kateri, what happens to you inside? Have you ever experienced favors or miracles due to Kateri's intercession?

ALBRING: I feel very good [and] I … had a miracle happen due to her prayer. She saved my grandson's life…. In 2009 my granddaughter Stephanie and her family went on vacation. They went to the store to pick up some stuff where she found baby Jorge not breathing. She screamed out for her husband and she ran to the baby to do CPR. Baby Jorge was rushed by Flight for Life to the hospital in Madison. That's when my granddaughter called … and told me the baby stopped breathing. So I told my daughter, "Let's go!" When I got to [North] 27th Street near the freeway, [the] traffic was bumper to bumper. So I said, "Kateri and the Blessed Mother of God! Please guide me through this traffic to get to our baby!" And before you knew it, the road just opened up like Noah did to the ocean. I also asked, "Virgin Mary! Please don't take our baby away like they took yours." So when I got onto the road, I followed a car that was speeding and [it] took me through the traffic all the way to

Madison. When we got there, baby Jorge was all hooked up with wires. They also found out he had a stroke in his mother's womb.

THIEL: What does Kateri mean to your parish?

ALBRING: She means a lot to us. We say a prayer for her every Sunday [at mass] and [on] Monday at the Kateri Circle. They are learning who she is and what she has become....

THIEL: Tell us about your participation in the Tekakwitha Conference.

ALBRING: I go to the Conference every year to learn [Kateri's] way of living and how she suffered.... When I came to Milwaukee ... I didn't know what it was. But [I] was missing something, so then I joined [the forerunner of the] Congregation of the Great Spirit.... [T]hen we had service there, and our Kateri was something else. I first met [Kateri] probably in about, oh I'd say '88, and they had a traveling picture of her.... From then on, it was just like something you didn't forget. You just kept growing and growing looking for information, and [I] realized what her story was. And she had a very poor, interesting life, too.

THIEL: What do you think about having a Native American Saint?

ALBRING: I think we should've had one a long time ago. And, spiritually, you know you hear all this White Buffalo, she'd rolled over and then when she stood up she was a saint.... It just seemed to keep bothering me and, her spirit meant a lot.... When I got into Congregation of the Great Spirit—there she was. She was here waiting. So I am always looking for that spiritual space.... So we have the reading here in church, every Sunday, and I was really happy when Father asked me to do it.... Then on Monday nights we have our meetings, Kateri Circle, which has really helped ... and ... we go to the meetings once a year.... I've been going there for the last four or five years—to New York, to Washington [State], where they had this little boy [Jake Finkbonner], he was very, very sick.... Nobody could heal him until they... prayed over this little boy and he was healed.... Baby Jorge is now three years old and you couldn't tell there was anything wrong with him. We're not out of the woods though. They found out that he has a hole in his heart and needs breathing treatments. This is why I believe in [prayers to] the Virgin Mary and Kateri Tekakwitha. When I go to the Kateri Conference, [I am] always asking for prayer for baby Jorge. So we're always praying whenever we have here at the [Great Spirit] Congregation church, we always pray to her. Her spirit will help. So this is my home, and when I come back here, it's just like coming back home again, I find the spirituality here.

Marquette University,
Congregation of the Great Spirit Records.
Printed by permission.

LARRY RICHMOND
IN MILWAUKEE, WISCONSIN, JUNE 6, 2012

Born in 1931, Larry Richmond is a Menominee and Chippewa-Cree Indian and a life-long Catholic with an understanding of Menominee language and religious heritage. He was raised in Keshena and Neopit, Wisconsin, on the Menominee Indian Reservation where he attended St. Joseph's and St. Anthony's Catholic schools. He attended high school at the Haskell Institute (now the Haskell All Nations Indian University), Lawrence, Kansas; served in the Korean War; and was later employed as an electrical and telephone lineman. He married and has six children, and moved to Milwaukee while job hunting in 1964. There during the 1960s and 1970s, he joined the outreach programs and the Siggenauk Center of the Milwaukee Archdiocese, and its successor in 1988, the Congregation of the Great Spirit. Interviewed and edited by Mark G. Thiel.

THIEL: Let's talk about Kateri Tekakwitha.

RICHMOND: ... I was about in the ... second or third grade when the nuns [first] told us about Kateri.... Whatever we could learn about her, I was always open to learning about this Native American. Would saint to be, no she is a saint.

But I was always wondering [about] Juan Diego—Saint Juan Diego—why he wasn't a saint when the Virgin appeared to him 400 years ago, or almost 500 years ago? ... Why? That was one of the greatest miracles, involving the Virgin, and this Indian man.... When they had his celebration [in Mexico], the dancers, they could only dance outside. They couldn't come in the church like we do here [at Great Spirit Congregation]. We allow the dancers to come in, and I know on the Menominee Reservation, the dancers can come in [to church and dance at mass].

[I] remember when I was young ... that was [considered] pagan. They used to tell me, "Your grandfather was a pagan." Well so were a lot of my relatives.... I used to wonder about why, why they were different.... I could have joined them, but there was that something that held me back. I used to go to their [Medicine Lodge] ceremonies, [I was] very interested, and I took up dancing and singing at a young age.

What does Jesus mean to me? He is the savior; he is my savior. He's become very personal, personal, making a connection, you know, with the Holy Spirit and with the Creator, and with Jesus. You know—Jesus— it amazed [me] that when I read about Jesus appearing to the young [Lakota] Sioux warrior [Black Elk] who was in the Ghost Dance.... Sister Marie Therese Archambault, she was Black Elk's advocate, [and] she wrote a book on him.... I look for him to be a saint someday because ... in his adulthood he became a Catholic and a catechist....

That's what Jesus means to me, and knowing what Kateri—how she felt about Jesus—when she learned about him.... You learn [during] the years of your life about your faith [and] I'm still working on that—the faith. I kind of pray the old way—try to greet the sun every morning, and pray the Menominee way, put tobacco down and pray, and whoop when the sun comes up. Give a big whoop! That's old traditional way that males used to greet the day. You always hear about Indians, especially in South America, in Mexico, they worship the sun. I don't think so. I think they worship what they know ... lives behind the sun, beyond the sun.... Like I say, we are star children. All the elements in our bodies were found in outer space.... So my traditional stories tell about the heavens, the stars....

Marquette University,
Congregation of the Great Spirit Records.
Printed by permission.

JOHN CLIFFORD

IN MILWAUKEE, WISCONSIN, JUNE 20, 2012

John Clifford, age 73, is a life-long Catholic and member of the Rosebud Sioux Tribe of South Dakota with master's degrees in Latin and World History from Marquette University and The University of Notre Dame, respectively. He taught in Milwaukee Public Schools and administered its American Indian student programs. Since 1979 he has been active in the Siggenauk Ministry and its successor, the Congregation of the Great Spirit. Interviewed and edited by Mark G. Thiel.

THIEL: Let's talk about Kateri Tekakwitha. When did you first learn about her?

CLIFFORD: We first learned about her when I was going to school at St. Francis [Mission, on the Rosebud Indian Reservation].... [W]e had the saints' feast days, but one of the feast days—when you're a kid you don't know the difference between blessed and saint, or whatever, so you just regard it, well that's one of the saints—was Blessed Kateri Tekakwitha. So we've heard about that, or we've been involved with her and prayed to her, throughout my years at St. Francis.

THIEL: How often do you think of her?

CLIFFORD: ... In [1985], we had our ... Siggenauk Indian Ministry, and my wife and my daughter went with [their delegation] to a Tekakwitha Conference in Syracuse, New York, and so that was our first long term engagement.... We didn't go to each one ... and then the following year we couldn't make it, maybe the third year we did, and so forth. So all that time, of course, we were praying for her sainthood, ... [which] was one of the main themes of the conference.... And that she needed miracles....

We had a Tekakwitha Conference here at Marquette ... in 1997.... Our congregation, by that time we had become Congregation of the Great Spirit ... was kind of the coordinator.... They latched into the local area providing the different workshops and so forth.... We were always constantly praying.... I was ... also asked to present a ... youth workshop.... I titled [it], "Making and Breaking Fry Bread at the Last

Supper." ... [But] when the people here reviewed that, they thought [it] might be too, somewhat sacrilegious ... so they shortened ... [it] to "Fry bread Making." ... [Then] ... one of the [local] nuns ... was somewhat incensed that they would shorten it ... to just "Fry Bread Making." So she ... put up a banner ... where we were having the workshop.... When I came in, expecting only youth ... we had ... about thirty or forty participants ... and the place was packed with more than youth, with adults. People were even sitting in the hallway listening ... and I also had ... the workshop that following day ... and again the place was packed.... Well, anyway, it was a very good presentation [and] people participated. In fact, one of the ladies ... grabbed some of the dough, ... used the microwave [in her room] and made a big loaf of fry bread and brought it back so that everybody could have a sample. So anyway, everything was rather spontaneous.... So that was probably the work of Kateri.

... [T]he last one I attended was ... in Albuquerque, ... about two years ago [2010].... People [there] were ... wondering why it was taking so long for her to get her sainthood.... We were told that the Church has implemented ... stringent guidelines, on how they arrive at establishing a miracle. So, one of the two criteria that they had mentioned was that ... [when a presumptive] miracle took place ... there ... [had to be] no way to explain how it could have happened, medically. So it had to go beyond, beyond medical science. And the other ... [criterion] was that the person, saint in question, or the person, candidate in question had to have exclusively been the person being prayed to for the miracle.... [W]hen I eventually got word this past year ... that she was going to be canonized, ... I thought to myself, well, here we have [an] instance where ... the miracle takes place beyond ... the laws of natural science.... Everything supersedes ... and that it would be exclusively prayers to that particular saint.... Over the years ... [I had] read different things, one was that ... [Isaac] Newton chased the angels and saints out of heaven. So I thought, well, Kateri's brought them all back, bringing all the angels and saints back into Heaven.

THIEL: ... [H]ow do you see this affecting Native people, both locally and elsewhere?

CLIFFORD: ... [W]e also had people from Canada and Alaska come to these conferences too, and even North and South America. In fact one year we even had people from Australia.... So its impact is going to be throughout the hemisphere.... It's probably going to lift a lot of Indian spirits, because of what happened, and … finally they can feel that all of the prayers were answered, because I don't know how many years we've had that conference, I understand that they were first started in 1939. So that must be almost seventy-three years before, in fact 1939, that was the year I was born, I can remember from then, seventy-three years. So, anyway, it took that long for the prayers to get answered. I suppose the impact there, too, you … got to just keep praying for an outcome. Never give up. And so, and I'm sure that with this, there will be probably be more … Native American saints being proposed, or become blessed, or whatever. In fact, a lot of the people that worked in the conference I think are saints, too….

THIEL: Absolutely there are people that have passed on.

CLIFFORD: Even … now there are people working, that organized it, they're saints. As far as I am concerned they are saints…. But when they pass on we pray to them and ask for more miracles.…

I think it's something about children in there, too. Children will now have a saint to pray to, … at least in [our parish] our children will probably be there to lead some of the prayers. And now after the canonization, they'll be praying, not for canonization, but for her to help different people. Of course they've always been praying for that. But that will just become more intense.

Marquette University,
Congregation of the Great Spirit Records.
Printed by permission.

PHOTOGRAPHS

Ca. 1890: Mother M. Catherine Sacred White Buffalo (Josephine Crow Feather), first Prioress-General of The Congregation of American Sisters. Published in the *Irish World*, August 16, 1890. BCIM 00242.

1893: Sculpted bust of Mother M. Catherine Sacred White Buffalo by James E. Kelley. BCIM 00246.

1893: Sketch by James E. Kelley depicting the death of Mother M. Catherine Sacred White Buffalo. Published in Terrance Kardong, *Catholic Life at Fort Berthold, 1889-1989,* Assumption Abbey Press, Richardson, North Dakota, 1989. Printed by permission.

Ca. 1896: The Congregation of American Sisters. Published in the newspaper *Sina Sapa Wocekiye Taeyanpaha*, February 1, 1897. BCIM 00240.

Ca. 1933: The cast of the "Lily of the Mohawks" school play at St. Anthony's Mission, Zuni Pueblo, New Mexico. Rev. Clement Druehe, O.F.M., photographer. BCIM 11443.

1934: Missionaries and Choctaw children with a poster of Kateri Tekakwitha at Holy Rosary Mission, Tucker, Mississippi. BCIM 01892.

1938: Pearl Brewer and Seth Irving in the school play, "Princess of the Mohawks". The students reenacted the life of Kateri Tekakwitha at the Golden Jubilee Catholic Sioux Congress at Holy Rosary Mission (now Red Cloud Indian School), Pine Ridge, South Dakota, on the Pine Ridge Reservation. Rev. Joseph A. Zimmerman, S.J., photographer. BCIM 01880.

Ca. 1940: The Kateri Club praying for benefactors, Sacred Heart Mission, Coeur d'Alene Reservation, DeSmet, Idaho. This picture illustrated "Our Tekakwitha Club" in *The Indian Sentinel*, 20, no. 6 (1940): 87. Sister Providencia Tolan, S.P., photographer. BCIM 01890.

Ca. 1950: Mohawk structural steel workers returned from New York City and elsewhere presenting a miniature bridge as a gift to Kateri Tekakwitha, St. Francis Xavier Church, Kahnawake, Québec. Rev. Jacques Bruyere, S.J., photographer. BCIM 01884.

1985: Sister Kateri Mitchell, S.S.A., singing praises to Blessed Kateri at the 46th annual Tekakwitha Conference, LeMoyne College, Syracuse, New York. The rainbow banner, over a statue of Blessed Kateri read, "Blessed Kateri Tekakwitha 1656-1680." TC 5-1 01-07 1985b:238.

1989: Joe and Juana Pecos leading the procession to enshrine Blessed Kateri in San Diego Mission, Jemez Pueblo, New Mexico. This was her first enshrinement in a church among the Pueblo tribes of the Southwest. KTP 01-38-1.

1989: The grand entry procession at the 50th Annual Tekakwitha Conference, Fargo, North Dakota. The banners identify the Kateri circles of St. Regis Mission, Akwesasne Mohawk Reservation, Hogansburg, New York-Quebec, and St. Ann's Church, Penobscot Reservation, Indian Island, Maine. AMS 3356-10.

1990: A basket dance (Tohono O'odham) within mass at the 51ˢᵗ annual Tekakwitha Conference, Tucson, Arizona. AMS 3570-07.

1990: Smudging with fragrant smoke for a first-class relic of Blessed Kateri (in the cross-shaped reliquary) at the 51ˢᵗ annual Tekakwitha Conference, Tucson, Arizona. AMS 3640-25.

1990: Mohawk ladies at a statue of Blessed Kateri, Martyrs' Shrine, Auriesville, New York. AMS 3556-27.

1991: Left to right: Deacon Ralph Partida (Tarahumara), San Bernardino Diocese, California, Rev. Diego Mazon, O.F.M. (Apache-Zuni-Mexican), Gallup Diocese, Arizona-New Mexico, Rev. Georges Mathieu (Potawatomi), La Crosse Diocese, Wisconsin, and Sister Theresa Chato (Navajo), S.B.S., Gallup Diocese, Arizona-New Mexico, of the Association of Native Religious and Clergy, processing in the grand entry at the 52nd annual Tekakwitha Conference, Norman, Oklahoma. AMS 3831-04.

1992: An eagle dance (Laguna Pueblo, New Mexico) within mass at the 53rd annual Tekakwitha Conference, Orono, Maine. AMS 3976-23.

1992: A Mohawk choir singing at Blessed Kateri's feast day celebration, National Kateri Shrine, Fonda, New York. AMS 4115-03.

1993: Julie Degonzack-Daniels (Mohawk) re-enacting the life of Blessed Kateri at the 54th annual Tekakwitha Conference, Seattle, Washington. AMS 4287-14.

1993: A mass by Archbishop Thomas Murphy at St. James Cathedral themed, "A Time for Reconciling Ourselves as the People," at the 54th annual Tekakwitha Conference, Seattle, Washington. AMS 4295-10.

1994: Members of the Eastern Cherokee Kateri Circle (Our Lady of Guadalupe Church, Cherokee Reservation, Cherokee, North Carolina), with their banner at the 55ᵗʰ annual Tekakwitha Conference, Bemidji, Minnesota. AMS 4378-15.

1995: The tomb of Blessed Kateri, St. Francis Xavier Church, Kahnawake, Québec. AMS 4493-04.

1996: A Pima family with a poster of Blessed Kateri, near Yécora, Sonora, Mexico. Rev. David J. Beaumont, O.F.M.Cap., photographer. KTP 01-45-1.

1997: Bishop Donald E. Pelotte (Abenaki), S.S.S., with vestments depicting Blessed Kateri at the 58th annual Tekakwitha Conference, Milwaukee, Wisconsin. AMS TC97-05-09.

2003: A shrine to Blessed Kateri at the 64th annual Tekakwitha Conference,
Sioux Falls, South Dakota. AMS TC03-06-08.

July 21, 2006: Seattle Archbishop Alexander J. Brunett (right) announcing the Vatican's investigation of Jake Finkbonner's miracle. Jake and his parents, Donny and Elsa Finkbonner, sisters Malia and Miranda (older), and Rev. Timothy Sauer gathered with Archbishop Brunett at the 67th annual Tekakwitha Conference on the Lummi Reservation, near Ferndale, Washington. AMS TC06-07-10.

July 21, 2012: Jake Finkbonner transferring the reliquary with Blessed Kateri's first class relic to a host committee representative for next year's conference at the 73rd annual Tekakwitha Conference at the Martyrs' Shrine, near Auriesville, New York, which is the site of Kateri Tekakwitha's birth. Looking on is Sister Kateri Mitchell, S.S.A. HDR120721-325.

INDEX

Algonquin- 89-90

   Kateri's Heritage- 50, 130

   See also Kahenta (Kateri's Mother), Mary Elizabeth Lagoy, and Theresa   Steele

Apache

   Response to Kateri- 31

   Interviewees and Contributors- 49, 233, 239

Archambault, Marie Therese- 26, 250

Auriesville, New York (Birthplace) - 14, 19, 26, 33, 61, 79, 82, 101, 104, 116, 130, 174, 178

Baptism- 57, 182, 199-200, 243

   Kateri's- 14-15, 28, 39, 74, 91, 102, 104, 116

Beatification-99

   Papal Declaration of Kateri's- 21, 27, 30, 61, 87, 103, 107, 115, 123, 163-165, 181

   Evidence for- 16, 103

   Call For- 20

   Reaction to- 22-23, 137, 145, 149, 153, 159, 167, 185-186, 188, 190, 205, 211, 216-217, 229, 242

   of Junipero Serra- 32

Benedictines- 81, 85, 163

   See also Native Sisterhoods

Blindness,

   Kateri's Partial- 14, 54-55, 58, 102

   Prayers to Kateri to heal- 178

Bridget, Sister

   See Anna Pleets

Canonization- 99, 113

   Papal Declaration of Kateri's- 13, 30, 33, 48, 88, 114, 130, 157, 252-253

   Evidence for- 21, 218

   Investigation into- 75, 98, 101-102

   Call for Kateri's- 18-20, 32, 69, 81, 103, 109, 174, 197, 212, 216-217, 222, 233

   Prayers for- 22, 26, 124, 146, 150, 160-161, 191, 198, 223, 231, 244

   Of Jesuit Martyrs- 99

   Of Juan Diego- 235

Catherine, Sister

   See Josephine Crowfeather

Catholic Name- 14, 74, 76, 91

Charity- 15, 73, 98

Chauchetière, Claude- 16-17, 71-75, 84, 92

Cherokee- 31

Cholenec, Pierre- 14-17, 39, 71-72, 74-75, 83, 93

Clark, Ellen- 77, 79-80, 85

Communion-146-147, 165-166, 182, 197

   Kateri's attitude toward- 41, 44,

   Kateri's first- 15, 40-41, 63, 74, 102

   Historical Context of- 102

Convent

See Native Sisterhoods

Craft, Francis M.- 26-27, 72, 76-86

Relationship with Sioux- 77-78, 85

Crowfeather, Josephine- 26, 77-82, 258

Cuauhtlatoatzin, St. Juan Diego

See Juan Diego

Disfigurement

Kateri's- 14, 16, 24, 26, 54, 94, 102, 110

Dominicans- 74

Father (Kateri's)- 14, 39, 89, 102, 163

Finkbonner, Jake

See Miracles

Fonda, New York- 130, 225-226

National Kateri Tekakwitha Shrine in - 23, 33, 61, 81, 104-104, 116-117

Ganadawage (Kateri's home)- 14

Franciscans- 32, 74, 99, 116, 215, 219, 233

Fur Trade- 14, 18, 89-90

Ganadwage (Kateri's Home)

See Fonda, New York

Gregory, Sister

See Ellen Clark

Hagiography- 16, 18, 71-72, 106, 114

Intercession- 105, 123

of Kateri- 13, 19, 25, 31-32, 47, 69, 94, 98, 106, 121-122, 126, 130

of Josephine Crowfeather- 84

in Lives of Interviewees- 142, 153-156, 161, 166, 192, 212, 218, 229-230, 232, 241, 245

Jesuit- 19-20, 89, 123, 164

Order- 13-14, 17-18, 21, 72-77, 81, 93, 100, 115, 163, 186

Martyrs- 19, 26, 75, 82, 99, 116, 174, 177

Biographers- 13, 15-18, 71, 74, 88, 90-92, 95, 101

Missions/Reductions- 14, 18-19, 39, 56-57, 90, 99, 102, 107

Archives- 75

Juan Diego- 13, 100, 114, 185, 188-190, 222, 233-235, 249

Junipero, Father Serra- 32

Kahenta (Kateri's Mother)- 14, 39, 54-55, 60, 89, 102, 163

Kahnawake (Home of Uncle)- 17-19, 22, 24-25, 27-28, 31, 39, 74, 103-104, 107-108, 117, 165, 174, 225-226

Kateri Circles- 21-25, 27, 29-31, 50-51, 63, 117, 151, 178-179, 225

Lagoy, Sister Mary Elizabeth- 23

Lamberville, James de- 14, 90-91, 102

Marriage- 56, 74, 89, 91, 92, 102, 110, 163, 222

Miracles- 94, 138, 142, 160, 166, 168, 182, 212, 218-219, 232

Healings- 17, 31, 147, 150, 154, 176, 245

Healing of Addiction- 28-29, 150

Canonization Miracle (Jake Finkbonner)- 32, 121-127, 246

Transfiguration- 16, 24, 75, 94, 102

Mohawk

Response to Kateri- 17-18, 22-25, 33, 106-112

Mortification of the Flesh-15, 40, 42-43, 93-94, 102

Bed of Thorns- 93, 95

Mother (Kateri's)

See Kahenta

National Kateri Tekakwitha Shrine

See Fonda, New York

Natives Sisterhoods

Kateri's Dream of- 15, 72-75, 92, 102

Benedictine Sister's Novitiate- 26, 77-86

Companions of Kateri Tekakwitha- 27

Oblate Sisters of Blessed Sacrament- 86

Sisters of the Snows- 86

Navajo

Response to Kateri- 19, 30-31

Interviewees- 195-198, 200-201, 205, 208-209, 211, 215, 217, 219, 221-222, 235-237

Ossernon

See Auriesville, New York

Penobscot- 31

Pilgrimage- 17, 19, 25, 27-28, 30, 98-99, 103-105, 107, 116-117

Pima

Response to Kateri- 31

Interviewees- 239-242

Pleets, Anna - 77, 79-80, 85

Pope Benedict XVI- 88, 126-127, 129

Pope Leo XIII- 45, 84

Pope John Paul II- 21, 32, 87, 99-100, 104, 113, 165, 168, 176, 202

Pope Pius XII- 19, 87, 106

Potawatomi- 31

Pueblo

Response to Kateri- 27-31, 53, 115

Interviewees- 225, 227-228, 235-237

Relics- 16-18, 30, 105, 107, 123-124

Sioux

Response to Kateri- 19, 26, 30

Interviewees- 133, 137, 139, 145, 149, 153-154, 159, 163-164, 167-168, 173, 181-182, 185, 187, 190-192, 221, 250-251

Sky World- 95

Smallpox- 14, 16-17, 39, 54, 58, 89, 94, 102

St. Francis Xavier Church- 17, 25, 91, 102, 104, 123, 165, 174, 225

Referenced as Sault- 40, 43, 92, 95

See also Kahnawake

Steele, Theresa - 25

Tegaiaguenta, Marie Thérèse- 15-16, 72, 75

Tekakwitha Conference- 21, 25, 30-33, 50, 53, 65, 67, 103, 107, 116-117, 125, 229

Founding- 20

Future- 130

Leaders- 61, 114, 123, 129, 130, 163, 195

Regional- 113, 143, 147, 149, 156, 222

Interviewees Perspective on- 28-29, 68, 137, 140-145, 147, 149, 151, 153-154, 156-157, 159-160, 163-167, 173-174, 181-182, 185, 191-192, 195-197, 204-205, 108, 109, 211-212, 215-216, 218, 220-223, 225-226, 230-231, 233, 239-241, 246, 251-253

Third Plenary Council- 18-19, 75

See also Veneration

Turtle Clan/ Turtle Island- 61-63, 65, 89, 123, 130

Veneration-13, 23, 83, 98-100, 105, 112

Call for Kateri's- 18, 45

Papal Declaration of Kateri's- 19, 27, 87, 102

by Interviewees- 31, 188

of Jesuit Martyrs- 46, 116

Virginity/Chastity

Kateri's- 15, 26, 39, 43, 45, 56, 72, 74, 92, 98, 110, 163

Josephine Crowfeather's- 78

See also Marriage

Visions, Spectral- 17, 29, 53-55, 75, 94, 125

White Buffalo- 77-78, 82-83, 183, 246